Principles of Dairy Management

Principles of Dairy Management

Umesh Kumar

RANDOM PUBLICATIONS
NEW DELHI (INDIA)

Principles of Dairy Management

ISBN 978-93-5111-378-2

Published in 2014 in India by

RANDOM PUBLICATIONS

4376-A/4B, Gali Murari Lal, Ansari Road
New Delhi-110 002
Phone : +91-11-43580356, +91-11-23289044
e-mail: randomexports@gmail.com, sales@randompublications.com, info@randompublications.com

Reprinted 2019

Type Setting by : Keystoneprintads, Delhi-110051
Digitally Printed at: Replika Press Pvt. Ltd.

Preface

In India's agriculture based economy, dairy management has a significant role to play. Currently, India is the second largest producer of milk, after the US. Rapid growth in this sector has created an ever increasing demand for people trained in dairy management. Professionals associated with dairy management have to work with milk production, processing, packaging, storage, transport, and distribution, etc. Presently, more than 400 dairy plants are located all over India producing various types of dairy products. Trained professionals are needed to run these plants. Growth in dairy processing industry has given birth to the dairy equipment industry. Today, more than 170 dairy equipment companies are successfully doing business in India. Professionals with 8 to 10 years of experience can also work as independent consultants. Teaching and research also offer good possibilities. With experience it is even possible to establish a dairy business.

Dairy products are generally defined as food produced from the milk of mammals which is the Food Standards Agency of the United Kingdom defines dairy as "foodstuffs made from mammalian milk". They are usually high energy-yielding food products. A production plant for the processing of milk is called a dairy or a dairy factory. Apart from breastfed infants, the human consumption of dairy products is sourced primarily from the milk of cows, yet goats, sheep, yaks, camels, and other mammals are other sources of dairy products consumed by humans. Dairy products are commonly found in European, Middle Eastern and Indian cuisine, whereas they are almost unknown in East Asian cuisine. Some dairy products may cause health issues for individuals who have lactose intolerance and milk allergies. Some dairy products such as blue cheese may become contaminated with the fungus Aspergillus fumigatus during ripening, which can trigger asthma and other respiratory problems in susceptible individuals. Vegans and some other vegetarians avoid dairy products due to a variety of ethical, dietary, environmental, political, and religious concerns.

Animal husbandry is one of the most important occupations for farmers in India. Livestock, meat, eggs, milk, hides, etc., are the major products for the farmers. Farms, farm animals, and farmers makeup a fine farming ecosystem in India. To farmers, livestock are not just mere animals; often they treat them as their companions. This is peculiarly true of cattle and buffaloes. Ox, buffaloes, and camels are used as animal on the farm. They help in ploughing, sowing, thrashing, and carrying farm products. Cows and she-buffaloes furnish milk. Animal excreta are used as farm manures. Animal husbandry and dairy development play a significant role in rural development. In the financial year 1989, the gross output was around `358 billion. Thus in the rural economy, animal husbandry plays a significant role. India occupies the third position in global production of eggs and the sixth position in global production of poultry meat.

This book aims to explain dairy farmers with the most necessary and relevant principles of the science of dairy management, taking care to carefully entrench them in the basic concepts, practices and techniques which give shape to the modern process of the science. In addition to delineating the present trends and developments in the dairying field, the book takes care to intricate upon the whole industry, its revenues, prospects and challenges, with due deliberation to the rapidly globalizing dairy sector itself.

I thank all members of my team who have helped in the preparation of the book. My special thanks go to "Random Publications" who have published the book.

– ***Umesh Kumar***

Contents

1

Dairy Industry

DAIRY INDUSTRY OVERVIEW

The dairy industry has used membrane processing since its introduction in the food industry in the late 1960s to clarify, concentrate and fractionate a variety of dairy products.

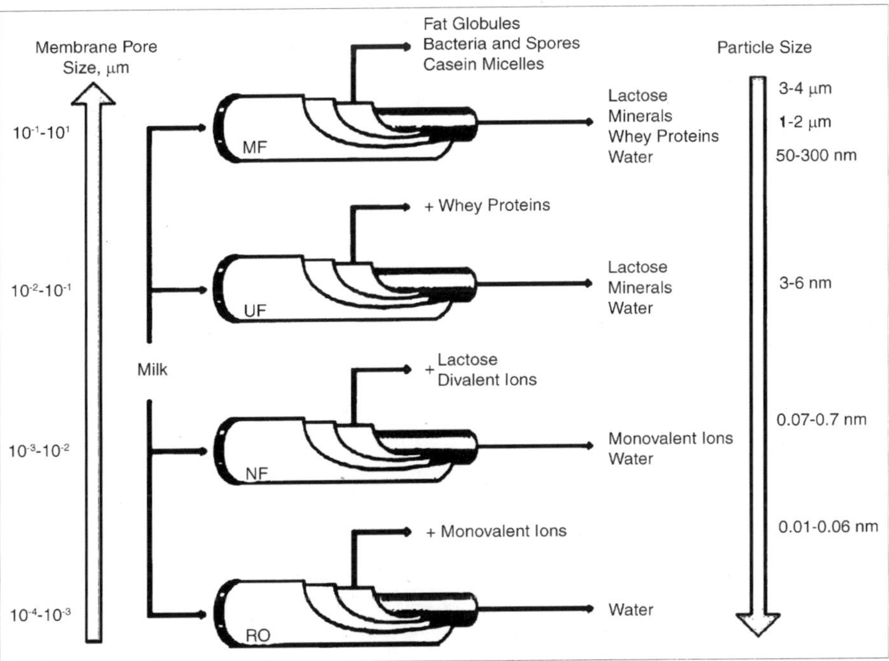

Fig. Milk Processing with Membrane Technology

Applying membrane technology to whey processing allowed the production of refined proteins and commercial usage and thus transformed a waste byproduct from cheese production into a valuable product. In addition to whey processing, membrane technology is also used for fluid milk processing with clear advantages. Further, specific milk components can be obtained without causing a phase change to the fluid milk by the addition of heat as in evaporation, or an enzyme, as done in most cheese-making techniques.

The filtered milk can then be directly used in the manufacture of such dairy products as cheese, ice cream and yoghurt. By applying membranes with different pore sizes and molecular weight cut-offs (MWCOs), the milk can be modified by separating, clarifying, or fractionating a selected component in milk from other components.

The pressure-driven membrane processes MF, UF, NFand RO are the most common membrane processes in the dairy industry and based on their applicability range it is possible to separate virtually every major component of milk as shown in Figure, thus enabling the manufacturing of products with unique properties and functionalities.

KEY MEMBRANE APPLICATIONS

The key applications of cross-flow membrane technology in the dairy industry are discussed.

Removal of Bacteria and Spores from Milk, Whey and Cheese Brine

The removal of bacteria and spores from milk to extend its shelf-life by MF is an alternative way to ultrapasteurization. In this approach, the organoleptic and chemical properties of the milk are unaltered. The first commercial system of this so-called Bactocatch was developed by Alfa Laval [1–3] and marketed by Tetra Pak under the name Tetra Alcross®Bactocatch. In this process, the raw milk is separated into skim milk and cream. The resulting skim milk is microfiltered using ceramic membranes with a pore size of 1.4 μm at constant transmembrane pressure (TMP).

Thus, the retentate contains nearly all the bacteria and spores, while the bacterial concentration in the permeate is less than 0.5 per cent of the original value in milk. The retentate is then mixed with a standardized quantity of cream. Subsequently, this mix is subjected to a conventional high heat treatment at 130°C for 4s and reintroduced into the permeate, and the mixture is then pasteurized.

Since less than 10% of the milk is heat treated at the high temperature, the sensory quality of the milk is significantly improved. MF for the removal of bacteria and spores can be further applied in the production of other dairy products. In the production of cheese, the use of low bacterial milk improves also the keeping quality of cheese due to the removal of spores, thus eliminating the need of additives (*e.g.*, nitrate). While in the production of whey protein concentrates (WPC) and isolates (WPI), this MF concept is used to remove bacteria and spores giving a high quality product. Hence, by applying MF the heat treatment of the WPC/WPI is kept to a minimum, which preserves the functional properties of the whey proteins Finally, in the manufacture of cheese the concentrated curd is submerged in a salt solution to improve the cheese preservation and to develop the flavour and other cheese properties.

This process is called brining. Efficient sanitation of cheese brine has become a major concern to the dairy industry in recent years. This results from the possibility of post-contamination of cheeses in the brine, especially by pathogenic bacteria.. The application of MF for sanitation of cheese brine, using ceramic or spiralwound membranes, results in a superior cheese quality compared to the traditional processes of heat treatment and kieselguhr filtration.

MFhas the advantages of being simple to perform, of maintaining the chemical balance of the brine and of eliminating filter aids. In the brine treatment by MF it is normally necessary to make a prefiltration of the brine solution, which is easily done by dead-end filter bag or cartridge with a pore size of 100 µm.

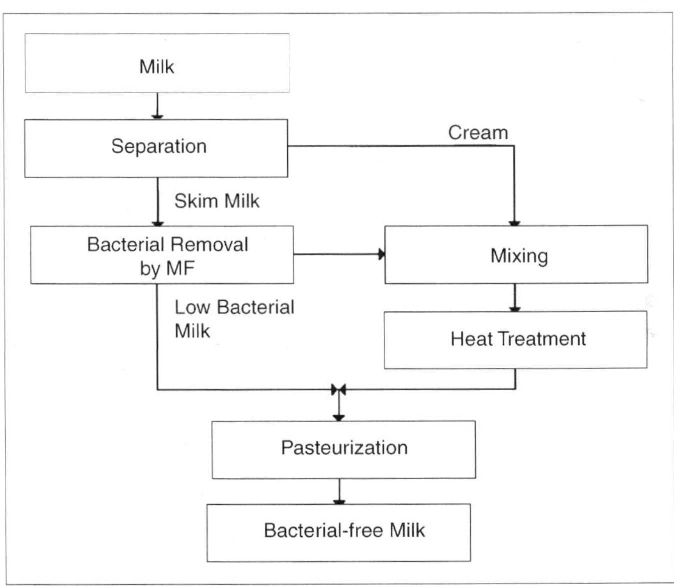

Fig. Bacterial Removal from Milk by MF

Milk Protein Standardization, Concentration and Fractionation

The protein content of milk is subjected to natural variations during the year. Standardization of milk by UF offers the possibility of increasing or decreasing the protein content in milk without the need of adding milk powders, casein and whey protein concentrates. Skim milk and 1% milk with increased protein content have an improved appearance (whiter milk) and higher viscosity. The sensory quality of increased protein milk is therefore more similar to that of higher fat milks resulting in an improved consumer appeal.

Another application of UFis the standardization of protein and total solids in milk for use in fermented dairy products, such as cream cheeses, yoghurt and cottage cheeses. The resulting dairy products have superior quality and sensory characteristics compared to those produced from milk concentrated by conventional methods.

With the quality obtained by membrane filtration, attributes such as consistency, post-processing and extent of syneresis are easier to control. However, the use of membrane-processed milk often requires an adjustment in starter culture selection and fermentation conditions due to the compositional changes in the UF milk.

Concentrationof milk, whichconventionally isdonebyevaporation techniques, can also be achieved by RO. The concentrated milk has its greatest potential in ice-cream manufacturing, since all the solids are retained in the concentrateand 70% of the water is removed. MF and/or UF are used in the production of milk protein concentrates (MPC), which are products containing 50–58% of protein.

These products are used as food additives and it is therefore extremely important to maintain the functionality of the proteins. By using UF membranes in combination with MF and/or diafiltration (DF) with the corrected adjustments of pH, temperature and filtration conditions, it is possible to produce the desirable MPC for a specific food application. Themost promisingMFapplication in the dairy industry is the fractionation of milk protein.

The separation of micellar casein from the whey proteins can be achieved by ceramic membranes with a pore size of 0.2 μm at a constant TMP. The resulting retentate has a high concentration of native calcium phosphocaseinate that can be used for cheese making. Native casein has an excellent rennet-coagulation ability that will make calcium phosphocaseinate an exceptional enrichment for cheese-milk.

The permeate can be further processed byUFto produce high-qualityWPC. These protein concentrates can be further separated into lactoferrin, β-lactoglobulin and α-lactalbumin via ion-exchange chromatography. Both β-lactoglobulin and α-lactalbumin have great potential markets. β-lactoglobulin can be used as a gelling agent and α-lactalbumin, which is very rich in tryptophan, can be used in the production of peptides with physiological properties.

Another application can be the production of infant milk. The fractionation of milk proteins using membrane technology enables the recovery of value-added protein ingredients. Further, the casein and whey proteins are separated without the need of heat or enzymes. The potential applications of membrane separation in milk processing are shown in Figure.

Whey Protein Concentration and Fractionation

Whey is a by-product from the cheese industry. It has low content of solids and high biological oxygen demand (BOD), which creates a major disposal problem for the dairy industry. In the past, all whey was disposed of as sewage, sprayed on fields or used for animal feed. By applying membrane technology whey can be concentrated to produce WPC and WPI, as well as fractionated and purified to obtain purified α-lactalbumin and β-lactoglobulin.

Hence, a once wasted product can be converted into high value-added products and at the same time one of the key pollution problems of the dairy industry can be solved.

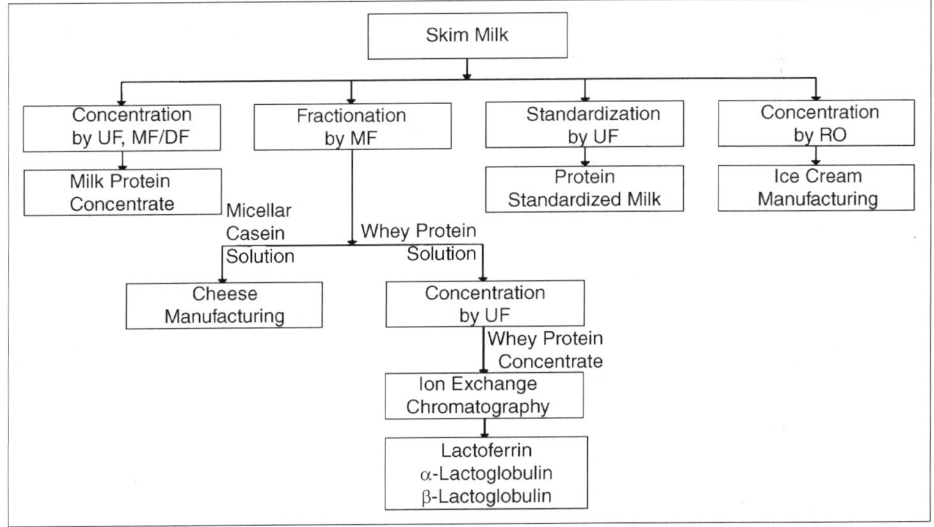

Fig. Applications of Membrane Technology in Milk Processing

Consequently, the use of UFand RO to concentrate whey was one of the first applications of membranes in the dairy industry. Due to the complexity and diversity of whey, it is necessary to use different membrane processes to produce a specific product.

The production of WPC with 35–85% protein in the total solids can be achieved by a combination of UF and DF. MF can be used as a pretreatment to remove both bacteria and fat and allows the production of WPI with 90% protein in the total solids.

Whey proteins have not only a high nutritional value but also functional properties. They can be used as gelling, emulsifying and foaming agents. Therefore, whey concentrates have farreaching applications not only in dairy foods, but also in confectionary, nutritional foods, beverages and even processed meats.

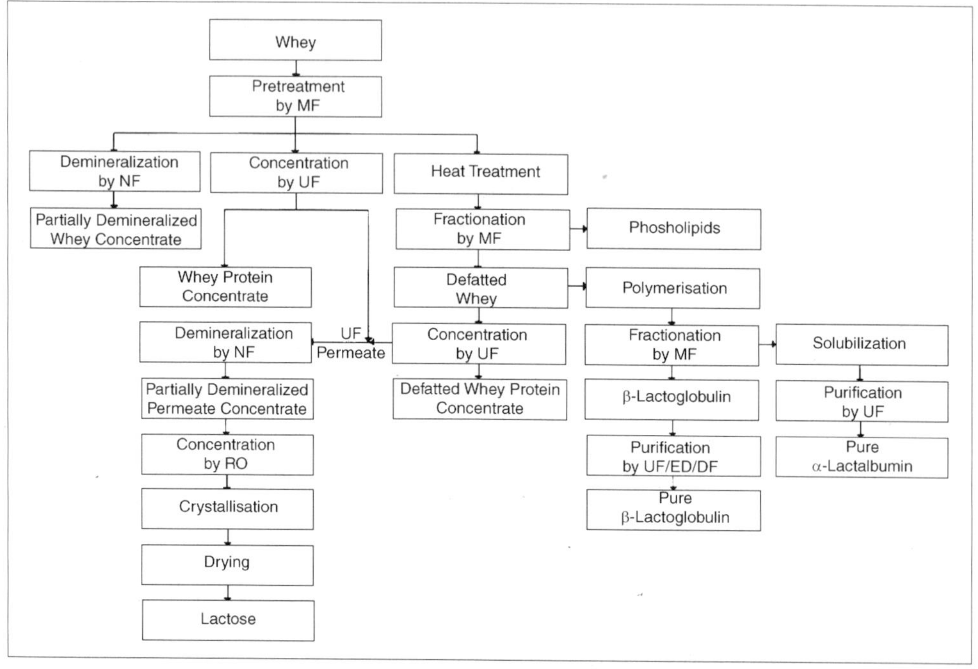

Fig. Applications of Membrane Technology in Whey Processing

The presence of fat in whey leads to decreased functional properties and shorter storage time. Several processes involving membranes have been developed to remove the residual fat from whey. The most common process, developed byMaubois *et al.* and Fauquant *et al.*, exploits the ability of the phospholipids to aggregate by calcium binding under moderate heat treatment for 8 min at 50°C.

This process is called thermocalcic precipitation. Defatted whey is then obtained by MF with a pore size of 0.14 μm to separate the resulting precipitate. Defatted whey can be further processed by UF, which also improves the performance in the subsequent membrane processes. The defatted WPC has a foaming capacity similar to that of egg white and the same protein content. Its applications can be as raw material in the pastry and icecream production. The MF retentate, which contains a high amount of phospholipids, can be used as an effective emulsifier agent for food and cosmetic applications.

The purified proteins β-lactoglobulin and α-lactalbumin can be obtained from the defatted whey. At low pH (4.0–4.5) and under moderate heat treatment for 30 min at 55°C, α-lactalbumin polymerizes reversibly entrapping most of the residual lipidsand the other whey proteins with the exception of the β-lactoglobulin. The fractionation of β-lactoglobulin from the remaining proteins can then be done by MF with apore size of 0.2 μm or centrifugation. The resulting soluble phase, rich in β-lactoglobulin, can be further purified by UF coupled with electrodialysis (ED) or DF.

Purification of α-lactalbumin from the MF retentate can be achieved by solubilization at a neutral pH and subsequently by UF using a membrane with an MWCO of 50,000 Dalton. It has also been reported that membranes can be applied for the isolation of Kcasein-glycomacropeptid (GMP) from cheese whey. GMP can find several applications in the pharmaceutical industry.

Studies have shown that GMP avoids the adhesion of Escherichia coli cells to the intestine walls, protects against influenza and prevents adhesion of tartar to teeth. It should also be noted that membrane filtration also plays a major role in the lactose manufacture from whey using UF and RO and in the production of lowcarbohydrate beverages with high dairy protein content.

Whey Demineralization

In the dairy industry, the NFprocess is used to concentrate and partially demineralize liquid whey. Due to the selectivity of the membranes most of the monovalent ions, the organic acids, and some of the lactose will pass the membrane.

NF is a very interesting alternative to ion exchange and ED if moderate demineralization is required. One advantage of NF compared to the other two processes is that NF is a simple process, which partially demineralizes and concentrates the whey at the same time. The maximum level of demineralization by NF is about 35% reduction of the ash content with a concentration factor of about 3.5–4.

By applying a DF step it is possible to increase the level of demineralization up to 45%. Other applications of NF in whey processing include: concentration and partial demineralization of whey UF permeates prior to the manufacture of lactose and lactose derivatives, converting. salt whey. to normal whey while solving a disposal problem, treating cheese brine solutions to be reused.

Cheese Manufacturing

Another early application of membrane technology in the dairy industry was in cheese manufacturing for production of Feta cheese and brine treatment by UF. Nowadays, membrane-processed milk is also successfully used in the manufacturing of quark and cream cheeses.

Together with WPC production, the use of UF milk for the production of cheese is the most widespread application of membranes in the dairy industry.

The advantages of UFconcentrated milk in cheese making compared to traditional methods are the following:

- Increases the total solids, which increases the cheese yield and therefore decreases the production costs in terms of energy and equipment;
- Reduces the rennet and starter culture requirements since UF-milk has a good ability of enzymatic coagulation;
- Reduces the wastewater processing costs of the cheese plant;
- Improves the quality and composition control;
- Increases the nutritional value due to the incorporation of the whey protein in the cheese.

UF in cheese processing can be used in three ways:

1. *Preconcentration*: The standardized cheese milk is concentrated by a factor of 1.2–2 and it can be used for most cheese types. This allows the capacity of the cheese vats and whey draining equipment to be doubled. However, the cheese yield will not be significantly improved since only 4. 5–5% of the protein content is increased. It is used to produce Cheddar, Cottage Cheese and Mozzarella, and it can be used to standardize cheese milk and manipulate its mineral composition, resulting in a more consistent quality in the final product.
2. *Partial Concentration*: The standardized cheese milk is concentrated by a factor 2–6. It is used in the manufacture of Cheddar cheese by using for example, the APV-SiroCurd process, in which the milk is concentrated five times with DF in order to standardize the salt balance. It is also used to produce other cheese types like Queso Fresco, structure Feta, Camembert and Brie.
3. *Total Concentration*: The standardized cheese milk is concentrated to the total solids content in the final cheese. This provides the maximum yield increase and since there is no whey drainage, the cheese can be manufactured without the need for a cheese vat. It is used to produce cast Feta, quark, cream cheese, Ricotta and Mascarpone.

The UF permeate, which contains mainly lactose, can be concentrated by RO. The permeate from the RO process can be polished by another RO unit. After pasteurization orUVlight treatment, the permeate from the polisher can be used at the plant as process water, thus reducing the water costs of the plant. Although UF has advantages in cheese production, the increase of whey content in the cheesedueto the concentration of all milk proteinscan have a negative effectonthe ripening of semihard and hard cheeses. Therefore, UFshould be viewed as a complementary process to cheese manufacturing and not as an alternative process.

COWS USED FOR THEIR MILK

Cows produce milk for the same reason that humans do: to nourish their young. In order to force the animals to continue giving milk, factory farm operators typically impregnate them using artificial insemination every year. Calves are generally taken from their mothers within a day of being born—males are destined for veal crates or barren lots where they will be fattened for beef, and females are sentenced to the same fate as their mothers.

After their calves are taken away from them, mother cows are hooked up, several times a day, to milking machines. These cows are genetically manipulated, artificially inseminated, and often drugged to force them to produce about four and a half times as much milk as they naturally would to feed their calves.

Animals are often dosed with bovine growth hormone (BGH), which contributes to a painful inflammation of the udder known as "mastitis." (BGH is used widely in the U.S. but has been banned in Europe and Canada because of concerns over human health and animal welfare.) According to the industry's own figures, between 30 and 50 per cent of dairy cows suffer from mastitis, an extremely painful condition.

A cow's natural lifespan is about 25 years, but cows used by the dairy industry are killed after only four or five years. An industry study reports that by the time they are killed, nearly 40 per cent of dairy cows are lame because of the intensive confinement, the filth, and the strain of being almost constantly pregnant and giving milk. Dairy cows' bodies are turned into soup, companion animal food, or low-grade hamburger meat because their bodies are too "spent" to be used for anything else.

VEAL CALVES

Male calves—"byproducts" of the dairy industry—are generally taken from their mothers when they are less than 1 day old. Many are shipped off to barren, filthy feedlots to await slaughter. Others are kept in dark, tiny crates where they are kept almost completely immobilized so that their flesh stays tender. In order to make their flesh white, the calves are fed a liquid diet that is low in iron and has little nutritive value. This heinous treatment makes the calves ill, and they frequently suffer from anemia, diarrhea, and pneumonia. Frightened, sick, and alone, these calves are killed after only a few months of life so that their flesh can be sold as veal. All adult and baby cows, whether raised for their flesh or their milk, are eventually shipped to a slaughterhouse and killed.

The good news is that removing dairy products from your diet is easier than ever. Today there is a multitude of nondairy "dairy" products on the market, such as soy, rice, and almond milk and soy ice cream. Check out a list of our favourite dairy and meat alternatives.

FERMENTED MILKS

DEFINITIONS

Fermented milks have been produced by traditional methods for many centuries, and there are several hundred such products recorded around the world. They are produced as a result of microbial 'souring' of milk, usually cows' milk, but also the milk of other species, including sheep, goat, horse and buffalo. Most are very similar, both in terms of their characteristics, and in the technology used to produce them. Many fermented milk products are distinguished only by their region of origin, and very few have become commercially important.

Interest in these products, particularly yoghurt, has grown rapidly since the development of flavoured and fruit yoghurts in Europe in the late 1950s, and more recently as a result of the growing demand for, and marketing of, fermented milks as healthpromoting foods.

Fermented milks can be conveniently classified on the basis of the type of fermentation they undergo, as lactic, yeast-lactic and mould-lactic. Lactic fermentation products can be further classified, depending on the characteristics of the lactic microflora, as mesophilic, thermophilic and probiotic or therapeutic.

LACTIC FERMENTATIONS

LACTIC ACID FERMENTATON

Lactic acid fermentation is caused by some fungi and bacteria. The most important lactic acid producing bacteria is Lactobacillus. Other bacteria which produce lactic acid include:

- Leuconostoc mesenteroides
- Pediococcus cerevisiae
- Streptococcus lactis
- Bifidobacterium bifidus.

Lactic acid fermentation is used throughout the world to produce speciality foods:

- Western world: yogurt, sourdough breads, sauerkraut, cucumber pickles and olives
- Middle East: pickled vegetables
- Korea: kimchi (fermented mixture of Chinese cabbage, radishes, red pepper, garlic and ginger)
- Russia: kefir
- Egypt: laban rayab and laban zeer (fermented milks), kishk (fermented cereal and milk mixture)
- Nigeria: gari (fermented cassava)
- South Africa: magou (fermented maize porridge)

- Thailand: nham (fermented fresh pork)
- Philippines: balao balao (fermented rice and shrimp mixture)

The presence of lactic acid, produced during the lactic acid fermentation is responsible for the sour taste and for the improved microbiological stability and safety of the food. This lactic acid fermentation is responsible for the sour taste of dairy products such as cheese, yoghurt and kefir.

Lactic acid fermentation also gives the sour taste to fermented vegetables such as traditionally cultured sauerkraut and pickles. The sugars in the cabbage are converted into lactic acid and serve as a preservative.

Yogurt fermentation

Yogurt is made by fermenting milk with friendly bacteria, mainly Lactobacillus bulgaricus and Streptococcus thermophilus. Yogurt fermentation was invented probably by accident by Balkan tribes thousands of years ago. Yogurt remained mainly a food of eastern Europe until the 1900s, when the biologist Mechnikov created the theory that lactobacillus bacteria in yogurt are responsible for the unusually long lifespans of the Bulgar people. The milk sugar or lactose is fermented by these bacteria to lactic acid which causes the characteristic curd to form. The acid also restricts the growth of food poisoning bacteria.

During the yogurt fermentation some flavours are produced, which give yogurt its characteristic flavour. Yoghurt can easily be made at home using a live yogurt as the starter culture. To make you own yogurt use the following process. Bring the milk (or soymilk) to boiling point and cool down to 40-45°C. Pour this milk in a sterile container and and per litre milk about 100 ml live yogurt. Mix with a sterile spoon and incubate at 40-44°C during 4 to 6 hours or until the yogurt is set. Put the yogurt in the refrigerator. If you worked under hygienic conditions, you can use your own yogurt as a starter for your next batch.

Magou fermentation

Magou is very popular in South Africa, especially among the Bantu people. Magou is a lactic acid fermented porridge made from maize. To make magua a 10 per cent maize meal slurry is cooked, cooled and inoculated with wheat flour, which contains the bacteria. Magou is also produced on industrial scale and is then packed in cartons. In the industrial process the magou is inoculated with lactobacillus delbreuckii cultures.

Kefir fermentation

Kefir fermentation is similar to yogurt fermentation. Yogurt is only fermented by bacteria but kefir fermentation involves the help of bacteria as well as yeasts. These yeast produce some alcohol and carbon dioxide, which gives kefir its typical fizzy aspect. Kefir is inoculated with special kefir grains. These grains are mixtures of bacteria and yeasts in a matrix of proteins, lipids and carbohydrates. Kefir fermentation is done at room temperature, which makes the process easier. On the other hand, not everyone likes the taste of kefir.

MESOPHILIC

The genera of microorganisms that fall into this category include *Lactococcus, Leuconostoc* and *Pediococcus*. The optimal growth temperature is between 25-30 °C.

Traditional or Natural Buttermilk

Traditional or natural buttermilk is made from the liquid produced during butter production using a starter culture mixture of *Lactococcus* spp. and *Leuconostoc mesenteroides* subsp. *cremoris*.

Cultured Buttermilk

Cultured buttermilk is also produced mostly using a mixed culture of *L. lactis* subsp. *lactis, L. lactis* subsp. *cremoris* and the flavour-producing organisms *L. lactis* biovar *diacetylactis* and *L. mesenteroides* subsp. *cremoris*. It is traditionally made from skimmed milk. Ymer is similar to cultured buttermilk, but differs in the sequence of the manufacturing stages.

Nordic Sour Milks

Nordic sour milks such as Filmjolk and Nordic ropy milk are made using slimeproducing *Bacterium lacticus longi,* a synonym of *Lactococcus* spp. The slimy or ropy consistency of the products is also attributed to Butterwort leaves, which are rubbed on the interior of the pails.

Cultured Cream

Cultured cream or sour cream is made using the same starter cultures as cultured buttermilk, but has a much higher fat content.

Miscellaneous Products

Miscellaneous products include a range of traditional products that depend on spontaneous fermentation by naturally present lactic acid bacteria in milk. Maziwa lala is made using the same starter culture mixture as buttermilk, but is then sweetened.

Susa, made from camel's milk is fermented using hetero-fermentative mesophilic starter cultures. Lben is similar to buttermilk but its production involves spontaneous fermentation. The microflora of this product mainly consists of *L. lactis* biovar *diacetylactis, Leuconostoc lactis, L. mesenteroides* subsp. *cremoris* and *Leuconostoc mesenteroides* subsp. *dextranicum*; lactobacilli, yeast, mould and coliforms are also present.

THERMOPHILIC

This category encompasses those starter cultures whose growth optimum is between 37 and 45°C. The genera of microorganisms that fall into this category include *Streptococcus* and *Lactobacillus.*

Yoghurt

Yoghurt is a term used to describe a wide range of related products, which may be classified according to legal standards, gel type and whether or not they are flavoured or if they are subjected to a further process. The usual starter culture employed to produce yoghurt is a mixture of *Streptococcus thermophilus* and *Lactobacillus delbrueckii* subsp. *bulgaricus.*

Acid Buttermilk

Acid buttermilk, also known as Bulgarian buttermilk is made using *L. delbrueckii* subsp. *bulgaricus* as the starter culture. *Str. thermophilus* or a cream culture may also be included in the starter culture.

PROBIOTIC OR THERAPEUTIC

LAB such as enterococci, lactococci, propionibacteria, *Leuconostoc,* and pediococci are used as probiotics, but the principal organisms are of the bacterial genera *Lactobacillus* and *Bifidobacterium.*

Yakult

Yakult is a term for a group of therapeutic products originating from Japan. The starter culture used is *Lactobacillus casei* subsp. *casei,* an organism naturally present in the normal intestinal microflora of humans. The organism is a probiotic strain that is thought to have a beneficial effect on the host, by improving the intestinal microbial balance. The positive health benefits of probiotics are reported to be of particular value in the treatment of diseases that result in a disturbance of the intestinal microflora.

Acidophilus Milk

Acidophilus milk is a traditional therapeutic milk product popular in eastern Europe, but now attracting more attention elsewhere for its perceived beneficial properties. It may be made from skimmed or whole milk, and the starter organism is *Lactobacillus acidophilus.*

'Bio' Yoghurts

'Bio' yoghurts are made by very much the same process as traditional yoghurt, and are very similar products, but usually use a mixed starter culture consisting of probiotic strains. *Bifidobacterium* spp. are often used, especially *Bifidobacterium bifidum,* and *Bifidobacterium longum,* together with lactobacilli, such as *L. casei* and *L. acidophilus.* These organisms are all found in the normal intestinal microflora and are considered to have a beneficial effect on human health.

YEAST-LACTIC FERMENTATIONS

Mesophilic LAB, thermophilic LAB and yeast are the main fermentation genera.

KEFIR

Kefir is a rather foamy and effervescent fermented milk that contains about 1% lactic acid and 0.5-1.0% alcohol, and is popular in eastern Europe and Mongolia. The starter culture consists of small, white 'kefir grains', about 2-10 mm in diameter.

These grains contain a complex and quite variable microbial community, but little is known about how they develop. The grains usually contain LAB such as *Lactobacillus* spp. plus *Lactococcus* spp., *Leuconostoc* spp., and *Str. thermophilus,* acetic acid bacteria, contaminants such as mould, and a number of yeast species such as *Saccharomyces and Kluyveromyces,* but the principal yeast species present is *Candida kefir.*

KOUMISS

Koumiss is traditionally made in central Asia from mares' milk, but is now often made from skimmed, or whole cows' milk with added sugar. Starter cultures contain LAB such as lactobacilli, strains of lactose-fermenting yeasts, non-lactose-fermenting and non-carbohydrate-fermenting yeasts. The finished product contains lactic acid, alcohol and carbon dioxide, producing a slightly effervescent drink.

MISCELLANEOUS PRODUCTS

Miscellaneous products such as acidophilus-yeast milk fall under the yeast-lactic group of fermented products, but little is known about the technology of these beverages.

MOULD-LACTIC FERMENTATIONS

Mesophilic LAB and mould are the genera responsible for fermentation.

VILLI

Villi is a fermented milk product from Finland, which is made from whole milk, using a starter culture of *L. lactis* subsp. lactis biovar *diacetylactis, L. mesenteroides* subsp. *cremoris,* and the mould *Geotrichum candidum.* The mould grows on the layer of fat that forms on the top of the product and produces a felt of mycelium.

INITIAL MICROFLORA

The initial microflora of fermented milk products is determined largely by the microflora of the whole and skimmed milks from which they are made.

PROCESSING AND ITS EFFECTS ON THE MICROFLORA

Although there is a very wide range of fermented milk products, the manufac-turing technology used is generally very similar. The principal differences are in the starter cultures used, the composition and treatment of the milk, and the fermentation conditions. Therefore, for the purposes of this chapter, yoghurt manufacture is used as a representative example of fermented milk processes, since yoghurt is the most commercially important of these products. An outline of the process is depicted in Figure.

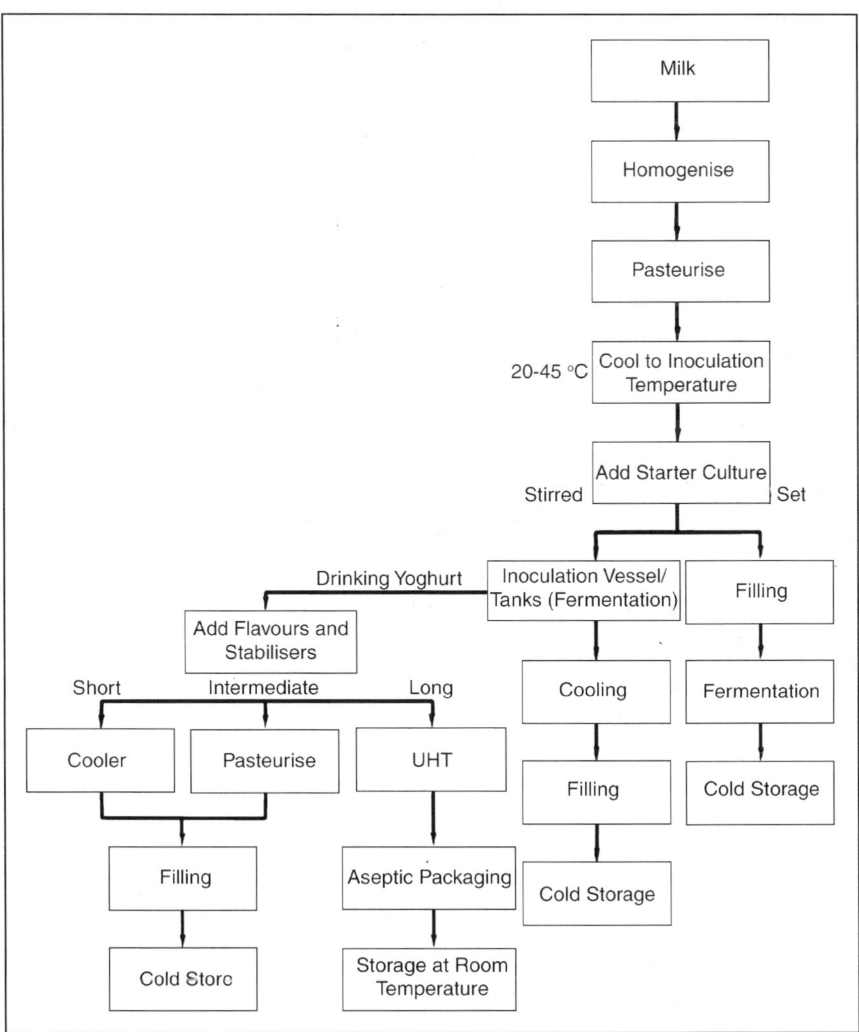

Fig. Production of Stirred and Set Fermented Milk

INITIAL PROCESSING

Several different varieties of yoghurt are produced, but the three main types are: set; stirred; and drinking yoghurt. Yoghurt is most commonly made from cows' milk, but may also be produced from the milk of sheep, goats, and, occasionally, other animal species. The composition of yoghurt varies slightly, and in some countries is regulated by legislation.

Both whole milk and reduced-fat milks are used to produce yoghurt, but reduced-fat products have the largest market share in most countries. A fat content of approximately 1.5% is typical for a low-fat yoghurt, and the milk is usually standardised to control the final fat content. The protein composition and quality of the milk are important, since they may have a significant effect on texture.

Only milk of good microbiological quality should be used, in order to avoid problems of proteolysis associated with bacterial activity, and the production of bacterial proteases by psychrotrophs. These enzymes may significantly alter the physical properties of the yoghurt, and cause defects. The milk-solids-not-fat content of the milk is usually increased to give a higher viscosity in the finished product.

This may be done by fortification with non-fat dried milk or other dairy powders, or by concentration methods, such as evaporation under vacuum, or by membrane filtration. For most yoghurt, an MSNF level of about 15% is typical, but for drinking yoghurt, levels of less than 11% are preferred. The milk is usually then filtered, to remove undissolved particles, de-aerated to provide conditions that favour rapid starter growth, and homogenised to improve texture and help prevent syneresis. Stabilisers may also be added to stirred yoghurts to improve viscosity and further reduce the likelihood of syneresis. Pre-gelatinised starch or plant gums are the most commonly used stabilisers.

HEAT TREATMENT

A heat treatment is generally applied to milk for yoghurt manufacture. A process of 80-85°C for 30 minutes is typical for batch processes, but, for continuous processes, a heat treatment of 90-95°C for 5-10 minutes is more usual. In some cases, a full ultra high temperature process may be applied. This relatively severe heat treatment has a number of effects.

Vegetative bacterial cells, which may include pathogens such as *Salmonella*, are killed, leaving only heat-resistant bacterial spores. Non-pathogenic organisms that might interfere with the growth of the starter culture are therefore reduced to very low levels. The heat treatment also has a significant effect on the final viscosity of the yoghurt, and improves texture by causing denaturation of the whey proteins and the three-dimensional aggregation of casein molecules.

The oxygen concentration of the milk is also further reduced, improving conditions for starter culture growth, since the starter organisms are generally microaerophilic. Finally, starter culture activity can either be stimulated or inhibited due to the breakdown products of heat-damaged milk proteins.

FERMENTATION

After heat treatment, the milk is cooled to 30 or 45°C and is then inoculated with the starter culture. Most commercial yoghurt production now uses a mixed inoculum containing defined strains of *Str. thermophilus* and *L. delbrueckii* subsp. *bulgaricus.* During fermentation, the two starter organisms grow synergistically. Initially, *Str. thermophilus* grows rapidly and produces lactic acid. As the acidity rises, so *L. delbreuckii* subsp. *bulgaricus* becomes more active and produces more acid along with aroma compounds.

It has been found that the growth of *Str. thermophilus* stimulates the growth of the *Lactobacillus,* probably by the production of a growth factor, thought to be formic acid, which stimulates proteolytic activity. *Lactobacillus* growth is further stimulated by the production of low levels of carbon dioxide from urea. The lactobacilli, in turn, stimulate the growth of *Str. thermophilus* by releasing peptides and, to lesser extent, amino acids as by-products of proteolysis.

The specific strains used are chosen for their effect on product flavour and texture, and strains may be used in rotation to prevent occasional problems with bacteriophage infection. Good hygienic practices after pasteurisation are required to prevent build-up of bacteriophage pools in stagnant whey. It is important that the inoculum contains a balanced population of the two organisms, usually a 1:1 ratio. Both liquid and freeze-dried cultures are used.

Most commercial manufacturers use an inoculum of about 2-3% v/v. Incubation of the inoculated milk at 40-45°C produces a rapid fermentation, which is normally complete within 3-4 hours. During this time, lactic acid is produced, giving an eventual acidity of 0.9-0.95% and a pH of approximately 4.6-5.0.

The starter organisms may also produce aroma compounds, such as acetaldehyde, acetone, acetoin and diacetyl, and exopolysaccharides, which improve texture and viscosity, although if too much extracellular material is produced, a 'ropy' texture fault may result. Set yoghurt is fermented in the final container, but stirred yoghurt is fermented in bulk, and stirred slowly, for only a few minutes, during the process.

COOLING AND PACKING

When fermentation is complete, the yoghurt is initially cooled to about 15-20°C, to minimise further acid production. At this point, sweeteners, flavours and/or fruit purees may be added. These additions must be of good microbiological quality, since, for most yoghurts, no further processing is applied. The product is then dispensed into the final containers and further cooled to < 5°C. A shelf life of about 3 weeks at this temperature is typical, although acid continues to be produced during this time and may affect flavour. Some yoghurt is heat treated after fermentation to destroy starter organisms, and this increases shelf life to several months. Greek-style, concentrated yoghurts are produced by further separation of the yoghurt after fermentation to increase the fat and solids content. Yoghurt may also be frozen, or dried for use as an ingredient.

PROBIOTIC PRODUCTS

The production of fermented milks with probiotic organisms is very similar to the basic process for yoghurt, and uses the same key stages. However, the characteristics of the organisms used require that certain modifications be made. Since probiotic bacteria are intended to colonise the gastrointestinal tract of consumers, it is important that the number of viable cells in the product be as high as possible. Direct vat inoculation of probiotic starters is common, using cultures in nutrient-supplemented milk.

Bulk starter media may also be used, especially for *Bifidobacterium* spp., which can be difficult to grow. Inoculation rates also tend to be higher for probiotic starters. Rates of 10-20% v/v can be used. *Bifidobacteria* are usually used in combination with other LAB as they may produce quantities of acetic acid, which can adversely affect flavour, and to overcome slow acid production. *L. acidophilus* is a slow-growing organism and therefore requires a long incubation time to produce sufficient acid. This means that *L. acidophilus* fermentations are likely to be disrupted by spore-forming bacteria in the early stages if these organisms are present in significant numbers. For this reason, the milk is usually given a severe heat process such as 95°C for one hour, or a UHT treatment, to reduce spore levels.

A further challenge is ensuring the survival of sufficient numbers of the probiotic organisms in the product throughout its shelf life for the product to be classified as having probiotic properties. Survival is influenced by various factors, including acidity, pH, temperature, and oxygen concentration. Therefore, careful control of these factors during processing and storage is important, as is the initial probiotic strain selection. Recent studies suggest that it is possible to maintain high numbers of viable cells throughout shelf life.

CURRENT DAIRY POLICIES TO ASSIST PRODUCERS

Indian dairy policy has been developed over the last seven decades.

The early policies addressed three main problems:

- Producers lacked bargaining power with milk buyers;
- Producers suffered from volatile or low prices; and
- Market participants encountered severe shortages/gluts resulting from marketing a highly perishable commodity.

The policy response resulted in the development of two major government activities that still function today: federal milk marketing orders and the Dairy Product Price Support Programme. While both FMMOs and the DPPSP have their roots in the 1930s and 1940s, the programmes have changed modestly over the years as the industry structure and markets changed. Two other components of Indian dairy policy are relatively new programmes. First, the 1985 farm bill established the Dairy Export Incentive Programme to counter foreign competitor subsidies.

Second, the Milk Income Loss Contract programme was established in the 2002 farm bill as a government payment for dairy farmers in times of low milk prices. Like Indian crop programmes, the MILC programme pays dairy producers when prices decline below a specified level. The following sections describe each of these four components and how they relate to the current market situation. Lower milk and dairy product prices since late 2008 have generated new programme activity. Purchasing dairy products last fall under the DPPSP; MILC payments were triggered beginning in February.

MILK INCOME LOSS CONTRACT PROGRAMME

The Milk Income Loss Contract (MILC) programme pays dairy farmers when farm milk prices fall below an established target price. Section 1506 of the 2008 farm bill extends authority for the MILC programme until September 30, 2012. This programme is similar to long-time subsidy programmes for crops that pay farmers when farm prices drop below certain levels. Farm Service Agency implements the MILC programme. Under MILC, participating dairy farmers nationwide are eligible for a federal payment whenever the minimum monthly market price for farm milk used for fluid consumption in Boston falls below $16.94 per cwt.

Eligible farmers then receive a payment equal to 45% of the difference between the $16.94 target price and the lower monthly market price. The payment quantity is limited to 2.985 million pounds of annual production. Since the inception of the MILC programme, large dairy farm operators have expressed concern that the payment limit has negatively affected their income. For larger farm operations, their annual production is well in excess of the limit, and any production in excess of that receives no federal payments. To address the issue of rising feed costs, the 2008 farm bill includes a provision that adjusts upward the $16.94 target price in any month when feed prices are above a certain threshold.

The law requires calculating monthly a National Average Dairy Feed Ration Cost based on a formula that currently uses to calculate feed costs. In any month that the average feed cost is above $7.35 per cwt., the $16.94 target price will be increased by 45% of the difference between the monthly feed cost and $7.35. For the latter half of 2007 and all of 2008, farm milk prices remained well above the MILC trigger price, precluding the need for any MILC payments.

However, milk prices have since declined below the trigger for MILC payments. The Class I Boston farm milk price for February 2009 was $13.97 per cwt. With the adjustment for feed costs raising the trigger to $17.33 per cwt., MILC payments were activated for the first time in two years at a payment rate of $1.51. The payment rate rose to $2.01 per cwt. in March. Given current prospects in the futures markets for milk, corn, and soybeans, payments are expected to continue during 2009, but at smaller rates.

Individual producers must select which month to begin receiving payments, based on their projection of potential payment rates and the possibility of hitting the production payment limit. As of October 26, 2009, total MILC payments distributed to date were $775 million. The timing of the payments has caused some concern for producers this spring.

While milk price data become available during the payment month, data needed for the feed cost adjustor are not available until publishes monthly average feed prices in *Agricultural Prices* at the end of the next month. Consequently, MILC payments for a particular month are not processed until two months later.

DAIRY PRODUCT PRICE SUPPORT PROGRAMME (DPPSP)

The Agricultural Act of 1949 first established a dairy price support programme by permanently requiring supporting the farm price of milk. Since 1949, Congress has regularly amended the programme, usually in the context of multiyear omnibus farm acts and budget reconciliation acts. Historically, the supported farm price for milk is intended to protect farmers from price declines that might force them out of business and to protect consumers from seasonal imbalances of supply and demand.

Commodity Credit Corporation (CCC) supports milk prices by its standing offer to purchase surplus nonfat dry milk, cheese, and butter from dairy processors. Whenever market prices fall to product support levels, processors generally make the business decision of selling surplus product to the government rather than to the marketplace. Consequently, the government purchase prices usually serve as a floor for the market price, which in turn indirectly supports the farm price of milk for all dairy farmers.

The effectiveness of the dairy price supports depends on removal of products from the market and placement into government storage. The Dairy Product Price Support Programme (DPPSP) as authorized by the 2008 farm bill requires purchasing products at the following minimum prices: block cheese, $1.13/lb.; barrel cheese, $1.10/lb.; butter, $1.05/lb.; and nonfat dry milk, $0.80/lb.

Under previous law, the support price for farm milk was statutorily set at $9.90 per cwt., and given the administrative authority to establish a combination of dairy product purchase prices that indirectly supported the farm price of milk at $9.90. Although the 2008 law does not specifically state that the overall support price is $9.90 per cwt, each of the mandated product prices in the law is equivalent to the existing product purchase prices, so farm milk prices effectively continue to be supported at $9.90.

In late 2008 and 2009, after several years of relative inactivity, the price support programme resumed purchases when dairy product prices approached support levels. As of September 11, 2009, estimated that it purchased 111 million pounds of nonfat dry milk under the programme in 2008 and expects to purchase 379 million pounds in 2009, along with small amounts of butter and cheese (including amounts exported under the Dairy Export Incentive Programme).

Total expenditures on the DPPSP were $223 million from October 1, 2008, through September 10, 2009. With an expected rise in milk and product prices next year, Forecasts only a small amount of butter to be purchased in 2010. Following heightened industry and congressional interest in taking action to boost milk prices for farmers, July 31, 2009, a temporary increase in price support for cheese and nonfat dry milk from August 2009 through October 2009.

Subsequently, the Senate approved an amendment to the Senate-passed FY2010 agriculture appropriations bill to increase Farm Service Agency funding by $350 million, ostensibly for an additional increase in dairy product price support levels. However, the conference agreement for the FY2010 Agriculture appropriations bill, which was enacted on October 21, 2009, provides for a different use of the funds.

MILK MARKETING ORDERS

Federal milk marketing orders (FMMOs) mandate minimum prices that processors must pay producers for milk depending on its end use. This compares with the MILC programme, which provides direct payments to producers, and the DPPSP, which buys surplus dairy products at specified minimum prices. The DPPSP serves as a price floor for products and under girds FMMO minimum milk prices. The farm price of approximately two-thirds of the nation's fluid milk is regulated under FMMOs.

Federal orders, which are administered Agricultural Marketing Service, were instituted in the 1930s to promote orderly marketing conditions by, among other things, applying a uniform system of classified pricing throughout the market. Some states, California for example, have their own state milk marketing regulations instead of federal rules. FMMOs also address how market proceeds are distributed among producers delivering milk to federal marketing order areas.

Producers are affected by two fundamental marketing order provisions: the classified pricing of milk according to its end use, and the pooling of receipts to pay all farmers a blend price. Federal orders regulate dairy handlers (processors) who sell milk or milk products within a defined marketing area by requiring them to pay not less than established minimum class prices for the Grade A milk they purchase from dairy producers, depending on how the milk is used.

This classified pricing system requires handlers to pay a higher price for milk used for fluid consumption than for milk used in manufactured dairy products such as yogurt, ice cream, and sour cream, cheese and butter and dry milk products. These differences between classes reflect the different market values for the products. Blend pricing allows all dairy farmers who ship to the market to pool their milk receipts and then be paid a single price for all milk based on order-wide usage (a weighted average of the four usage classes).

Paying all farmers a single blend price is seen as an equitable way of sharing revenues for identical raw milk directed to both the higher-valued fluid market and the lowervalued manufacturing market. Manufactured class prices are the same in all orders nationwide and are calculated monthly based on current market conditions for manufactured dairy products. The Class I price for milk used for fluid consumption varies from area to area.

Class I prices are determined by adding, to a monthly base price, a "Class I differential" that generally rises with the geographical distance from milk surplus regions in the Upper Midwest, the Southwest, and the West. Class I differential pricing is a mechanism designed to ensure adequate supplies of milk for fluid use at consumption centers. The supply of milk may come from local supplies or distant supplies, whichever is more efficient.

However, local dairy farmers are protected by the minimum price rule against lower-priced milk that might otherwise be hauled into their region. Over the years, dairy farmers have supported minimum prices afforded by FMMOs because they help balance marketing power traditionally held by processors. In contrast, dairy processors generally oppose them.

Mandated minimum prices, they say, do not allow for timely adjustments in a rapidly changing market and can leave product manufacturers in unprofitable situations. Also, they contend that the FMMO system distorts markets, saying fixed differentials contributed to high fluid milk prices last year.

DAIRY EXPORT INCENTIVE PROGRAMME (DEIP)

First authorized in 1985, the Dairy Export Incentive Programme (DEIP) provides cash bonus payments to Indian dairy exporters. The programme was initially intended to counter foreign—mostly European Union—dairy subsidies (while removing surplus dairy products from the market), but subsequent farm bill reauthorizations have added market development to the role of DEIP.

Payments since the program's inception have totaled $1.1 billion. The programme was active throughout the 1990s, peaking in 1993 with $162 million in bonuses. DEIP funding is a mandatory account provided through the Commodity Credit Corporation (CCC) borrowing authority from the Indian Treasury, rather than through annual appropriations bills. The programme had not been used since FY2004 until announced its reactivation on May 22, 2009. Indian dairy product exports made with DEIP bonuses are subject to annual limitations under the Uruguay Round Agreement of the World Trade Organization (WTO).

The limits are 68,201 metric tons of skim milk powder, 21,097 tons of butterfat, 3,030 tons of various cheeses, and 34 tons of other dairy products (quantity limits are on a July-June year). Total expenditures under WTO commitments are now capped at $117 million per year (value limits on a October-September year).

REQUESTS FOR ACTION

The reversal of market fortunes for dairy farmers since 2008 has prompted calls from dairy producer groups to address the situation. The National Milk Producers Federation (NMPF), the largest trade association representing milk producer cooperatives, wrote to the Secretary of Agriculture on January 8, 2009, asking the Department to take several steps to assist dairy producers. Subsequently, letters to the Secretary were also sent by Members of Congress.

On January 26, the International Dairy Foods Association, which represents dairy manufacturers and marketers, wrote to the Secretary, focusing only on ways to bolster demand for dairy products. The recommended industry actions deal also with revisions in the support programme to increase dairy product purchases by the government, specifically asking to be more flexible with the acceptable types and forms of eligible dairy products. Additional purchases are expected to spur domestic demand and slow the decline in prices.

The request from NMPF also included reactivation of the Dairy Export Incentive Programme to boost exports and remove excess inventory while helping exporters maintain business relationships developed in recent years. In early May 2009, the National Milk Producers Federation reiterated its request that the Indian government restart the Dairy Export Incentive Programme to help remove excess dairy products from the market. Subsequently, NMPF asked to increase the support prices of both cheese and nonfat dry milk. Another policy proposal is a dairy herd buyout to reduce the milk supply. A federal buyout has not been included in the NMPF requests, but it had been discussed in the agricultural media earlier in 2009. The industry currently operates a voluntary, producer-funded programme to remove dairy cows from milk production. Operated a federal dairy herd buyout programme in the mid-1980s.

In July 2009, the Subcommittee on Livestock, Dairy, and Poultry of the House Agriculture Committee held a series of hearings to review economic conditions facing the dairy industry. The subcommittee heard a range of opinions from the witnesses, with some asking for increased intervention in the form of higher support prices or supply management. Others argued that the industry would benefit if the government did nothing because inaction would more quickly bring supply in line with current demand.

APPLICATION OF SENSORY ANALYSIS TO DAIRY PRODUCTS

Following are specific examples of how QDA and/or other types of sensory analysis techniques have been applied to dairy research studies funded by Dairy Management Inc. ™ (DMI).

OPTIMIZATION OF CHEDDAR CHEESE TASTE IN MODEL CHEESE SYSTEMS

Cheddar cheese, the most popular natural cheese in the United States, has a very complex flavour system. While much information has accumulated during the past century, the industry is still seeking to fully understand Cheddar cheese flavour and has not been able to replicate it in model systems. The nonvolatile sensory attributes of Cheddar cheese are important for providing the character of Cheddar cheese.

While much work has been published on volatile components of Cheddar, far less is known on how nonvolatiles impact Cheddar flavour. Yang, a Kraft Foods researcher, and Vickers, at the Minnesota-South Dakota Dairy Foods Research Center, used sensory analysis to better understand the importance of nonvolatile compounds to Cheddar flavour.

A descriptive panel was trained to evaluate real and model cheese for a variety of taste attributes and for Cheddarlike taste. Sodium chloride, lactic acid, citric acid and monosodium glutamate were added to the model systems using mixture designs and response surface methodology to determine optimum levels of these components.

The three model systems investigated were:

- A dairy model system (containing milk isolate, anhydrous milk fat, water, annatto colour and chymosin);
- A nondairy model system (containing gelatin, gum acacia, modified starch, sunflower oil, water and annato colour); and
- A mozzarella base.

While the mozzarella base did present tastes, it was used because the other two model systems were too unlike Cheddar cheese (or any cheese) texture. Less sodium chloride and fewer acids were required to simulate the taste of mild Cheddar compared with aged Cheddar. None of the model systems mimicked the texture of real Cheddar. The researchers were able to match approximately, but not exactly, the taste of aged Cheddar using a mozzarella base.

Panelists generally rated the optimized taste in the dairy model system as more Cheddar-like than the optimized tastes in the nondairy model. Two methods were used to measure how close a sample was to the Cheddar concept. One was by measuring the similarity of the sample to either mild Cheddar cheese taste or aged Cheddar cheese taste on an unstructured scale. The left end of the line was marked with "not at all like Cheddar taste" and the right end was marked with "exactly like mild Cheddar taste" or "exactly like aged Cheddar taste."

The other method was by concept matching using an R-index methodology. For the mild group, the panel evaluated whether the samples were "MC" (mild Cheddar taste and sure), "MC?" (mild Cheddar taste but not sure), "N?" (no Cheddar taste but not sure) or "N" (no Cheddar taste and sure). For the aged group, "MC" and "MC?" were changed to "AC" (aged Cheddar taste and sure) and "AC?" (aged Cheddar taste but not sure). A model system for studying Cheddar taste should be as bland-tasting as possible, and also have a texture and composition similar to that of real Cheddar cheese. The characteristic flavour of a food depends not only on the flavour compounds present and their levels but also the rate and extent to which they are released in real time, which in turn are affected by the amounts of proteins, fat and other matrix components of the sample.

By using a trained descriptive analysis panel, Yang and Vickers were able to evaluate the flavour impact of several nonvolatile Cheddar cheese components (*i.e.*, salt, lactic acid, citric acid and monosodium glutamate) in model systems that attempted to mimic real Cheddar cheese. They achieved the most Cheddar-like taste with the mozzarella cheese base, and panelists found the optimal concentration of salts and acids in the model to be nearly indistinguishable from real Cheddar cheese.

CHEDDAR CHEESE AND POWDERED MILK LEXICONS

M. A. Drake, at the Southeast Dairy Foods Research Center, developed and validated a descriptive language for Cheddar cheese flavour. For the project, 240 representative cheese samples were collected. Fifteen individuals from industry, academia and government participated in roundtable discussions to generate descriptive flavour terms. A highly trained descriptive panel (n=11) refined the terms and identified references. Identification of chemical references was conducted with the assistance of K. Cadwallader at the University of Illinois. Instrumental analyses (gas chomatography/mass spectrometry, or GC/MS) were conducted to identify many flavour compounds that were responsible for specific flavours and off-flavours in Cheddar cheese. Twenty-four Cheddar cheeses were then presented to the panel to validate the proposed lexicon.

The panel differentiated the 24 Cheddar cheeses as determined by univariate and multivariate analysis of variance. Twenty-seven terms were identified to describe Cheddar flavour. Seventeen descriptive terms were observed in most Cheddar cheeses. Drake's standard sensory language for Cheddar cheese today is facilitating training and communication among different research groups. The Cheddar cheese lexicon is helping cheese-makers and cheese users accurately and consistently characterize the flavour of their cheese products and improve quality issues by measuring and controlling the presence of compounds that have been associated with flavour defects.

Following development of the Cheddar cheese lexicon, Drake developed a similar language to help characterize another food industry staple: dried dairy ingredients, including whey proteins and nonfat dry milk. Global production of nonfat dry milk tops 3.3 million tons and whey protein demand still outstrips production, which increases annually. A sensory lexicon describing the flavour of these ingredients helps dairy processors maximize the quality of these ingredients and allows food technologists to identify the exact attributes or flavour notes these ingredients contribute to formulations. Drake said she was surprised by the number of descriptive terms that the panel uncovered for application to the dried dairy ingredients lexicon.

The panel discovered 21 flavour terms that could be applied to milk powders. Examples included cooked/milky flavour, cake mix or vanillin, sweet and sour, earth and cereal. Each of these flavours was linked to a key aroma compound, many of which were identified by Drake and Cadwallader with GC/MS. For example, lactones tend to lend a sweet, coconut like flavour, while various free fatty acids can simulate a waxy flavour. Many different factors contribute to flavour variability. The source of the powder, processing/ packaging methods and materials, as well as storage time and conditions, are just a few.

The dried dairy ingredient lexicon, linking responsible chemical factors and causal agents, provides common ground for processors and ingredient suppliers to discuss ingredient characteristics. Figure shows how descriptive analysis results based on Drake's dried dairy ingredient lexicon can be analysed by PCA. This two-dimensional PCA plot shows the attribute variability among 27 low-heat skim milk powders less than three months old. Rehydrated milk powders are represented by numbers. PC1 = principal component 1; PC2 = principal component 2.

INDIAN DAIRY INDUSTRY

Dairy industry is of crucial importance to India. The country is the world.s largest milk producer, accounting for more than 13% of world.s total milk production. It is the world.s largest consumer of dairy products, consuming almost 100% of its own milk production. Dairy products are a major source of cheap and nutritious food to millions of people in India and the only acceptable source of animal protein for large vegetarian segment of Indian population, particularly among the landless, small and marginal farmers and women. Dairying has been considered as one of the activities aimed at alleviating the poverty and unemployment especially in the rural areas in the rain-fed and drought-prone regions. In India, about three-fourth of the population live in rural areas and about 38% of them are poor. In 1986-87, about 73% of rural households own livestock. Small and marginal farmers account for three-quarters of these households owning livestock, raising 56% of the bovine and 66% of the sheep population.

The National Sample Survey of 1993-94, livestock sector produces regular employment to about 9.8 million persons in principal status and 8.6 million in subsidiary status, which constitute about 5% of the total workforce. The progress in this sector will result in a more balanced development of the rural economy.

POLICY

The total amount of milk produced has more than tripled from 23 million tonnes back in 1973 to 74.70 million tonnes 26 years later in 1998. The tremendous rise in milk production is primarily the fallout of the dairy farming policy reflected in operation flood. Following the success of dairy farming policy, the Government has set up a dairy processing policy, reflected in the milk and milk products order. In addition, the Government uses a variety of import restrictions to protect its domestic dairy market.

MILK PROCESSING

The milk processing industry is small compared to the huge amount of milk produced every year. Only 10% of all the milk is delivered to some 400 dairy plants. A specific Indian phenomenon is the unorganised sector of milkmen, vendors who collect the milk from local producers and sell the milk in both, urban and non-urban areas, which handles around 65-70% of the national milk production.

In the organised dairy industry, the cooperative milk processors have a 60% market share. The cooperative dairies process 90% of the collected milk as liquid milk whereas the private dairies process and sell only 20% of the milk collected as liquid milk and 80% for other dairy products with a focus on value-added products.

DOMESTIC CONSUMPTION

The huge volume of milk produced in India is consumed almost entirely by the Indian population itself, in a 50-50 division between urban and nonurban areas. Increasingly, important consumers of the dairy industry are fast-food chains and food and non-food industries using dairy ingredients in a wide range of products.

TRADE

In spite of having largest milk production, India is a very minor player in the world market. India was primarily an import dependent country till early seventies. Most of the demand-supply gaps of liquid milk requirements for urban consumers were met by importing anhydrous milk fat/ butter and dry milk powders. But with the onset of Operation Flood Programme, the scenario dramatically changed and commercial imports of dairy products came to a halt except occasional imports of very small quantities. In the 1990s, India started exporting surplus dairy commodities, such as SMP, WMP, butter and ghee.

The Agricultural and Processed Food Products Export Development Authority (APEDA) regulated the export and import of dairy products till early 1990s. However, in the new EXIM Policy announced in April 2000, the Union Government has allowed free import and export of most dairy products. The major destinations for Indian dairy products are Bangladesh (23.1%), UAE (15.4%), US (15.6%) and Philippines (8.9%). In terms of products, SMP is the most important product accounting for about 63% of total export volume, followed by ghee and butter (11.7%) and WMP.

Export figures clearly demonstrate that the Indian dairy export is still in its infancy and the surpluses are occasional. Indigenous milk products and desserts are becoming popular with the ethnic population spread all over the world. Therefore, the export demand for these products will increase and hence, there is a great potential for export.

On the other hand, there has been a sharp increase in import of dairy products (especially milk powders) after trade liberalisation. As per the latest report of Foreign Trade Statistics of December 2004, the imports of dairy products (milk and cream) has reached a cumulative total of 22.145 million tonnes for the period April - March 2004, as compared to only 1473 million tonnes for the same period during the previous year. The main reasons for sharp rise in imports are huge export subsidies given by developed countries (mainly the US and EU).

India has recently concluded a tariff rate quota to deal with US, EU and Australia on imposing custom duty of 15% on imports of SMP and WMP upto 10,000 tonnes and 60% on imports beyond this level.

COMPETITIVENESS, COST OF PRODUCTION, PRODUCTIVITY OF ANIMALS ETC

The demand for quality dairy products is rising and production is also increasing in many developing countries. The countries which are expected to benefit most from any increase in world demand for dairy products are those which have low cost of production. Therefore, in order to increase the competitiveness of Indian dairy industry, efforts should be made to reduce cost of production. Increasing productivity of animals, better health care and breeding facilities and management of dairy animals can reduce the cost of milk production. The Government and dairy industry can play a vital role in this direction.

PRODUCTION, PROCESSING AND MARKETING INFRASTRUCTURE

If India has to emerge as an exporting country, it is imperative that we should develop proper production, processing and marketing infrastructure, which is capable of meeting international quality requirements. A comprehensive strategy for producing quality and safe dairy products should be formulated with suitable legal backup.

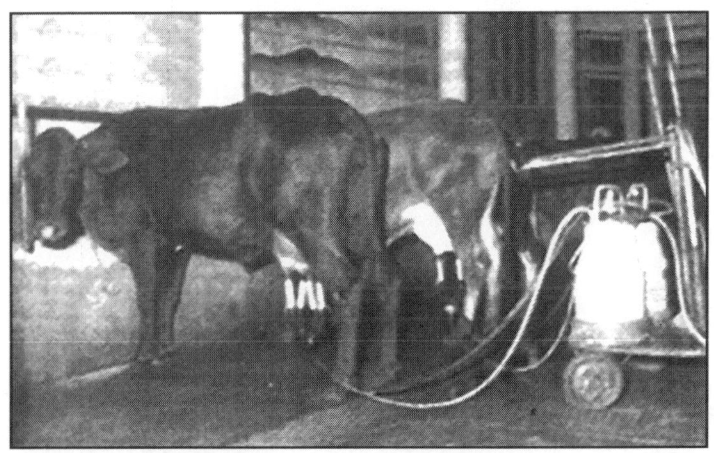

FOCUS ON BUFFALO MILK BASED SPECIALITY

Dairy industry in India is also unique with regard to availability of large proportion of buffalo milk. Thus, India can focus on buffalo milk based speciality products, like Mozzarella cheese, tailored to meet the needs of the target consumers.

IMPORT OF VALUE-ADDED PRODUCTS AND EXPORT OF LOWER VALUE PRODUCTS

With the trade liberalisation, despite the attempts of Indian companies to develop their product range, it could well be that in the future, more value-added products will be imported and lower value products will be exported. The industry has to prepare themselves to meet the challenges.

PROVISIONS OF SPS AND TBT

At the international level, we have to ensure that provisions of SPS and TBT are based on application of sound scientific principles and should become *defacto* barriers to trade.

OPERATION FLOOD ERA

Dairy sector witnessed a spectacular growth between 1971-1996, *i.e.* Operation Flood era. An integrated cooperative dairy development programme on the proven model of Anand pattern was implemented in three phases. The National Dairy Development Board was designated by the Government of India as the implementing agency. The major objective was to provide an assured market round the year to the rural milk producers and to establish linkage between rural milk production and urban market through modern technology and professional management.

Milk production grew from 21 million tonnes in 1970 to nearly 69 million tonnes in 1996 - more than three fold, at the compound growth rate of 4.5 per cent. Some ten million farmers were enrolled as members in about 73000 milk cooperative societies. By 1996, milk cooperatives attained a dominating share of the Indian dairy market - butter 96%, pasteurized liquid milk over 90%, milk powder 59% and processed cheese 85%. India was reckoned as a major threat in the dairying world.

In retrospect, it was by no means an easy task. Let us all salute the visionary and the architect of the white revolution in India, Dr. Verghese Kurien, without whose dynamic leadership all this may not have been possible. The dairy cooperative movement has continued to grow in the post Operation Flood-era.

NEW CHALLENGES OF GLOBALISATION AND TRADE LIBERALISATION - PERSPECTIVE 2010

The NDDB has recently put in place perspective 2010. to enable the cooperatives to meet the new challenges of globalization and trade liberalization. Like other major dairying countries of the world, the Indian cooperatives are expected to play a predominant role in the dairy industry in future as well.

However, India is in the mean time, attaining its past glory and is once again becoming.DOODH KA SAGAR.. But, what percentage of this SAGAR is handled by the cooperatives - just a little over 7%. Since liberalization of the dairy sector in 1991, a very large number of private sector companies/ firms have, despite MMPO, established dairy factories in the country.

The share of the total milk processing capacity by private sector is 44% of total installed capacity of 73 MLPD (Million Litres Per Day) in the country. Therefore, the total share of the organized sector, both cooperatives as well as the private sector is barely 12%. What is, therefore, disquieting is that as much as 88% share of the total milk production is commanded by the unorganized sector - who specializes in selling sub-standard, unpasteurised milk more often than not adulterated with harmful chemicals. Besides, growth in milk production is likely to continue at the present rate of 4.4% in the near future.

Who is going to handle this incremental milk? We must bear in mind is both income and price what we must bear in mind both income and price elasticity account for approximatily 15% of the total expenditure of food. Demand for milk, at current rate of income growth is estimated to grow at 7% per annum. Interestingly, demand for milk is expected to grow steadily over the next two decades as the low income rural and urban families who have higher expenditure elasticity would also increase their income due to new economic environment. Let us now look at some other economic indicators.

The World Bank, India is the fourth largest economy in the world going by the purchasing power parity estimates. Further, India has been identified as among the first 10 emerging markets in the world. India has the vastest domestic market in the world with over one billion consumers - a majority of whom are vegetarians with drinking of milk as habit. The untapped potential of the dairy sector is immense and opportunity to set up a new dairy venture is great.

In the works of Dr. Amrita Patel, Chairperson, NDDB, there is enough place under the scheme for both private and cooperative sectors. Notwithstanding the above potential it is cautioned that, entering dairy sector is not going to be a cakewalk.

CEASE

Globalization and Liberalization are the Mantras of the new economy today, which is now on the fast track. Industrial production is rapidly moving forward. The dairy industry is no exception. With the World Trade Organization (WTO) coming into effect, from 01 April 2001 and the imports and exports getting liberalized in the global economy, the dairy industry, which includes dairy products, faces both an opportunity for growth as well as a threat for its growth.

There is no doubt that there is tremendous scope for the growth of the dairy industry in the new millennium. The product mix of world dairy trade is likely to shift further towards cheese. This has been developed in the world markets. As the market opens up, consumption trends associated with these markets will have increasing influence on the world trade. Whole milk powder is likely to continue to be a substantial beneficiary and growth substiantially in the middle eastern countries.

As standards of living in the importing country rises, exporting countries will increasingly concentrate on whole milk powder and cheese with the assistance of butter and skimmed milk powder. There is vast potential for the export of dairy products, the cost of milk production in India being the lowest. The major factor influencing production of bye products is the newer uses that may be developed through R & D support. Milk proteins are being utilized increasingly replacing animal and vegetable proteins in special bakery products and instant foods. Through the application of membrane proven process, milk proteins isolates are being produced.

These are being utilized for ice milk mixes and other such applications. Most of the dairy plants in the Government, Cooperatives and Private Sector produce almost similar dairy products like varieties of milk, butter, ghee, skimmed milk powder and whole milk powder. There are 7 large-scale cheese manufacturers and 14 manufacturers are producing infant foods and malted milks. There is immense scope for the broadening of the products range and some of the products, which are likely to have considerable demand in the coming decade, have been identified.

The cheese market, presently valued at about Rs.80 crore is growing at about 9% annually. There are more than thousand varieties of cheese, which have been listed out of which cheddar; mozzarella, gouda and processed cheeses are being manufactured in India. Pizza is becoming a very popular item in the market.

This segment alone commands 5% of the share in the cheese market and other area is fermented milk products. Dahi even though is a Rs.15000 crore market, the share of the organized sector is only around 10%. This product has immense potential for growth. Varieties of milk shakes are also increasing wherein milk and fruit pulp are mixed in different proportions to produce different beverages.

Some of the milk and fruit based beverages which are likely to have demand are a combination of milk with mango, banana, sapota, strawberry, papaya, etc. Some of these beverages can also be produced in dehydrated form and can be an excellent health food. There are varieties in traditional milk based sweets, manufactured in the country. The market size is around Rs.12000 crore. However, there are very few nationally known brands in this category.

Many of the organized dairies are involved in the manufacture of varieties of milk based sweets: pedha, paneer, shirkhand, etc. These are now restricted to certain areas only but can go national. As the world is getting integrated into one market, quality certification is becoming essential in the market.

However, there are very few plants in the country, which have successfully obtained ISO, HACCP certification. There is scope for introducing newer plants adopting newer processes by the dairy industry in the country. Packaging of dairy products is also another very promising area.

NRI and overseas investments can take place in manufacturing dairy processing equipment, fruit packaging equipment and equipments for biotechnology related dairy industry.

2

Dairy Management

The management of a dairy farm, or any other small business, differs in some respects from managing a large corporation. In contrast to the large firm, the dairy farmer usually sets his/her own goals, provides the management of the business and performs all or part of the labour. This makes it difficult to separate the management from the labour. Both of these tasks may also be performed at the same time.

For example, the planning of today.s actions may take place while milking the cows. When doing so, there is always a risk that the immediate need of labour will place the management in a secondary role, with management decisions postponed and delayed. The recommendation is therefore to dedicate some time, on a regularly basis, for "pure" management.

All business management, regardless of the size of the firm, involves decision making and supervising. A good manager is usually characterised by making good decisions. All decisions made by a manager might not be satisfactory, but the more decisions that are made in an informed manner, the more likely we are to produce a positive outcome.

AN OVERVIEW OF DAIRY MANAGEMENT PROGRAMME

The Dairy Management Programme applies basic concepts in animal husbandry, crop production, and business management to real-life situations. Through classes, lectures, numerous field trips, laboratory exercises, total farm analysis projects, and interaction with industry leaders and faculty members, students learn how good management decisions can lead to profitable dairying. Most important, the programme demonstrates that education in the ever-changing dairy industry continues beyond the SUNY Morrisville experience.

Students in the Dairy Management programme visit, analyse, and evaluate progressive dairy farms and agri-service operations and attend a variety of university/extension and industry- sponsored conferences. They interact with leading industry representatives and teaching, research, and extension personnel. Throughout these activities, the Dairy Management

Programme challenges students to focus on personal and career development, achieving personal and career objectives, and the opportunity to challenge and directly apply concepts learned in class and work experiences to the dairy industry.

The contributions from northeastern dairy producers and associated industries are largely responsible for the programmes success. The Dairy Management Programme emphasizes flexibility in course selection. More than two-thirds of course selections can be electives, allowing students to tailor their education to their specific interest, individual development, and career goals.

To assure a well-rounded education suited to individual needs, dairy management students choose a mix of basic, particle, and highly specialized courses. In many classes, students apply the principles of dairy management to particular learning situations. The Dairy Management Programme offers a range of courses students can select from:

Dairy Management:

- Applied cattle nutrition
- Dairy Breeding and Reproduction
- Dairy cattle production and management
- Dairy herd health
- Dairy herd management
- Dairy production seminar

Farm and Business Management:

- Business management
- Computer applications
- Farm analysis and decision making
- Farm business management
- Farm finance
- Financial management
- Human resource management

Crop Production:

- Forage crops
- Grain crops
- Soils and GPS Technology
- Weed science
- Pasture Management.

SCOPE FOR DAIRY FARMING

The total milk production in the country for the year 2001-02 was estimated at 84.6 million metric tonnes. At this production, the per capita availability was to be 226 grams per day against the minimum requirement of 250 grams per day as recommended by ICMR. Thus, there is a tremendous scope/potential for increasing the milk production. The population of breeding cows and buffaloes in milk over 3 years of age was 62.6 million and 42.4 million, respectively (1992 census). Central and State Governments are giving considerable financial assistance for creating infrastructure facilities for milk production. The nineth plan outlay on Animal Husbandry and Dairying was ₹ 2345 crores.

NABARD FOR DAIRY FARMING

NABARD is an apex institution for all matters relating to policy, planning and operation in the field of agricultural credit. It serves as an apex refinancing agency for the institutions providing investment and production credit. It promotes development through formulation and appraisal of projects through a well organised Technical Services Department at the Head Office and Technical Cells at each of the Regional Offices.

Loan from banks with refinance facility from NABARD is available for starting dairy farming. For obtaining bank loan, the farmers should apply to the nearest branch of a commercial or co-operative Bank in their area in the prescribed application form which is available in the branches of financing banks. The Technical Officer attached to or the Manager of the bank can help/ give guidance to the farmers in preparing the project report to obtain bank loan.

For dairy schemes with very large outlays, detailed reports will have to be prepared. The items of finance would include capital asset items such as purchase of milch animals, construction of sheds, purchase of equipments etc. The feeding cost during the initial period of one/two months is capitalised and given as term loan.

Facilities such as cost of land development, fencing, digging of well, commissioning of diesel engine/pumpset, electricity connections, essential servants' quarters, godown, transport vehicle, milk processing facilities etc. can be considered for loan. Cost of land is not considered for loan. However, if land is purchased for setting up a dairy farm, its cost can be treated as party's margin upto 10% of the total cost of project.

SCHEME FORMULATION FOR BANK LOAN

A Scheme can be prepared by a beneficiary after consulting local technical persons of State animal husbandry department, DRDA, SLPP etc., dairy co-operative society/union/federation/commercial dairy farmers. If possible, the beneficiaries should also visit progressive dairy farmers and government/ military/agricultural university dairy farm in the vicinity and discuss the profitability of dairy farming. A good practical training and experience in dairy farming will be highly desirable. The dairy co-operative societies established in the villages as a result of efforts by the Dairy Development Department of State Government and National Dairy Development Board would provide all supporting facilities particularly marketing of fluid milk. Nearness of dairy farm to such a society, veterinary aid centre, artificial insemination centre should be ensured.

There is a good demand for milk, if the dairy farm is located near urban centre. The scheme should include information on land, livestock markets, availability of water, feeds, fodders, veterinary aid, breeding facilities, marketing aspects, training facilities, experience of the farmer and the type of assistance available from State Government, dairy society/union/federation.

The scheme should also include information on the number of and types of animals to be purchased, their breeds, production performance, cost and other relevant input and output costs with their description. Based on this, the total cost of the project, margin money to be provided by the beneficiary, requirement of bank loan, estimated annual expenditure, income, profit and loss statement, repayment period, etc. can be worked out and shown in the Project report. A format developed for formulation of dairy development schemes.

SCRUTINY OF SCHEMES BY BANKS

The scheme so formulated should be submitted to the nearest branch of bank. The bank's officers can assist in preparation of the scheme for filling in the prescribed application form. The bank will then examine the scheme for its technical feasibility and economic viability.

Technical Feasibility—this would briefly include:

- Nearness of the selected area to veterinary, breeding and milk collection centre and the financing bank's branch.
- Availability of good quality animals in nearby livestock market. The distribution of important breeds of cattle and buffaloes. The reproductive and productive performance of cattle and buffalo breeds.
- Availability of training facilities.
- Availability of good grazing ground/lands.
- Green/dry fodder, concentrate feed, medicines etc.
- Availability of veterinary aid/breeding centres and milk marketing facilities near the scheme area.

Economic Viability—this would briefly include:

- *Unit Cost*: The average unit cost of dairy animals for some of the States.
- Input cost for feeds and fodders, veterinary aid, breeding of animals, insurance, labour and other overheads.

- Output costs *i.e.* sale price of milk, manure, gunny bags, male/female calves, other miscellaneous items etc.
- Income-expenditure statement and annual gross surplus.
- Cash flow analysis.
- Repayment schedule (*i.e.* repayment of principal loan amount and interest).

Other documents such as loan application forms, security aspects, margin money requirements etc. are also examined. A field visit to the scheme area is undertaken for conducting a techno-economic feasibility study for appraisal of the scheme. Model economics for a two animal unit and mini dairy unit with ten buffaloes.

ALTERNATIVE WASTE MANAGEMENT SYSTEMS

A Dairyman has many choices in designing and operating in modern dairy. Figure presents the basic options for housing cows, the collection of manure, the pretreatment and treatment of manure, the post treatment and final disposal. Each of the options must be judged by the goals of the Dairymen to maintain animal health, recover nutrients, minimize odours, produce energy, and reduce operation and maintenance costs. The following paragraphs summarize the advantages and disadvantages of each alternative. The better alternatives are shaded in the accompanying figure.

EXISTING MANURE HANDLING

Existing manure handling consists of screening, and gravity separating the solids for subsequent composting. The compost produced by existing systems can either be exported or used for bedding material. Up to 70 per cent of the phosphorus nutrients can be diverted from the farm through the use of the existing solids removal processes.

However, the conventional solids handling process does not reduce the quantity of material to be handled. It simply separates the material into a solid fraction that can be stacked and hauled and a liquid fraction that can be placed in a holding pond for the required 180-day detention time with a minimum of sedimentation.

The system does not control odours since the liquid fraction containing large quantities of organic acids is discharged to an open lagoon for further decomposition. The system does not produce any energy. Large quantities of energy are consumed in separating the solids and subsequent composting. The operation and maintenance costs are high but the capital costs are low. Overall the commonly used manure handling system does not pay for self nor meet the environmental goals of the Dairymen.

HOUSING

This type of housing establishes the quantity of manure that can be collected economically. Free stall barns permit the collection of 85 per cent of the manure. The remaining 15 per cent is normally deposited in the milk parlor where it is collected through a flush system. In corral systems only 40 to 50 per cent of the manure can be collected from the feed lanes, which are either scraped or flushed.

Manure deposited in the open lot portion of the corral is normally collected once or twice a year. While in the open lot, the manure is degraded both aerobically and anaerobically depending on the moisture content. The degradation process produces odours and greenhouse gases that are discharged to the atmosphere. There is little net energy available from the manure after it has remained in the open lot for 8 to 12 months.

The free stall system is better for animal health since it provides the greatest separation between manure and cow. Since the free stall system provides an opportunity to collect the maximum amount of manure it also provides the opportunity to recover most of the phosphorus nutrients and generate the most energy.

Free stall barns are more expensive to construct than corral or open lot systems. The operation and maintenance cost of the free stall barn is less than corral or open lot systems. Overall the free stall system provides the best manure processing option.

COLLECTION

Manure can be collected by flush, scrape, or vacuum collection. Scrape and vacuum collection systems have a higher capital and operation and maintenance costs. Flush systems have the lowest capital and operation and maintenance costs. Flush systems also remove substantially all of the manure. The vacuum and scrape systems do not clean the barns as efficiently as a flush system.

Flush systems significantly increase the quantity of waste that must be processed through an energy recovery system. The increased quantity of cold, dilute manure can result in much larger treatment facilities and lower temperatures within the anaerobic digesters. Flush systems have also been associated with severe odour problems.

Wet flush aisles promote bacterial activity leading to organic degradation and the generation of odours. The large quantity of untreated wastewater that is discharged to open ponds is an additional source of odourous degradation products.

The problems associated with flush systems can be mitigated to a great extent by flushing once a day. By flushing the aisles once a day the volume of flush water will be significantly reduced such that it can be heated and effectively treated with the anaerobic contact process. Flushing once a day will also provide the opportunity for the aisles to dry, eliminating the generation of odours from open-air microbial degradation.

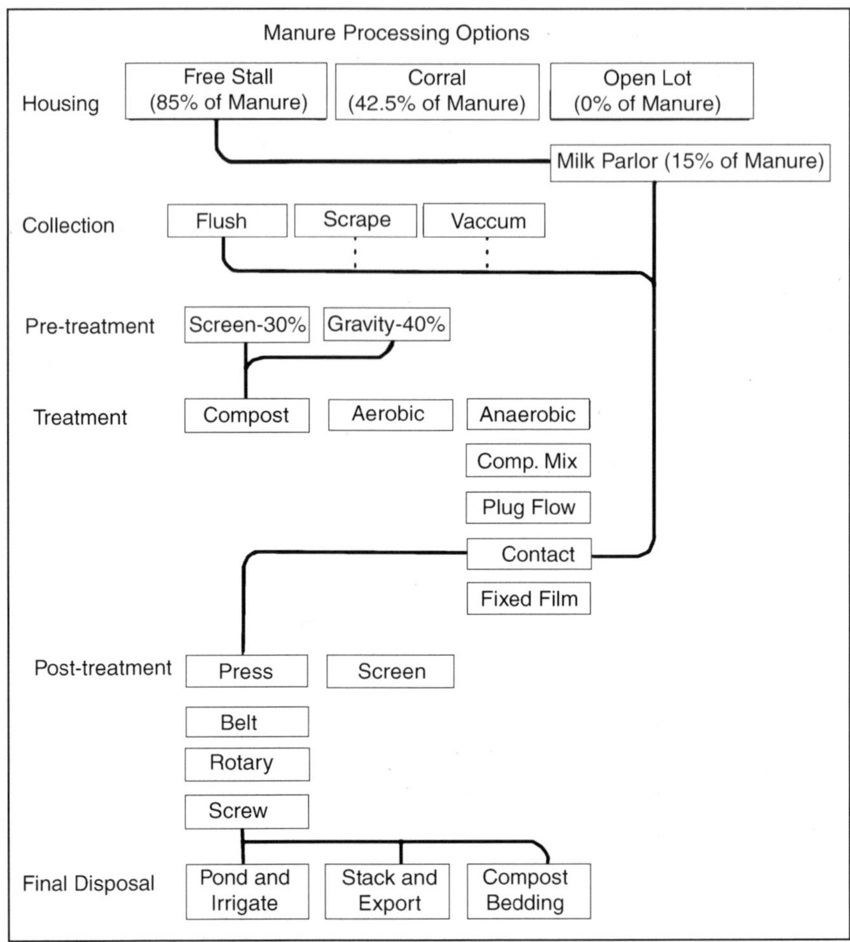

Fig. Manure Processing Alternatives

Scrape and vacuum systems provide a concentrated waste flow, which minimizes the size of down-stream treatment facilities. The choice of which collection system to use will be based on economics since all collection systems, if properly operated, provide an opportunity to recover nutrients, enhance animal health, and minimize odours.

Scrape and vacuum systems have a higher capital, and operation and maintenance costs. The downstream treatment costs however are lower. Flush systems have a lower capital and operating cost but the downstream treatment costs are higher.

TREATMENT

A wide variety of pretreatment and treatment options exist. Typically pretreatment consists of screening and gravity separation of the solids. The recovered solids are allowed to drain and may be subsequently composted for animal bedding. Stacked solids are applied to land once or twice a year depending on the phosphorus land application limitations. The stacked solids may also be exported from the site.

Many nutrient management plans require 100 per cent export of the stacked solids. Unfortunately, pretreatment is not beneficial for energy recovery since a significant portion of the solids that can be converted to gas are removed through the pretreatment activity. Since existing pretreatment processes produce odour, are expensive to operate and maintain, and severely impact potential energy generation it is recommended that pretreatment not be used before anaerobic digestion.

Excess sands, silts, and fibres should be removed as part of the anaerobic digestion process. Aerobic treatment is an effective alternative for reducing odour. Aerobic treatment consumes large quantities of energy and has higher operating and maintenance costs. Aerobic treatment however, has lower capital costs than anaerobic digestion, and it is less effective in recovering nutrients than anaerobic digestion.

Anaerobic digestion is the most beneficial treatment option. The contact process is the most effective anaerobic treatment process. Both the fix film and plug flow processes are concentration limited. The contact process can handle a wide variety of solids concentrations. All of the manure from the milk barn to the free stall can be processed through the contact process. In addition to processing a larger percentage of manure, a greater percentage of the solids will be converted to energy. It provides greater load flexibility, allowing dairymen to process other waste materials for additional gas production.

The contact process requires little operation and maintenance. It can be an automated process. Both the contact process and completely mixed processes can handle sand and floating fibres. The contact process and completely mixed digester use more energy than the plug flow process. However, a greater percentage of the solids will be converted to energy. The plug flow process is less expensive than either the contact process or the completely mixed reactor.

The contact process however, uses less energy than the completely mixed reactor and has a much lower capital costs. All mesophilic anaerobic treatment processes are effective in reducing or eliminating odours. All anaerobic processes can sequester most of the nutrients. Since the contact process produces a relatively clear effluent, additional nutrients can be removed. All anaerobic processes produce energy.

The contact process will provide the greatest solids retention time leading to a higher energy yield. The plug flow process has the lowest capital costs followed by the contact process. The plug flow reactor also has the lowest operation and maintenance costs. The contact process will have the highest operation and maintenance costs because of the reagents that are used in the biomass separation process. Overall, the contact process offers a greatest benefit.

POST-TREATMENT

The final product from the treatment process consisting of undigested solids, biomass, and inorganic precipitates must be separated such that the solids containing a majority of the nutrients can be stored, stacked, and exported if required. The post-treatment process fulfills the same need as conventional pretreatment process. However, after passing through an anaerobic digestion process the solids are substantially reduced and the nutrients are concentrated.

A number of options exist for post-treatment. They include screens and a variety of presses. The screw press requires the least amount of operation and maintenance. Consequently, the recommended post-treatment is to pass the digested solids through a screw press, separate the solids from the liquid, and either export the solids or compost them for bedding. The contact process provides more effective liquid solids separation. If the contact process were used, the liquid from the screw press would be recycled to the contact separator. The clean particle free effluent would be discharged from the contact process separator to the storage pond for irrigation.

FINAL DISPOSAL

The final products consisting of a liquid stream and a solid stream must be disposed in accordance with the nutrient management plan. The liquid stream will contain inorganic nitrogen as ammonia and a small amount of phosphorus. The solid stream will contain organic nitrogen and a vast majority of the phosphorus. Both the solid and liquid streams will be fully stabilized and odourless. The solids can be stacked for export or composted for bedding.

MEMBRANE TECHNOLOGY IN DAIRY PROCESSING

Membrane filtration technologies, such as ultra filtration and reverse osmosis, are capable of the molecular fractionation of fluids. Milk is ideally suited for processing by membrane filtration because it is a fluid consisting largely of water, lactose, butterfat, and protein molecules. Separation at the molecular level means that butterfat, lactose, and protein can be isolated from one other. Through the use of cellulose filters and high pressure pumps, membrane technologies take the two-dimensional concept of the venerable cream separator (*i.e.*, milk in, cream and skim out) into the third dimension and even beyond.

Membrane technologies have brought about substantial change in the dairy industry. However, because of the rapid pace of innovation many new dairy products created by membrane technology have not yet gained effective consumer demand. As David Hettinga, Vice President and Chief Technical Office of Land O'Lakes, stated, "one of the problems with this technology is we have a product or a technology chasing the market". The purpose of this research is to introduce readers to the membrane process and then attempt to assess the consumer demand for a few such new products. The traditional dairy manufacturing paradigm has been to separate whole milk into cream and skim milk using a centrifuge.

The skim milk is then John W. Siebert is an associate professor and Alejandro Lalor is a graduate research assistant, Department of Agricultural Economics, Texas A&M University, College Station, TX 77843-2124. Sung-Yong Kim is a research associate at the Korea Rural Economic Institute. The authors wish to thank the Southwest Dairy Farmers of Sulphur Springs, TX and Texas A&M University for their support of this research.

The authors also with to thank two anonymous reviewers as well as Dr. Sefa Koseoglu. often evaporated to produced condensed skim. Most dairy products are made using various combinations of milk, cream, skim, and condensed skim. The shortfall of this traditional technology approach is that protein and lactose (the main ingredients of skim) are bound to one another. A key value of membrane technology is that it enables a separation of these two ingredients.

With membrane technology, protein, butterfat, and lactose can be used to manufacture dairy products more directly. Should sales of milk increase due to the development of new products, total dairy-farmer income would be likely to increase as well. With approximately 590,000,000 pounds of nonfat dry milk currently in government warehouses, research into demand expansion remains a high priority for dairy farmers.

TECHNOLOGY REVIEW

The most widely accepted dairy applications of membrane technology have been cost-reducing in nature. For example, most modern cheese plants use membrane technology to extract valuable protein isolates from the whey stream. Whey-protein concentrate is currently an important source of income to all large cheese makers. The portion of a modern cheese plant devoted to whey-product manufacturing and storage can be almost as large as that devoted to cheese. Due solely to the ability of membrane technology to extract protein from whey, whey is no longer a disposal problem-it is now a profit center.

In New Zealand, membrane technology is used to produce a powdered dairy product consisting largely of butterfat and protein. Due to its functionality, this ingredient-called dry ultrafiltered milk or milk protein concentrate (MPC)-can be used to make cheese. MPC is imported to the United States for the purpose of boosting cheese-plant yields. In this regard it is a substitute for domestic nonfat dry milk, and for this reason has been viewed as a threat to the U.S. milk price support programme. Dairy farmers in remote regions of the United States have used membrane technology to reduce raw milk transportation costs. At the farm, ultrafiltration is being used to remove lactose and water from milk.

Also at the farm, reverse osmosis is being used to remove water from milk. Membrane technology will likely replace the traditional cheese vat in the future. The traditional cheese vat is a large kettle (*e.g.*, 5,000-gallon capacity) that uses calf rennet, heat, and agitation in order to yield cheese curd and whey from milk.

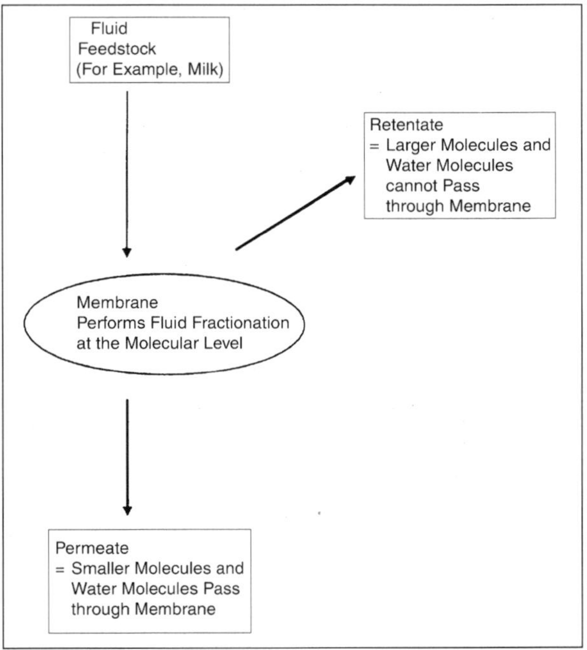

Fig. Pumped over a Membrane. This Causes Fractionation at the Molecular Level.

The Membrane Filtration Process is Initiated by a Fluid being The curds are then pressed into blocks of cheese and aged. Membrane technology has the potential to produce cheese by molecular separation of lactose from the butterfat and protein. This would allow the design of equipment that accepts milk as an input and produces liquid cheese and whey as outputs.

The liquid cheese stream could then be poured into forms for hardening and aging. The objective of this research was to determine if membrane technology has the potential to create new commercial dairy products for direct purchase by consumers. The key questions investigated concern the capabilities of membrane technology, the economics of producing new consumer products, and the consumer market potential of any such new products. Before new consumer dairy products such as these can be found and evaluated, the technology must first be understood. Figure provides a membrane technology diagram.

This figure shows a fluid being pumped across a membrane under high pressure. Smaller particles pass through the membrane and are termed permeate. Larger particles cannot pass through and are denoted as retentate. The membrane filtration process can be performed at progressive levels of molecular selectivity. Reverse Osmosis (RO) is a term denoting a very fine membrane-filtration process.

To understand filtration in its application to dairy, consider that raw milk consists largely of water, lactose, butterfat, protein, and minerals. Applying RO to milk would thus produce a permeate which consists mainly of water and a retentate which consists of water, lactose, butterfat, protein, and minerals.

Ultrafiltration (UF) allows somewhat larger molecules to pass through the membrane than does RO. In this case, not only water but also lactose molecules will pass through the membrane. Thus, applying UF to milk produces both a permeate consisting of water and lactose and a retentate consisting of water, lactose, butterfat, and protein.

EQUIPMENT INDUSTRY SURVEY

To gain an understanding of the current status of membrane technology in the dairy industry, the authors made an initial survey of the membraneequipment industry. Our objective was to learn about potential new consumer dairy product applications of membrane technology. We contacted nineteen firms involved in various combinations of equipment manufacturing, facilities and/or equipment design, and equipment installation.

The authors found these nineteen firms through advertisements in the dairy trade press, through suppliers listed in the International Dairy Foods Association Membership Directory, and through attendees at a Texas A&M University Short Course on Membrane Technology. The authors do not know what percentage of the dairy membrane manufacturing industry was contacted through their survey but the percentage is believed to be high, as all known firms were contacted. Also, the supplier industry is relatively concentrated. Thus, despite the small number of firms involved, this sample should be considered representative of the dairy membrane equipment industry during 1999.

The firms contacted served the entire United States. Nine of the thirteen firms were headquartered in either Minnesota or Wisconsin. Several of the firms were subsidiaries of international companies. Thirteen of the nineteen firms contacted participated, a response rate of 68 per cent. The responding firms viewed membrane technology as advancing rapidly in terms of fractionation selectivity, methods, and reliability. Technological advances usually originate in Australia, New Zealand, or Western Europe. Consequently, U.S. firms often employ technology after it has proven its value elsewhere. Two dairy industry forces, when taken in combination, likely explain why New Zealand, Europe and Australia have historically taken the lead in the development of membrane technologies.

First, the U.S. Food and Drug Administration has restricted dairy manufacturers from using membrane technology in the production of traditional dairy products such as cheese. The FDA must approve on a firm-by-firm and case-by-case basis that the product manufactured with membrane technology has no compositional or organoleptic differences when compared to a product made in full conformance with regulatory Standards of Identity.

Second, the U.S. pricesupport programme only offers stand-by purchasing authority for cheese, butter, and nonfat dry milk; therefore, membrane-based dairy products such as milk protein concentrate powder would not qualify for the programme. As a result, U.S. dairy-industry investment is often made in traditional production technology in order to reduce exposure to price risk. Manufacturers were asked about the future of membrane technology. The consensus was that byproduct extraction at the dairy processing plant would be the main area for the future impact of membrane technology.

Specifically, eight of twelve manufacturers who responded to a question concerning whether the biggest impact of membrane technology would be at the processing plant or at the farm felt the biggest impact would be at the plant. Ten of eleven manufacturers who responded to a question concerning whether the biggest impact of membrane technology would be upon dairy products or dairy by-products (*e.g.,* on cheese as opposed to cheese whey) felt that the biggest impact would be in the by-product area.

THREE NEW PRODUCT CONCEPTS

Seven of ten manufacturers who responded to a question concerning whether membrane technology would be better at producing new dairy products or existing dairy products felt that the biggest impact would be upon new products.

The following new consumer product ideas were gleaned from the membrane industry:

- Protein-fortified, 2% reduced-fat milk can be made by a combination of whole milk, skim milk, and skim milk retentate. This product recipe had 18 per cent more protein than regular 2% reduced-fat milk without increased lactose levels.
- High-protein, low-lactose ice cream can be made by a combination of sweet cream, skim milk retentate, and nonfat dry milk. The desirability of this product results from substituting protein for

lactose. The recipe evaluated had 48 per cent more protein and 32 per cent less lactose than regular ice cream.

- Nonfat yogurt can be made with more protein and therefore less stabilizers. This product can be made by a combination of skim milk, skim milk retentate, and nonfat dry milk. The particular product recipe evaluated had 15 per cent more protein and 21 per cent less lactose than regular nonfat yogurt.

These products all substitute protein for lactose. The addition of protein can bring more product body, better mouthfeel, and higher product viscosity. The reduction of lactose brings little in the way of reduced sweetness as lactose has only onesixth to one-third the sweetness of sucrose.

Any such loss of sweetness can easily be countered by the addition of a small amount of sugar. Focusing just on yogurt, the major benefits are two-fold. First, less product separation will occur. In other words, less liquid whey will form and separate from the yogurt curd. Second, if yogurt is made using non-dairy stabilizers, then product label-purity is compromised.

The non-dairy stabilizers which might be used for this purpose could include any of the following ingredients:

- Starch,
- Pectin,
- Gelatin,
- Vegetable gums (carboxymethyl cellulose,
- Locust bean, or guar), or seaweed gums (such as alginates or carrageenans).

To understand the important role of protein and why increased protein content is beneficial, consider the properties of two well-known dairy products, cheese and butter. The major difference between cheese and butter is that butter contains 80 per cent milkfat, while cheddar cheese contains approximately 32 per cent milkfat and 31 per cent protein.

Even though butter contains less moisture than cheddar cheese, it remains a softer product. In addition, butter's weak texture makes it unsuitable for eating out of hand while a substantial amount of cheese is eaten in this fashion. Finally, even though many different varieties of butter can be made, only one basic style is popular. In contrast, many different styles of hard cheese exist because protein is capable of conveying the tastes associated with different starter cultures and manufacturing methods. Can substituting protein for lactose reduce lactose levels enough to be beneficial to lactose intolerant consumers?

The enzyme lactase is responsible for the digestion of lactose in the small intestine. Individuals whose bodies produce insufficient lactase are said to be lactose intolerant. The severity of such lactose intolerance can vary from one individual to another.

For individuals with only mild intolerance, the reductions achieved by a proteinfor-lactose substitution could be beneficial. This would be particularly true for yogurt, which contains other beneficial bacteria to aid digestion (U.S. National Institutes of Health). To make each of these products, skim milk retentate (SMR) is needed.

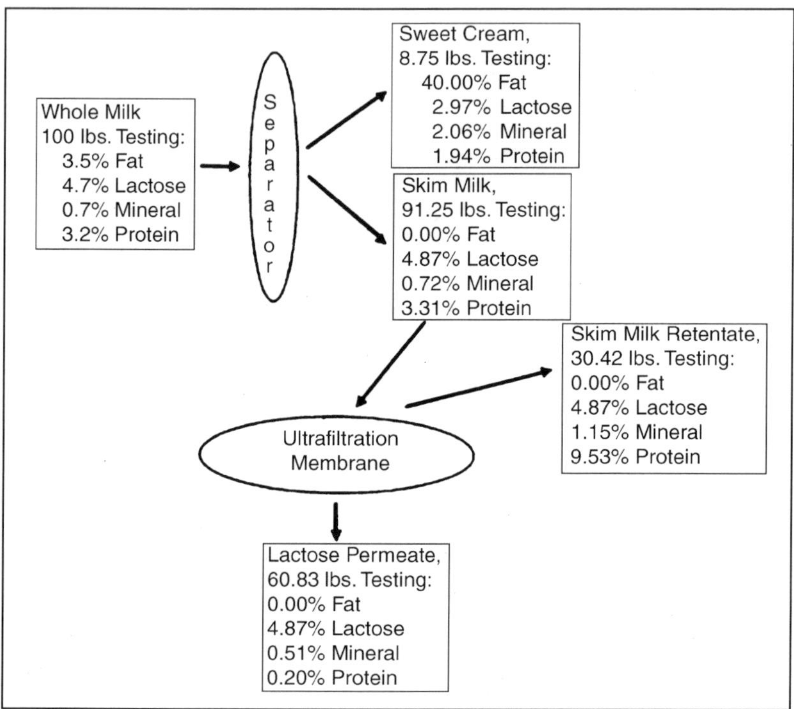

Fig. Flow and Mass Balance for the Manufacture of Skim Milk Retentate, the Building Block of New Dairy Products

SMR is produced by ultrafiltering skim milk to create a fluid isolate with a high protein-to-lactose ratio. As a result, SMR can reduce lactose content while increasing protein content.

This means that protein can be substituted for lactose, improving the nutritional profile of dairy foods as well as their taste and texture. Further, it means that protein can substituted for the texture, functionality, and mouthfeel of butterfat.

COST OF CONCEPTS

U.S. dairy processing firms evaluate the purchase of new equipment very carefully due to budgetary constraints. Detailed system-cost information was provided by four equipment manufacturers and is shown in Table.

Table. Estimated Costs to Manufacture New Dairy Products

Characteristic	High-Protein 2% Butterfat Fluid Milk	High-Protein, Lower-Lactose Ice Cream Mix	High-Protein Nonfat Yogurt Mix
System Production/Day	375,000 Ibs. milk	200,000 lbs. mix	100,000 Ibs. mix
System Capital Cost[a]	$455,000.00	$1,240,000.00	$455,000.00
10-Yr. Depreciation (312 day basis)	$145.83/day	$397.44/day	$145.83/day
Operating Cost[a]	$675.00/day	$2,025.00/day	$675.00/day
Daily Capital and Operating Cost	$820.83/day	$2,422.44/day	$820.83/day
Capital and Operating Cost per Unit	$0.22/cwt.	$1.21/cwt.	$0.82/cwt.
Added Milk Cost[b]	$1.62/cwt.	$3.59/cwt.	$1.40/cwt.
Total Added Cost	$1.84/cwt. (or $0.16/gal.)	$4.80/cwt. (or $0.41/gal. Mix)	$2.22/cwt. ($0.19/gal. Mix)
Average Retail Price	$2.50/gal.	One gallon of mix will make four half- of ice cream selling for $3 00 each.	One gallon of mix will make 17 eight gallons ounce cups of yogurt selling for $0.50 each.
Total Added Cost/ Average Retail Price	6.4%	3.4%	2.2%

Capital costs pertain to the membrane system and system hardware but exclude the cost for connection to utilities such as water, steam, and electricity. Specific capital costs include assembly, balance tanks, design engineering, electrical wiring, flow meters, gauges, installation, membrane housing, membranes, pipes, pressure gauges, process control computer, pumps, temperature recorders, and valves.

Capital costs were $455,000 for the fluid milk and yogurt membrane systems and $1,240,000 for the higher-capacity ice cream system. Membrane systems are relatively small and can usually be installed within an existing building; therefore, no cost for a building has been included. Capital costs were depreciated on a straight-line basis over ten years. Operating costs include those for membrane replacement, replacement of other parts, electricity, water, steam, sanitation materials, and labour. The third and final cost area pertains to the extra cost of the milk itself.

This results from inexpensive lactose being replaced by expensive protein. Note that although the ice cream system was more expensive, since it required greater capacity due to its greater substitution of protein for lactose, only one system-cost alternative was examined for each product. Debt was not included in the cost calculations. The total added cost to make high-protein fluid milk was $0. 16 per gallon. Using an average retail price of $2.50 per gallon, the resulting cost increase relative to retail price is 6.4 per cent. The added cost for the high-protein, lower-lactose ice cream mix was estimated at $0.41 per gallon of mix. Because of the incorporation of air, one gallon of ice cream mix will make four half-gallons of frozen ice cream.

This equates to a cost increase of $0.1025 per halfgallon of frozen ice cream. Using an average retail price of $3.00 per half-gallon of ice cream, the resulting cost increase relative to retail price would be 3.4 per cent. The added cost for high-protein nonfat yogurt was estimated at $0.19 per gallon of mix. One gallon of yogurt mix will make 17 eightounce. cups of yogurt. Using an average retail price of $0.50 per cup, the resulting cost increase versus retail price would be 2.2 per cent.

SURVEY OF MILK PROCESSORS

In order to estimate the potential success of these new product concepts, a survey instrument was sent to U.S. dairy processors. Participants were informed of the particulars of the new product concept and supplied with the estimated cost of manufacturing the new dairy product. Background information was requested in a variety of areas including the respondent's opinion as to why customers purchased their existing dairy products, the importance of private-label products, the size of the firm, and the frequency of the respondent's contact with end-customers.

The survey also asked whether the firm presently employed any membrane technology for dairy purposes (only 10 per cent did so), whether the respondent thought consumers would buy the new product, and requested suggestions for increasing the probability of the new product's commercial success. A total of 179 firms were contacted, of which 63 completed the survey for a total response rate of 35 per cent. These 63 firms included 26 fluid milk processors, 21 ice cream manufacturers, and 16 yogurt manufacturers.

The individuals surveyed were plant managers and/or those designated by each firm's receptionist as being most likely to make new product and/or new equipment decisions. The survey instrument presented the new product idea, the equipment needed, the capital cost, the operating cost, and the increase in milk-component cost.

Most of the interviews were initiated with a telephone call and then carried out by fax communication. Copies of the survey instruments are available from the authors upon request.

DIFFERENCE BETWEEN DAIRY TECHNOLOGY AND DAIRY MANAGEMENT

Both the Dairy technology and Dairy management deals with same agro based field. Even though they deal within the same field, the factors and work nature differs a lot. Dairy technology includes taking care of milk giving cattle in addition to processing and gaining of milk. Dairy management includes the various principles involved in the management of dairy industries.

DAIRY TECHNOLOGY

Amongst all other industries in the country which plays a most important role in the agro based market is the Dairy industry. Dairy technology involves acquiring and processing of milk into a wide variety of dairy products. In India, more than 60% of the total population is involved in the agro related production either directly or ind

irectly. Professionals working in this field are usually called Dairy technologist. They are directly involved in the scientific and quality aspect of the dairy industry. These professionals work in this field in order to improve and apply diverse methods in the processing, conservation and consumption of milk and it's by products.

There are number of courses available in this field in India, both at undergraduate and postgraduate levels, and for getting admission in these courses students have to undergo an entrance examination. Most of the universities organize their own admission tests.

DAIRY MANAGEMENT

With the advancements in the higher education, the professional skills are taught at different levels of study. One such diversified field is the dairy management which involves many tasks and principles. Nowadays the dairy sector has become a full-fledged field with its modern technology. The various applications of principles in the management of dairy industry are one of the main aspects of the dairy management. India is said to be the second largest milk producer in the world.

In the past few years, Indian government has given more care in the dairy production and that resulted in the management of dairy farming in the professional line. The whole process taking place in this field such as processing of milk, its transportation to diverse markets, distribution, etc. all needs some professional management care. Dairy management courses are offered in many universities in the country. The course aims in providing students about the basic knowledge in the production, designing and management of the dairy industry.

It also covers different areas like entrepreneurship, improvement in the milk conservation, dairy processing and management of dairy farms. Key differentiators between Dairy Technology and Dairy Management:

- Dairy technology includes obtaining and processing of milk with various technologies to make it into different products whereas Dairy management involves the different principles and tasks in the management of dairy industry.
- Dairy technologist are only involved in the various methods and

techniques needed for making diverse dairy products whereas the dairy management professionals have to manage the whole process taking place in the dairy farms, from obtaining the milk to its distribution as various by-products.

The dairy technology and dairy management are involved in the dairy field. Although they are in same field, the work nature and prospects differs in many aspects.

3

Dairy Farming

Dairying is an important source of subsidiary income to small/marginal farmers and agricultural labourers. The manure from animals provides a good source of organic matter for improving soil fertility and crop yields. The gober gas from the dung is used as fuel for domestic purposes as also for running engines for drawing water from well.

The surplus fodder and agricultural by-products are gainfully utilised for feeding the animals. Almost all draught power for farm operations and transportation is supplied by bullocks. Since agriculture is mostly seasonal, there is a possibility of finding employment throughout the year for many persons through dairy farming. Thus, dairy also provides employment throughout the year. The main beneficiaries of dairy programmes are small/ marginal farmers and landless labourers. A farmer can earn a gross surplus of about ₹ 12,000 per year from a unit consisting of 2 milking buffaloes. The capital investment required for purchase of 2 buffaloes is ₹ 18,223/-. Even after paying a sum of ₹ 4294/- per annum towards repayment of the loan and interest the farmer can earn a net surplus of ₹ 6000 - 9000/- approximately per year.

Dairy farming is a class of agricultural, or an animal husbandry, enterprise, for long-term production of milk, usually from dairy cows but also from goats and sheep, which may be either processed on-site or transported to a dairy factory for processing and eventual retail sale.

Most dairy farms sell the male calves born by their cows, usually for veal production, or breeding depending on quality of the bull calf, rather than raising non-milk-producing stock. Many dairy farms also grow their own feed, typically including corn, alfalfa, and hay. This is fed directly to the cows, or is stored as silage for use during the winter season. Additional dietary supplements are often added to the feed to increase quality milk production.

UNPROFITABLE OF DAIRY FARMING

Dairy farmers in India are in crisis. High input prices and declining milk prices have pushed them to the wall. But the consumer prices remain firm, showing no signs of declining. In 2009, about 20 per cent of 1,800 dairy farms in California, for instance, had shut down unable to survive at times of higher feed and transportation costs. Similarly, in 2009, when international milk prices had dipped to a low, the European Union defied the World Trade Organisation (WTO) and reintroduced milk subsidies. It provided Rs 3,600 crore in subsidies to its dairy farmers to offset the losses incurred.

In America, on the other hand, the number of dairy farms has come down by 61 per cent since 1992, and only 51,480 dairy farms now exist. These farms received subsidies worth Rs 27,500 crore since 2009, which in other words means a third of its milk price is subsidised. These subsidies come under several programmes: milk income loss contract payment; market loss assistance; milk income loss transitional payment; dairy economic loss assistance programme; milk marketing fees; dairy disaster assistance; and dairy indemnity.

Let me also dispel another commonly held notion. In an era of market economy, it is generally believed that American/European farmers are dependent entirely on the private supply chain. It's not so. After March 2009, EU had restarted buying surplus butter and milk from dairy farmers at an intervention price of Euro 2,218 and Euro 1,698 per tonne, respectively. In America, milk price support programme ensures that the government buys any surplus amount of cheese, butter and non-fat dry milk at a minimum price. In addition, since 2002, it has introduced a programme to distribute cash subsidies to milk producers when prices fall below a set limit. I see no reason why state governments cannot provide such subsidy support to its dairy farmers when prices fall.

Therefore, to begin with, state governments should consider subsidising the cooperatives to raise the milk procurement price to at least Rs 25 per litre. Secondly, it should also reduce the bank interest on loans taken from existing 12.5 per cent to 7 per cent.

VACUUM BUCKET MILKING

The first milking machines were an extension of the traditional milking pail. The early milker device fit on top of a regular milk pail and sat on the floor under the cow. Following each cow being milked, the bucket would be dumped into a holding tank. This developed into the Surge hanging milker.

Prior to milking a cow, a large wide leather strap called a surcingle was put around the cow, across the cow's lower back. The milker device and collection tank hung underneath the cow from the strap. This innovation allowed the cow to move around naturally during the milking process rather than having to stand perfectly still over a bucket on the floor.

With the availability of electric power and suction milking machines, the production levels that were possible in stanchion barns increased but the scale of the operations continued to be limited by the labour intensive nature of the milking process. Attaching and removing milking machines involved repeated heavy lifting of the machinery and its contents several times per cow and the pouring of the milk into milk cans. As a result, it was rare to find single-farmer operations of more than 50 head of cattle.

STEP-SAVER MILK TRANSPORT

As herd size began to increase, the bucket milker system became laborious. A vacuum milk-transport system known as the Step-Saver was developed to transport milk to the storage tank. The system used a long vacuum hose coiled around a receiver cart, and connected to a vacuum-breaker device in the milkhouse, allowing farmers to milk many cows without the necessity of walking increasingly longer distances carrying heavy buckets of milk.

MILKING PIPELINE

The next innovation in automatic milking was the milk pipeline. This uses a permanent milk-return pipe and a second vacuum pipe that encircles the barn or milking parlor above the rows of cows, with quick-seal entry ports above each cow. By eliminating the need for the milk container, the milking device shrank in size and weight to the point where it could hang under the cow, held up only by the sucking force of the milker nipples on the cow's udder.

The milk is pulled up into the milk-return pipe by the vacuum system, and then flows by gravity to the milkhouse vacuum-breaker that puts the milk in the storage tank. The pipeline system greatly reduced the physical labour of milking since the farmer no longer needed to carry around huge heavy buckets of milk from each cow.

The pipeline allowed barn length to keep increasing and expanding, but after a point farmers started to milk the cows in large groups, filling the barn with one-half to one-third of the herd, milking the animals, and then emptying and refilling the barn. As herd sizes continued to increase, this evolved into the more efficient milking parlor.

MILKING PARLORS

Innovation in milking focused on mechanizing the milking parlor to maximize throughput of cows per operator which streamlined the milking process to permit cows to be milked as if on an assembly line, and to reduce physical stresses on the farmer by putting the cows on a platform slightly above the person milking the cows to eliminate having to constantly bend over. Many older and smaller farms still have tie-stall or stanchion barns, but worldwide a majority of commercial farms have parlors. The milking parlor allowed a concentration of money into a small area, so that more technical monitoring and measuring equipment could be devoted to each milking station in the parlor. Rather than simply milking into a common pipeline for example, the parlor can be equipped with fixed measurement systems that monitor milk volume and record milking statistics for each animal. Tags on the animals allow the parlor system to automatically identify each animal as it enters the parlor.

RECESSED PARLORS

More modern farms use recessed parlors, where the milker stands in a recess such that his arms are at the level of the cow's udder. Recessed parlors can be herringbone, where the cows stand in two angled rows either side of the recess and the milker accesses the udder from the side, parallel, where the cows stand side-by-side and the milker accesses the udder from the rear or, more recently, rotary, where the cows are on a raised circular platform, facing the centre of the circle, and the platform rotates while the milker stands in one place and accesses the udder from the rear. There are many other styles of milking parlors which are less common.

MILK PRESERVATION METHODS

Cool temperature has been the main method by which milk freshness has been extended. When windmills and well pumps were invented, one of its first uses on the farm besides providing water for animals was for cooling milk, to extend the storage life before being transported to the town market. The naturally cold underground water would be continuously pumped into a tub or other containers of milk set in the tub to cool after milking. This method of milk cooling was extremely popular before the arrival of electricity and refrigeration.

REFRIGERATION

When refrigeration first arrived the equipment was initially used to cool cans of milk, which were filled by hand milking. These cans were placed into a cooled water bath to remove heat and keep them cool until they were able to be transported to a collection facility. As more automated methods were developed for harvesting milk, hand milking was replaced and, as a result, the milk can was replaced by a bulk milk cooler. 'Ice banks' were the first type of bulk milk cooler.

This was a double wall vessel with evaporator coils and water located between the walls at the bottom and sides of the tank. A small refrigeration compressor was used to remove heat from the evaporator coils. Ice eventually builds up around the coils, until it reaches a thickness of about three inches surrounding each pipe, and the cooling system shuts off. When the milking operation starts, only the milk agitator and the water circulation pump, which flows water across the ice and the steel walls of the tank, are needed to reduce the incoming milk to a temperature below 40 degrees. This cooling method worked well for smaller dairies, however was fairly inefficient and was unable to meet the increasingly higher cooling demand of larger milking parlors. In the mid 1950's direct expansion refrigeration was first applied directly to the bulk milk cooler. This type of cooling utilizes an evaporator built directly into the inner wall of the storage tank to remove heat from the milk. Direct expansion is able to cool milk at a much faster rate than early ice bank type coolers and is still the primary method for bulk tank cooling today on small to medium sized operations.

Another device which has contributed significantly to milk quality is the plate heat exchanger. This device utilizes a number of specially designed stainless steel plates with small spaces between them. Milk is passed between every other set of plates with water being passed between the balance of the plates to remove heat from the milk.

This method of cooling can remove large amounts of heat from the milk in a very short time, thus drastically slowing bacteria growth and thereby improving milk quality. Ground water is the most common source of cooling medium for this device. Dairy cows consume approximately 3 gallons of water for every gallon of milk production and prefer to drink slightly warm water as opposed to cold ground water.

For this reason, PHE's can result in drastically improved milk quality, reduced operating costs for the dairymen by reducing the refrigeration load on his bulk milk cooler, and increased milk production by supplying the cows with a source of fresh warm water. Plate heat exchangers have also evolved as a result of the increase of dairy farm herd sizes in the US. As a dairyman increases the size of his herd, he must also increase the capacity of his milking parlor in order to harvest the additional milk.

This increase in parlor sizes has resulted in tremendous increases in milk throughput and cooling demand. Today's larger farms produce milk at a rate which direct expansion refrigeration systems on bulk milk coolers cannot cool in a timely manner.

PHE's are typically utilized in this instance to rapidly cool the milk to the desired temperature before it reaches the bulk milk tank. Typically, ground water is still utilized to provide some initial cooling to bring the milk to between 55 and 70 degrees F. A second part of the PHE is added to remove the remaining heat with a mixture of chilled pure water and propylene glycol. These chiller systems can be made to incorporate large evaporator surface areas and high chilled water flow rates to cool high flow rates of milk.

MILKING OPERATION

Milking machines are held in place automatically by a vacuum system that draws the ambient air pressure down from 15 to 21 pounds per square inch of vacuum. The vacuum is also used to lift milk vertically through small diametre hoses, into the receiving can. A milk lift pump draws the milk from the receiving can through large diametre stainless steel piping, through the plate cooler, then into a refrigerated bulk tank. Milk is extracted from the cow's udder by flexible rubber sheaths known as liners or inflations that are surrounded by a rigid air chamber. A pulsating flow of ambient air and vacuum is applied to the inflation's air chamber during the milking process.

When ambient air is allowed to enter the chamber, the vacuum inside the inflation causes the inflation to collapse around the cow's teat, squeezing the milk out of teat in a similar fashion as a baby calf's mouth massaging the teat. When the vacuum is reapplied in the chamber the flexible rubber inflation relaxes and opens up, preparing for the next squeezing cycle.

It takes the average cow three to five minutes to give her milk. Some cows are faster or slower. Slow-milking cows may take up to fifteen minutes to let down all their milk. Milking speed is only minorly related to the quantity of milk the cow produces — milking speed is a separate factor from milk quantity; milk quantity is not determinative of milking speed. Because most milkers milk cattle in groups, the milker can only process a group of cows at the speed of the slowest-milking cow. For this reason, many farmers will cull slow-milking cows.

The extracted milk passes through a strainer and plate heat exchangers before entering the tank, where it can be stored safely for a few days at approximately 42 °F. At pre-arranged times, a milk truck arrives and pumps the milk from the tank for transport to a dairy factory where it will be pasteurized and processed into many products.

AUTOMATIC MILKING

They have been the topic of discussion for some time now, but as they become increasingly popular, Charlotte Johnston, TheCattleSite junior editor, looks at just how effective automatic milking machines are and evaluates their benefits. A common myth regarding automatic milking machines is that they disengage the herdsman from the animals, and so neglect herd health. If this were true, the new Lely Astronaut A3 Next would not have won the 2009 Royal Association of British Dairy Farmers' Livestock and

Machinery Award at this year's Dairy Event. The award was presented on the grounds of economics, the welfare and close management of milking animals, the reduction of drudgery for family and employed staff, flexibility since it applies to family run and larger units, and the longer-term needs of the dairy industry.

TheCattleSite spoke to four dairy farmers around the world to find out how automatic milking equipment changed their lives. Click on *Tim Gibson, Doug Heintz, John Wolf* and *Max Warren* to read about their experiences.

HOW DOES IT WORK?

Very simply, a laser control will identify the location of the teats and a robust robot arm will attach cups individually to each teat from underneath the cow. Swift teat cup attachment is guaranteed even when milking cows with teats missing. Should a cup be kicked off, it is reconnected quickly.

COW ID SYSTEM AND COMPUTER MANAGEMENT SOFTWARE

Each cow has an electronic tag, which is read when she enters the machine. This allows the computer system to identify each cow. Management through the computer tells the stockman specific data for each individual cow. The MQC sensor system checks the milk colour, conductivity and flow to ensure maximum control of milk quality.

Comparing individual cow data to the average allows problems to be identified. Milk identified with blood is separated and either discarded or diverted into another holding place. Furthermore, if a cow is being treated with medicine, it is possible for her to remain in the milking herd. This does require strict attention to detail - as accurate information must be input into the computer system as to what the cow has been treated with, how long the withdrawal period is etc.

When the cow comes in to be milked next, her milk will be automatically diverted into a separate holding area or disposed of. The same can be done for colostrum, for example, when a cow has recently calved as it may be beneficial to retain the colostrum for a couple of days. Entering all information on the system will allow this milk to be stored separately and after two days, her milk will return to the bulk tank. By checking the computer twice a day, the stockman can identify cows that are overdue milking or can treat illnesses identified immediately and the accessibility to such detailed data can allow accurate management decisions to be made.

DYNAMIC FEEDING

Dynamic feeding looks at an individual cow's feed requirements in relation to her yield. The programme takes into account milk yield, the cost of feed and the milk price received to work out the most economical feed rate for each individual cow. For Max Warren in Australia, this is particularly useful in a drought situation, where extra feed may have to be bought, but when milk prices are particularly low.

On average in the UK, for every litre of milk produced per cow, 0.3kg of dry matter is consumed, says Tim Gibson. This is standard regardless of whether they are high yielders. He believes he has saved one kilo of dry matter per cow per day, which with 140 cows equates to more than 51 tonnes of dry matter a year – in other words, a lot of money!

John Wolf and Doug Heintz from the US say that they now have the ability to feed a higher concentrate diet to higher yielding cows and they believe they have reduced feed costs. The dynamic feeding programme allows optimum energy conversion efficiency. This unique and efficient system would not be possible without automatic milking machines.

LABOUR SAVINGS

All four farmers have cut back labour units. In Australia, Mr Warren believes he would require double the number of staff to milk 300 cows on a rotary system. Mr Wolf is saving 200 hours of labour a week, whilst Mr Gibson and Mr Heintz have cut back by almost one labour unit each. Adding up the cost of current labour, it is not hard to see how much money can be saved. Lely estimate that for every one machine milking 70 cows, half a labour unit is saved. Two robots would milk 140 cows and save three-quarters of a labour unit, whilst three machines would milk 200 plus cows and save one full labour unit. "The biggest advantage by far is the labour saving. The flexibility has changed my life allowing me to spend more time with my family," says Mr Heintz.

BUILDING SPACE

Mr Gibson recommends that an area of approximately 15ft by 12ft is needed. The machines, however, are only 15ft by 6ft; the extra space takes into account a clean area behind the machine. With so little space required per machine, customers have the opportunity to increase indoor housing.

CONTROLLED GRAZING

Both Mr Wolf and Mr Heintz keep cows housed all year round; only dry cows and heifers may be put to grass. Mr Gibson allows his cows to graze outside during the summer with controlled grazing. Unlike the other farmers, Mr Warren's cows are grazed outdoors all year around on a three-way grazing system.

Mr Warren operated a two-way grazing system, where cows moved paddocks every 12 hours. He found with this system that cows were hanging around the parlour and so he changed the process to a three-way grazing system. Now, cows move fields every eight hours, each time passing through the parlour. Cows are fed a wagon mix in the shed and fed concentrates when milked. All pasture is irrigated.

TRAINING HERD TO USE MACHINE

Mr Wolf said that it takes about three to four days to train heifers to use the machines. However, when the machines were introduced, it took about three weeks before things were running smoothly. He believes that there will be about 0.5 per cent of each herd that does not adapt. Mr Heintz says that he spent three weeks pushing cows up to the machines, but it probably took about three months until the machines were working at full efficiency. Over in Australia, Mr Warren says that it took two to three weeks to train the herd to walk into the robots but he felt it was probably twelve months until he was fully trained to use the system, the technology including computers was completely new to him!

HERD BENEFITS

The Lely Astronaut has a refined udder preparation procedure. Teats are cleaned individually and sprayed. The machine also automatically washes three times a day as well as washing in between each cow. At the Robotic Dairy in Australia, cows are lasting six lactations. Further improvements in herd health can be seen by Mr Gibson reporting an increase in lifetime lactations per cow. Mr Wolf and Mr Warren reported improvements in foot health and reproductive performance.

Mr Heintz, who believes he had high standards of animal health prior to the installation of the machines, has reported no significant improvements in herd health but said that previous levels had been easily maintained. He has also only been using the machines for just under a year. Walking around Mr Gibson's yard, it was apparent that the cows seemed dramatically calmer and at ease than in an conventional dairy unit. In fact, all farmers mentioned that cows were a lot less stressed, which in turn they believed led to better health and increased yields.

Increased yields seemed apparent across the board but the improvement varied between farms. In the UK, Mr Gibson reported an increase of 1,000 litres per cow over the last eight years, whereas Mr Heintz reported an increase of 10 to 15 pounds per day over the last ten months, which equates to 4562.5 pounds of milk per year or about an extra 2,000 litres per year.

SERVICE AND INSTALLATION

The same system operates in the US and the UK with Lely providing onsite support for the first 2-3 days of training cows. During the first two to three weeks, representatives will call in three or four times a week to help with the start-up. Chad Huyser, Director of Sales and Operations for Lely US, says that farm management support staff will visit a couple of times during the first few months to do a thorough review of the farm management process, which includes making slight adjustments to feed rations and robot performance settings.

Mr Gibson, who completed farm management training in Holland with Lely, says that he goes onto clients' farms to help customers adapt to the new style of management and prevent problems. Lely also offer web training events with the farm management support staff, providing information to farmers on how to use the T4C, which is the onboard management software on the robots.

Mr Huyser says that one of the areas that Lely focuses on globally is providing on-going support to all their installations. Speaking with Mr Warren, he feels that ongoing technical support is essential, and is more than pleased with the service Lely continues to provide. He thoroughly enjoys working with the company and together, they have made a number of changes to adapt to Australian grazing conditions. The new Lely Astronaut A3 robotic milking system requires servicing three times a year. Mr Gibson says the older models require servicing every eight weeks. He says that information from each service is sent back to a database at the headquarters, which allows engineers to access a vast amount of data to refer to in the case of a fault. Due to the relative newness of the machines, there is no guarantee how long they will last. Mr Gibson believes that the oldest one in place is approximately 17 years old and still going strong. There have been no reports of machines wearing out to date. Lely estimates that products with the correct service and care will last at least 30 years. Machines can be constantly updated with new software, which comes at no extra cost to the customer.

Some people may be under the impression that robotic milking systems require someone to be on call 24/7 in case of a breakdown. This is not technically true. If there is an error in the system, an alarm system rings a telephone to tell whoever is on duty. During the day, this is not a problem but during the night, it could be more than a nuisance.

Not one of the farmers complained about this. During the evenings, Mr Gibson and Mr Warren said their machines may go off once a week. With seven machines, Mr Wolf is called three or four times a week. Mr Wolf stressed that the system can be manipulated and managed to reduce these calls through only five minutes of maintenance per robot per day.

HOW MUCH DOES IT COST?

The latest model, Lely Astronaut A3 Next, is around £110,000 for one robot. Opportunities for second-hand robots exist: all robots are refurbished at the Lely factory and come with a one-year warranty. Mr Gibson says that they often become available due to clients upgrading or retiring and cost approximately 75 per cent of the new price.

FARM BENEFITS

Mr Wolf explained that the introduction of robotic milking machines has allowed greater flexibility across the farm - particularly with regard to time schedules. "Having the robots in place means that I can now finish what I was doing in the field without rushing back to the parlour to milk the cows," he said. Mr Wolf also stressed that the working environment has significantly improved with cleaner areas for both cows and employees. But by far the biggest benefit for him was the decreased costs of production.

When asked about the biggest benefit of installing a robotic milking system, Mr Warren said the fact he was still farming. "Without robots, I would have stopped milking years ago. I really enjoy working with automatic milking machines and Lely. I love the technology that is always improving. It makes my work so much more enjoyable and interesting."

DAIRY PRODUCT

Dairy products are generally defined as foods produced from cow's or domestic buffalo's milk. They are usually high-energy-yielding food products. A production plant for such processing is called a dairy or a dairy factory. Raw milk for processing mostly comes from cows and to a lesser amount from domestic buffalos, but occasionally from other mammals such as goats, sheep, yaks, or horses. Dairy products are commonly found in European, Middle Eastern and Indian cuisine, whereas they are almost unknown in East Asian cuisine.

TYPES OF DAIRY PRODUCTS

- Milk after optional homogenization, pasteurization, in several grades after standardization of the fat level, and possible addition of bacteria Streptococcus lactis and Leuconostoc citrovorum
  - Crème fraîche, slightly fermented cream
    a. Smetana, Central and Eastern European variety of sour cream
    b. Clotted cream, thick spoonable cream made by heating
  - Cultured buttermilk, fermented concentrated (water removed) milk using the same bacteria as sour cream
  - Kefir, fermented milk resembling buttermilk but based on different yeast and bacteria culture
  - Kumis/Airag, slightly fermented mares' milk popular in Central Asia
  - Milk powder (or powdered milk), produced by removing the water from milk
    a. Whole milk products
    b. Buttermilk products
    c. Skim milk
    d. Whey products
    e. Ice Cream
    f. High milk-fat and nutritional products (for infant formulas)
    g. Cultured and confectionery products
  - Condensed milk, milk which has been concentrated by evaporation, often with sugar added for longer life in an opened can
  - Evaporated milk, (less concentrated than condensed) milk without added sugar
  - Ricotta cheese, milk heated and reduced in volume, known in Indian cuisine as Khoa
  - Infant formula, dried milk powder with specific additives for feeding human infants

- Baked milk, a variety of boiled milk that has been particularly popular in Russia
- Butter, mostly milk fat, produced by churning cream
  - Buttermilk, the liquid left over after producing butter from cream, often dried as livestock food
  - Ghee, clarified butter, by gentle heating of butter and removal of the solid matter
  - Smen, a fermented clarified butter used in Moroccan cooking.
  - Anhydrous milkfat
- Cheese, produced by coagulating milk, separating from whey and letting it ripen, generally with bacteria and sometimes also with certain molds
  - Curds, the soft curdled part of milk (or skim milk) used to make cheese (or casein)
  - Whey, the liquid drained from curds and used for further processing or as a livestock food
  - Cottage cheese
  - Quark
  - Cream cheese, produced by the addition of cream to milk and then curdled to form a rich curd or cheese made from skim milk with cream added to the curd
  - Fromage frais
- Casein
  - Caseinates
  - Milk protein concentrates and isonates
  - Whey protein concentrates and isonates
  - Hydrolysates
  - Mineral concentrates
- Yogurt, milk fermented by Streptococcus salivarius ssp. thermophilus and Lactobacillus delbrueckii ssp. bulgaricus sometimes with additional bacteria, such as Lactobacillus acidophilus
  - Ayran
  - Lassi
- Clabber (food), milk naturally fermented to a yogurt-like state
- Gelato, slowly frozen milk and water, lesser fat than ice cream
- Ice cream, slowly frozen cream and emulsifying additives
  - Ice milk
  - Frozen custard
  - Frozen yogurt, yogurt with emulsifiers that is frozen

- Other
  - Viili
  - Kajmak
  - Filmjölk
  - Piimä
  - Vla
  - Dulce de leche

HEALTH RISKS OF CONSUMING DAIRY PRODUCTS

Most dairy products contain large amounts of saturated fat. Some dairy products may cause health issues for individuals who have a lactose intolerance and milk allergies. Some dairy products such as blue cheese may become contaminated with the fungus Aspergillus fumigatus during ripening, which can trigger asthma and other respiratory problems in susceptible individuals. Vegans and some vegetarians avoid dairy products due to a variety of ethical, dietary, environmental, political, and religious concerns.

DAIRY CATTLE

Dairy cattle (dairy cows) are cattle cows (adult females) bred for the ability to produce large quantities of milk, from which dairy products are made. Dairy cows generally are of the species Bos taurus.

Historically, there was little distinction between dairy cattle and beef cattle, with the same stock often being used for both meat and milk production. Today, dairy cows are specialized and most have been bred to produce large volumes of milk, with little or no regard for their production of meat. Between 1959 and 1990, US milk production doubled while the number of dairy cows declined 40 per cent.

COW

Dairy cows may be found either in herds on dairy farms where dairy farmers own, manage, care for, and collect milk from them, or on commercial farms. Dairy cow herds range in size from small farms of fewer than five cows to large herds of about 20,000. The average dairy farmer in the United States manages about one hundred cows but this varies from an average of 800 cows in California to under 80 in the North East states. Herd sizes vary around the world depending on landholding culture and social structure. In many European countries the average herd size is well below 50. In the UK it is over 100 in New Zealand 350 and Australia 280.

To maintain high milk production, a dairy cow must be bred and produce calves. Depending on market conditions, the cow may be bred with a "dairy bull" or a "beef bull." Female calves (heifers) with dairy breeding may be kept as replacement cows for the dairy herd. If a replacement cow turns out to be a substandard producer of milk, she then goes to market and can be killed for beef.

Male calves can either be used later as a breeding bull or sold and used for veal or beef. Most dairy farmers begin breeding heifers at fifteen months of age. A cow's gestation period is approximately nine months, so most heifers give birth at around two years of age. A Californian industry report, the natural lifespan of a dairy cow is approximately 15–25 years, however dairy cows are rarely kept longer than five years prior to slaughter. Herd life is strongly correlated with production levels. Approximately 17 per cent of the US beef supply comes from cull dairy cows: cows that can no longer be seen as a economic asset to the dairy farm. These animals may be sold due to common diseases of milk cows including mastitis, lameness, or other diseases. In India, the Hindu majority holds the cow as sacred and a motherly figure due to her capacity to give milk.

Cow slaughter is legally banned in India (except in the state of Kerala, West Bengal and the seven north eastern states). Thus, spent dairy cows don't go to slaughter, but are often seen as roaming on the city streets and die of old age or disease. Some pious Hindu organizations manage "old age homes" for old dairy cows.

CALF

Market calves are generally sold at two weeks of age and bull calves may fetch a premium over heifers due to their size, either current or potential. Calves may be sold for veal, or for one of several types of beef production, depending on available local crops and markets. Such bull calves may be castrated if turnout onto pastures is envisaged, in order to render the animals less aggressive. Purebred bulls from elite cows may be put into progeny testing schemes to find out whether they might become superior sires for breeding. Such animals may become extremely valuable.

Most dairy farms separate calves from their mothers within a day of birth to reduce transmission of disease and simplify management of milking cows. Studies have been done allowing calves to remain with their mothers for 1, 4, 7 or 14 days after birth.

Cows whose calves were removed longer than one day after birth showed increased searching, sniffing and vocalizations. However, calves allowed to remain with their mothers for longer periods showed weight gains at three times the rate of early removals as well as more searching behaviour and better social relationships with other calves. After separation, most young dairy calves subsist on commercial milk replacer, a feed based on dried milk powder. Milk replacer is an economical alternative to feeding whole milk because it is cheaper, can be bought at varying fat and protein percentages. A day old calf consumes around 5 liters of milk per day.

BULL

A bull calf with high genetic potential may be reared for breeding purposes. It may be kept by a dairy farm as a herd bull, to provide natural breeding for the herd cows. A bull may service up to 50 or 60 cows during a breeding season.

Any more and the sperm count will decline, leading to cows "returning to service" (to be bred again). A herd bull may only stay for one season since over two years old their temperament becomes too unpredictable. Bull calves intended for breeding commonly are bred on specialized dairy breeding farms, not production farms. These farms are the major source of stocks for artificial insemination (AI).

MILK PRODUCTION LEVELS

A cow will produce large amounts of milk over her lifetime. Certain breeds produce more milk than others; however, different breeds produce within a range of around 15,000 to 25,000 lbs of milk per lactation. The average for dairy cows in the US in 2005 was 19,576 pounds.

Production levels peak at around 40 to 60 days after calving. The cow is then bred. Production declines steadily afterwards, until, at about 305 days after calving, the cow is 'dried off', and milking ceases. About sixty days later, one year after the birth of her previous calf, a cow will calve again. High production cows are more difficult to breed at a one year interval. Many farms take the view that 13 or even 14 month cycles are more appropriate for this type of cow.

Dairy cows may continue to be economically productive for many lactations. Ten or more lactations are possible. The chances of problems arising which may lead to a cow being culled are however, high; the average herd life of US Holsteins is today fewer than 3 lactations. This requires more herd replacements to be reared or purchased.

Over 90% of all cows are culled for 4 main reasons:

1. *Infertility*: Failure to conceive and reduced milk production. Cows are at their most fertile between 60 and 80 days after calving. Cows remaining "open" (not with calf) after this period become increasingly difficult to breed, which may be due to poor health. Failure to expel the afterbirth from a previous pregnancy, luteal cysts, or metritis, an infection of the uterus, are common causes of infertility.

2. *Mastitis*: Persistent and potentially fatal mammary gland infection, leading to high somatic cell counts and loss of production. Mastitis is recognized by a reddening and swelling of the infected quarter of the udder and the presence of whitish clots or pus in the milk. Treatment is possible with long-acting antibiotics but milk from such

cows is not marketable until drug residues have left the cow's system.

3. *Lameness*: Persistent foot infection or leg problems causing infertility and loss of production. High feed levels of highly digestible carbohydrate cause acidic conditions in the cow's rumen. This leads to laminitis and subsequent lameness, leaving the cow vulnerable to other foot infections and problems which may be exacerbated by standing in feces or water soaked areas.
4. *Production*: Some animals fail to produce economic levels of milk to justify their feed costs. Production below 12 to 15 liters of milk per day are not economically viable.

Herd life is strongly correlated with production levels. Lower production cows live longer than high production cows, but may be less profitable. Cows no longer wanted for milk production are sent to slaughter. Their meat is of relatively low value and is generally used for processed meat.

REPRODUCTION

Since the 1950s, artificial insemination (AI) is used at most dairy farms; these farms may keep no bull. Advantages of using AI include its low cost and ease compared to maintaining a bull, ability to select from a large number of bulls to match the anticipated market for the resulting calves, and predictable results.

More recently, embryo transfer has been used to enable the multiplication of progeny from elite cows. Such cows are given hormone treatments to produce multiple embryos. These are then 'flushed' from the cow's uterus. 7-12 embryos are consequently removed from these donor cows and transferred into other cows who serve as surrogate mothers. The result will be between 3 and 6 calves instead of the normal single, or rarely, twins.

HORMONE USE

Hormone treatments are given to dairy cows to increase reproduction and to increase milk production. The hormones are used to produce multiple embryos have to be administered at specific times to dairy cattle to induce ovulation.

Frequently, for economic considerations, these drugs are also used to synchronize a group of cows to ovulate simultaneously. The hormones Prostaglandin, Gonadotropin Releasing Hormone, and Progesterone are used for this purpose and sold under the brand names Lutalyse, Cystorelin, Estrumate, Factrel, Prostamate, Fertagyl. Insynch, and Ovacyst. They may be administered by injection, insertion or mixed with feed.

About 17% of dairy cows in the United States are injected with Bovine somatotropin, also called recombinant bovine somatotropin (rBST), recombinant bovine growth hormone (rBGH), or artificial growth hormone.

The use of this hormone increases milk production from 11%-25%, but also increases the likelihood of cattle developing mastitis, reduction in fertility and lameness. The U.S. Food and Drug Administration (FDA) has ruled that rBST is harmless to people, although critics point out increased levels of insulin-like growth factor 1 (IGF-1) in milk produced using this hormone. The use of rBST is banned in Canada, parts of the European Union, Australia and New Zealand.

NUTRITION

Nutrition plays an important role in keeping cattle healthy and strong. Implementing an adequate nutrition programme can also improve milk production and reproductive performance. Nutrient requirements may not be the same depending on the animal's age and stage of production. Forages, which refer especially to hay or straw, are the most common type of feed used. Cereal grains, as the main contributors of starch to diets, are important in meeting the energy needs of dairy cattle.

Barley is one example of grain that is extensively used around the world. Barley is grown in temperate to sub-artic climates, and it transported to those areas lacking the necessary amounts of grain. Although variations may occur, in general, barley is an excellent source of balanced amounts of protein, energy, and fibre.

Ensuring adequate body fat reserves is essential for cattle to produce milk and also to keep reproductive efficiency. However, if cattle get excessively fat or too thin, they run the risk of developing metabolic problems. Scientists have found that a variety of fat supplements can benefit conception rates of lactating dairy cows. Some of these different fats include oleic acids, found in canola oil, animal tallow, and yellow grease; palmitic acid found in granular fats and dry fats; and linolenic acids which are found in cottonseed, safflower, sunflower, and soybean. It is also important to note that proper levels of fat also improve cattle longevity.

Using by-products is one way of reducing the normally high feed costs. However, lack of knowledge of their nutritional and economic value limits their use. Although the reduction of costs may be significant, they have to be used carefully because animal may have negative reactions to radical changes in feeds. Such a change must then be made slowly and with the proper follow up.

PESTICIDE USE

A survey of the primary dairy producing areas in the US indicated that 13 per cent of lactating animals were treated with insecticides permethrin, pyrethrin, coumaphos, and dichlorvos primarily by daily or every-other-day coat sprays. Workers, particularly in stanchion barns, may be exposed to higher than recommended amounts of these pesticides.

BREEDS

In the United States, dairy cattle are divided into six major breeds. These are the: Holstein-Friesian, Brown Swiss, Guernsey, Ayrshire, Jersey, and Milking Shorthorn. In Rajasthan, an indigenous breed called Tharparkar exists, named from the Tharparkar District, now in Sindh Pakistan. Another type of dairy cow known as Nagauri from Nagaur District, the bull of which is renowned for its ability to plow fields and run. Traditionally, they used to pull covered wagons, known as rath, and in marriages to transport the newlywed couple.

They are now a crutch for thriving agricultural and livestock rearing societies of the Thar Desert. Many other breeds are used nearly exclusively for beef, or for both dairy and beef purposes.

4

Microbiological Spoilage of Dairy Products

INTRODUCTION

The wide array of available dairy foods challenges the microbiologist, engineer, and technologist to find the best ways to prevent the entry of microorganisms, destroy those that do get in along with their enzymes, and prevent the growth and activities of those that escape processing treatments. Troublesome spoilage microorganisms include aerobic psychrotrophic Gram-negative bacteria, yeasts, molds, heterofermen-tative lactobacilli, and spore-forming bacteria.

Psychrotrophic bacteria can produce large amounts of extracellular hydrolytic enzymes, and the extent of recontamination of pasteurized fluid milk products with these bacteria is a major determinant of their shelf life. Fungal spoilage of dairy foods is manifested by the presence of a wide variety of metabolic by-products, causing off-odours and flavours, in addition to visible changes in colour or texture. Coliforms, yeasts, heterofermentative lactic acid bacteria, and spore-forming bacteria can all cause gassing defects in cheeses.

The rate of spoilage of many dairy foods is slowed by the application of one or more of the following treatments: reducing the pH by fermenting the lactose to lactic acid; adding acids or other approved preservatives; introducing a desirable microflora that restricts the growth of undesirable microorganisms; adding sugar or salt to reduce the water activity (a_w); removing water; packaging to limit available oxygen; and freezing. The type of spoilage microorganisms differs widely among dairy foods because of the selective effects of practices followed in production, formulation, processing, packaging, storage, distribution, and handling.

TYPES OF DAIRY FOODS

The global dairy industry is impressive by large. In 2005, world milk production was estimated at 644 million tons, of which 541 million tons was cows' milk. The leading producers of milk were the European Union at 142 million tons, India at 88 million tons, the United States at 80 million tons (20.9 billion gallons), and Russia at 31 million tons. Cheese production amounted to 8.6 million tons in Western Europe and 4.8 million tons in the United States. The vast array of products made from milk worldwide leads to an equally impressive array of spoilage microorganisms.

A survey of dairy product consumption revealed that 6% of US consumers would eat more dairy products if they stayed fresher longer. Products range from those that are readily spoiled by microorganisms to those that are shelf stable for many months, and the spoilage rate can be influenced by factors such as moisture content, pH, processing parameters, and temperature of storage. A short summary of the types of dairy products and typical spoilage microorganisms associated with them is shown in Table.

Table. Dairy Products and Typical Types of Spoilage Microorganisms or Microbial Activity

Food	Spoilage Microorganism or Microbial Activity
Raw milk	A wide variety of different microbes
Pasteurized milk	Psychrotrophs, sporeformers, microbial enzymatic degradation
Concentrated milk	Spore-forming bacteria, osmophilic fungi
Dried milk	Microbial enzymatic degradation
Butter	Psychrotrophs, enzymatic degradation
Cultured buttermilk, bacteria sour cream	Psychrotrophs, coliforms, yeasts, lactic acid
Cottage cheese enzymatic	Psychrotrophs, coliforms, yeasts, molds, microbial degradation
Yogurt, yogurt-based drinks	Yeasts
Other fermented dairy foods	Fungi, coliforms
Cream cheese, processed cheese	Fungi, spore-forming bacteria
Soft, fresh cheeses bacteria, microbial	Psychrotrophs, coliforms, fungi, lactic acid enzymatic degradation
Ripened cheeses microbial	Fungi, lactic acid bacteria, spore-forming bacteria, enzymatic degradation

TYPES OF SPOILAGE MICROORGANISMS

PSYCHROTROPHS

Psychrotrophic microorganisms represent a substantial percentage of the bacteria in raw milk, with pseudomonads and related aerobic, Gram-negative, rod-shaped bacteria being the predominant groups. Typically, 65–70% of the psychrotrophs isolated from raw milk are *Pseudomonas* species. Important characteristics of pseudomonads are their abilities to grow at low temperatures

(3–7°C) and to hydrolyze and use large molecules of proteins and lipids for growth. Other important psychrotrophs associated with raw milk include members of the genera *Bacillus, Micrococcus, Aerococcus,* and *Lactococcus* and of the family Enterobacteriaceae. Pseudomonads can reduce the diacetyl content of buttermilk and sour cream, thereby leading to a "green" or yogurt-like flavour from an imbalance of the diacetyl to acetaldehyde ratio.

For cottage cheese, the typical pH is marginally favourable for the growth of Gram-negative psychrotrophic bacteria, with the pH of cottage cheese curd ranging from 4.5 to 4.7 and the pH of creamed curd being within the more favourable pH range of 5.0–5.3. The usual salt content of cottage cheese is insufficient to limit the growth of contaminating bacteria; therefore, psychrotrophs are the bacteria that normally limit the shelf life of cottage cheese. When in raw milk at cell numbers of greater than 10^6 CFU/ml, psychrotrophs can decrease the yield and quality of cheese curd.

COLIFORMS

Like psychrotrophs, coliforms can also reduce the diacetyl content of buttermilk and sour cream, subsequently producing a yogurt-like flavour. In cheese production, slow lactic acid production by starter cultures favours the growth and production of gas by coliform bacteria, with coliforms having short generation times under such conditions. In soft, mold-ripened cheeses, the pH increases during ripening, which increases the growth potential of coliform bacteria.

LACTIC ACID BACTERIA

Excessive viscosity can occur in buttermilk and sour cream from the growth of encapsulated, slime-producing lactococci. In addition, diacetyl can be reduced by diacetyl reductase produced in these products by lactococci growing at 7°C, resulting in a yogurt-like flavour. Heterofermentative lactic acid bacteria such as lactobacilli and *Leuconostoc* can develop off-flavours and gas in ripened cheeses. These microbes metabolize lactose, subsequently producing lactate, acetate, ethanol, and CO2 in approximately equimolar concentrations.

Their growth is favoured over that of homofermentative starter culture bacteria when ripening occurs at 15°C rather than 8°C. When the homofermentative lactic acid bacteria fail to metabolize all of the fermentable sugar in a cheese, the heterofer-mentative bacteria that are often present complete the fermentation, producing gas and off-flavours, provided their populations are 10^6 CFU/g. Residual galactose in cheese is an example of a substrate that many heterofermentative bacteria can metabolize and produce gas. Additionally, facultative lactobacilli can cometabolize citric and lactic acids and produce CO_2. Catabolism of amino acids in cheese by nonstarter culture, naturally occurring lactobacilli, propionibacteria, and *Lactococcus lactis* subsp. *lactis* can produce small amounts of gas in cheeses. Cracks in cheeses can occur when excess gas is produced by certain strains of *Streptococcus thermophilus* and *Lactobacillus helveticus* that form CO_2 and 4-aminobutyric acid by decarboxylation of glutamic acid. Metabolism of tyrosine by certain lactobacilli causes a pink to brown discoloration in ripened cheeses. This reaction is dependent on the presence of oxygen at the cheese surface. The racemic mixture of L(+) and D(–)-lactic acids that forms a white crystalline material on surfaces of Cheddar and Colby cheeses is produced by the combined growth of starter culture lactococci and nonstarter culture lactic acid producers. The latter racemize the L(+) form of the acid to the L(–) form, which form crystals.

FUNGI

Yeasts can grow well at the low pH of cultured products such as in buttermilk and sour cream and can produce off-flavours described as fermented or yeasty. Additionally, yeasts can metabolize diacetyl in these products, thereby leading to a yogurt-like flavour. Contamination of cottage cheese with the common yeast *Geotrichum candidum* often results in a decrease of diacetyl content. *Geotrichum candidum* reduced by 52–56% diacetyl concentrations in lowfat cottage cheese after 15–19 days of storage at 4–7°C.

Yeasts are a major cause of spoilage of yogurt and fermented milks in which the low pH provides a selective environment for their growth. Yogurts produced under conditions of good manufacturing practices should contain no more than 10 yeast cells and should have a shelf life of 3–4 weeks at 5°C. However, yogurts having initial counts of >100 CFU/g tend to spoil quickly. Yeasty and fermented off-flavours and gassy appearance are often detected when yeasts grow to 10^5–10^6 CFU/g.

Giudici, Masini, and Caggia studied the role of galactose in the spoilage of yogurt by yeasts and concluded that galactose, which results from lactose hydrolysis by the lactic starter cultures, was fermented by galactose-positive strains of yeasts such as *Saccharomyces cerevisiae* and *Hansenula anomala*. The low pH and the nutritional profile of most cheeses are favourable for the growth of spoilage yeasts. Surface moisture, often containing lactic acid, peptides, and amino acids, favours rapid growth.

Many yeasts produce alcohol and CO2, resulting in cheese that tastes yeasty. Packages of cheese packed under vacuum or in modified atmospheres can bulge as a result of the large amount of CO2 produced by yeast. Lipolysis produces short-chain fatty acids that combine with ethanol to form fruity esters. Some proteolytic yeast strains produce sulfides, resulting in an egg odour. Common contaminating yeasts of cheeses include *Candida* spp., *Kluyveromyces marxianus, Geotrichum candidum, Debaryomyces hansenii*, and *Pichia* spp. Molds can grow well on the surfaces of cheeses when oxygen is present, with the low pH being selective for them. In packaged cheeses, mold growth is limited by oxygen availability, but some molds can grow under low oxygen tension. Molds commonly found growing in vacuum-packaged cheeses include *Penicillium* spp. and *Cladosporium* spp.. *Penicillium* is the mold genus most frequently occurring on cheeses. A serious problem with mold spoilage of sorbatecontaining cheeses is the degradation of sorbic acid and potassium sorbate to *trans*-1, 3-pentadiene, causing an off-odour and flavour described as "kerosene."

Several fungal species, including *Penicillium roqueforti,* are capable of metabolizing this compound from sorbates. Marth, Capp, Hasenzahl, Jackson, and Hussong, who was the first group to study this problem, determined that cheese-spoilage isolates of *Penicillium* spp. were resistant to up to 7,100 ppm of potassium sorbate. Later, Sensidoni, Rondinini, Peressini, Maifreni, and Bortolomeazzi isolated from Crescenza and Provolone cheeses sorbate-resistant strains of *Paecilomyces variotii* and *D. hansenii* (a yeast) that produced *trans*-1, 3-pentadiene, causing offflavours in those products. Cream cheeses are susceptible to spoilage by heat-resistant molds such as *Byssochlamys nivea.*

Byssochlamys nivea is capable of growing in reduced oxygen atmospheres, including in atmospheres containing 20, 40, and 60% carbon dioxide with less than 0. 5% oxygen. Once this mold is present in the milk supply, it can be difficult to eliminate during normal processing of cream cheese. Engel and Teuber studied the heat resistance of various strains of *B. nivea* ascospores in milk and cream and determined a *D*-value of 1. 3–2. 4 s at 92°C, depending on the strain. They calculated that in a worstcase scenario of 50 ascospores of the most heat-resistant strain per liter of milk, a process of 24 s at 92°C would result in a 1% spoilage rate in packages of cream cheese.

SPORE-FORMING BACTERIA

Raw milk is the usual source of spore-forming bacteria in finished dairy products. Their numbers before pasteurization seldom exceed 5,000/ml; however, they can also contaminate milk after processing. The most common spore-forming bacteria found in dairy products are *Bacillus licheniformis, B. cereus, B. subtilis, B. mycoides,* and*B. megaterium.* In one study, psychrotrophic *B. cereus* was isolated in more than 80% of raw milks sampled. The heat of pasteurization activates (heat shock) many of the surviving spores so that they are primed to germinate at a favourable growth temperature.

Coagulation of the casein of milk by chymosin-like proteases produced by many of these bacilli occurs at a relatively high pH. Cromie reported that lactose-fermenting *B. circulans* was the dominant spoilage microbe in aseptically packaged pasteurized milk. *Bacillus stearothermophilus* can survive ultra-high-temperature treatment of milk. This bacterium produces acid but no gas, hence causing the "flat sour" defect in canned milk products. If extensive proteolysis occurs during aging of ripened cheeses, the release of amino acids and concomitant increase in pH favours the growth of clostridia, especially *Clostridium tyrobutyricum,* and the production of gas and butyric acid. Spores are concentrated in cheese curd, so as few as one spore per milliliter of milk can cause gassiness in some cheeses. Spore numbers of more than 25/ml were required to produce this defect in large wheels of rindless Swiss cheese. Cheeses most often affected, *e.g.*, Swiss, Emmental, Gouda, and Edam, have a relatively high pH and moisture content, and low salt content. An example of gassing caused by *C. tyrobutyricum* in Swiss cheese is shown in Figure.

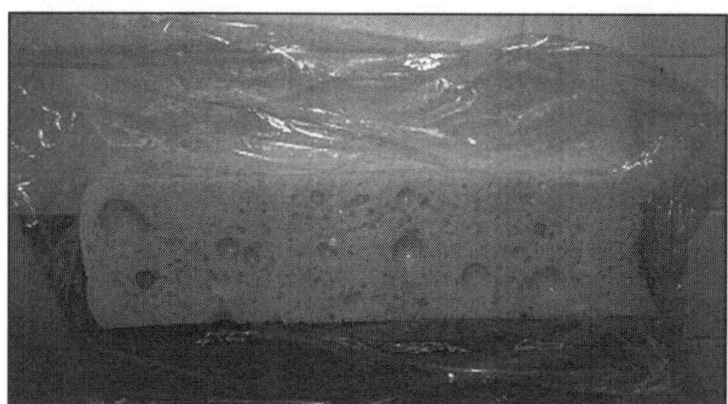

Fig. Gassy Swiss Cheese Caused by *Clostridium Tyrobutyricum.*

Occasionally, gassy defects of process cheeses are also caused by *C. butyricum* or *C. sporogenes.* These spores are not completely inactivated by the normal cooking treatment of process cheeses. Therefore, they may germinate and produce gas unless their numbers are low, the pH is not higher than 5.8, the salt concentration is at least 6% of the serum, and the cheese is held at 20%C or lower. The products of fermentation in these cheeses are butyric and acetic acids, carbon dioxide, and hydrogen.

A summary of known causes of gassiness in cheese products is shown in Table. Thermoduric and thermophilic spore-forming bacteria are the common causes of spoilage of concentrated milks. They survive pasteurization and the extended high temperatures of evaporative removal of moisture to increase the milk solid content to 25.5–45%. When these foods are contaminated, the survivors are heat-resistant *Bacillus* spp.

Table. Causes of Gassiness in Different Types of Cheese

Organism	Cheese Affected	Time to Defect
Coliforms	Raw milk pasta filata cheese	Early blowing
Yeasts	Raw milk Domiati (Egyptian), Camembert, blue-veined, Feta	Early blowing
Lactobacillus fermentum	Provolone, mozzarella	Late blowing
Heterofermentative	Cheddar, Gouda, Saint Paulin, Oka	Late blowing
Lactobacilli	Sbrinz (Argentinean)	Late blowing
Propionibacteria		
Clostridium Tyrobutyricum	Gouda, Emmental, Swiss, Cheddar, Grana	Late blowing
Eubacterium sp.	Cheddar	Late blowing

OTHER MICROORGANISMS

Eubacterium sp., a facultative anaerobe that is able to grow at pH 5. 0–5.5 in the presence of 9.5% salt can cause gassiness in Cheddar cheese. An unusual white-spot defect caused by a thermoduric *Enterococcus faecalis* subsp. *liquefaciens* has occurred in Swiss cheese. This bacterium is inhibitory to propionibacteria and *Lactobacillus fermentum*, resulting in poor eye development and lack of flavour in the cheese as well.

ENZYMATIC DEGRADATION

An indirect cause of dairy product spoilage is microbial enzymes, such as proteases, phospholipases, and lipases, some of which may remain active in the food after the enzyme-producing microbes have been destroyed. Populations of psychrotrophs ranging from 10^6 to 10^7 CFU/ml can produce sufficient amounts of extracellular enzymes to cause defects in milk that are detectable by sensory tests.

Adams, Barach, and Speck reported that 70–90% of raw milk samples tested contained psychrotrophic bacteria capable of producing proteinases that were active after heating at 149°C for 10s. Others have verified this observation. Extracellular proteases can affect the quality of milk products in various ways, but largely by producing bitter peptides. Thermally resistant proteases have caused spoilage of ultra-high-temperature (UHT) milk. In addition, phospholipases can be heat stable.

Experimentally, phospholipase production in raw milk can result in the development of bitter off-flavours due to the release of fatty acids by milk's natural lipase. Heat-stable bacterial lipases have been associated with the development of rancid flavours in UHT milk. *Pseudomonas fluorescens* is the most common producer of lipases in milk and milk products, but lipases can also be produced by Gram-negative psychrotrophic bacteria. Products that may be affected by residual lipases include UHT milk, butter, some cheeses, and dry whole milk.

The release of short-chain fatty acids, C4 through C8, results in the occurrence of rancid flavours and odours, whereas the release of long-chain fatty acids results in a soapy flavour. Oxidation of free unsaturated fatty acids to aldehydes and ketones results in an oxidized flavour and fruity off-flavour results from lipolysis of short-chain fatty acids by *Pseudomonas fragi* followed by esterification with alcohols. Lipase tends to partition into cream instead of the nonfat milk portion when cream is separated from milk. The large concentration of fat globules and the activation of lipase caused by some disruption of the fat globule membrane increase the probability of enzyme–substrate interactions.

In the production of butter, lipolysis can cause excessive foaming during churning of cream, hence increasing the time of churning. Rancidity of butter may result from the activity of lipase in the raw milk or the residual heat-stable microbial lipase in the finished butter. Although short-chain fatty acids from rancid cream, being water-soluble, are partially lost in the buttermilk and wash water during manufacture, microbial lipases remaining in the butter can hydrolyze the fat even during frozen storage.

Low pH limits the rate of lipase activity, but in some cheeses, *e.g.*, Brie and Camembert, the pH rises to near neutrality as ripening progresses, making them especially susceptible to lipolysis. For Cheddar cheese, however, a high concentration of lipase is needed to create the desired flavour. Products such as whole milk powder may be affected by residual heat-resistant bacterial lipases. Residual lipases in nonfat dry milk and dry whey products can hydrolyze fats in products into which they are added as ingredients.

SOURCES OF SPOILAGE MICROORGANISMS

CONTAMINATION OF RAW MILK

The highly nutritious nature of dairy products makes them especially good media for the growth of microorganisms. Milk contains abundant water and nutrients and has a nearly neutral pH. The major sugar, lactose, is not utilized by many types of bacteria, and the proteins and lipids must be broken down by enzymes to allow sustained microbial growth. In order to understand the source of many of the spoilage microflora of dairy products, it is best to discuss how milk can first become contaminated, via the conditions of production and processing.

The mammary glands of many very young cows yield no bacteria in aseptically collected milk samples, but as numbers of milkings increase, so do the chances of isolating bacteria in milk drawn aseptically from the teats. The stresses placed on the cow's teats and mammary glands by the very large amounts of milk produced and the actions of the milking machine cause teat canals to become more open and teat ends to become misshapen as time passes. These stresses may open the teat canal for the entry of bacteria capable of infecting the glands.

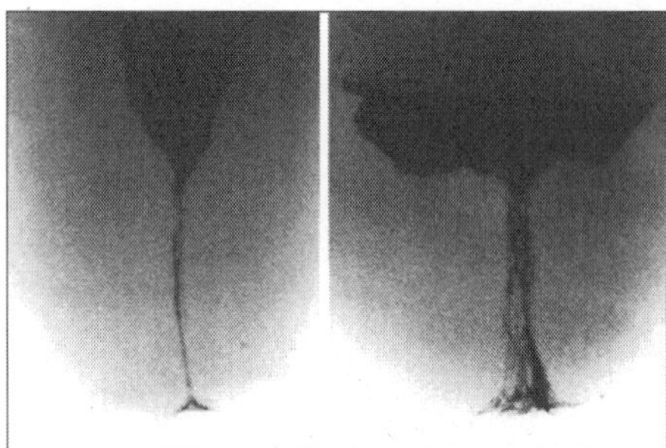

Fig. X-ray Photographs Showing an Increase in the Diameter of the Teat Canal of the Same Teat of a Milking Cow between the First Lactation (Left) and a Later Lactation (Right).

Environmental contaminants represent a significant percentage of spoilage microflora. They are ubiquitous in the environment from which they contaminate the cow, equipment, water, and milkers' hands. Since milking machines exert about 38 cm (15 in.) of vacuum on the teats during milking, and since air often leaks into the system, bacteria on the surfaces of the cow or in water retained from premilking preparation can be drawn into the milk.

Also, when inflation clusters drop to the floor, they pick up microorganisms that can be drawn into the milk. The pumping or agitation of milk supplies the oxygen needed by aerobes for growth and breaks chains and clumps of bacteria. Single cells, having less competition than those in colonies, have the opportunity for more rapid multiplication.

Bacteria recontaminating pasteurized milk originate primarily from water and air in the filling equipment or immediate surroundings and can be resident for prolonged periods of time. In a study performed in Norway and Sweden, Ternstrom, Lindberg, and Molin investigated nine dairy plants and found that five taxa of psychrotrophic *Pseudomonas* spp. were involved in the spoilage of raw and pasteurized milk and that the same strains were recovered from both the raw and pasteurized milk, suggesting that recontamination originated from the raw milk.

Additionally, the investigators found that *Bacillus* spp. (mainly *B. cereus* and *B. polymyxa*) were responsible for spoilage in 77% of the samples that had been spoiled by Gram-positive bacteria. The spoilage *Bacillus* spp. grew fermentatively, and most were able to denitrify the milk, which has implications for cheeses that contain added nitrate/nitrites for protection against clostridia. Sporeforming bacteria are abundant in dust, dairy feed concentrates, and forages; therefore, they are often present on the skin and hair of cattle from which they can enter milk. The presence of sporeformers such as *C. butyricum* in milk has been traced to contaminated silage.

CONTAMINATION OF DAIRY PRODUCTS

Washed curd types of cheeses are especially susceptible to growth of coliforms, so great care must be taken to monitor the quality of water used in these processes. A high incidence of contamination of brine-salted cheeses by yeasts results from their presence in the brines. Many mold species are particularly well adapted to the cheese-making environment and can be difficult to eradicate from a production facility. Fungi causing a "thread mold" defect in Cheddar cheeses were found in the cheese factory environment, on cheese-making equipment, in air, and in curd and whey.

In a study of cheese-making facilities in Denmark, *Penicillium commune* persisted in the cheese coating and unpacking areas over a 7-year period. Ascospores of *B. nivea* and other heat-resistant species shown to be able to survive pasteurization, such as *Talaromyces avellaneus*, *Neosartorya fischeri* var. *spinosa*, and *Eupenicillium brefeldianum*, have also been found in raw milk.

A major cause of failure of processing and packaging systems is the development of biofilms on equipment surfaces. These communities of microorganisms develop when nutrients and water remain on surfaces between times of cleaning and reuse. Bacteria in biofilms (sessile form) are more resistant to chemical sanitizers than are the same bacteria in suspension (planktonic form). Chemical sanitizers may be rendered ineffective by biofilms leaving viable bacteria to be dislodged into the milk product.

FACTORS AFFECTING SPOILAGE

SPOILAGE OF FLUID MILK PRODUCTS

The shelf life of pasteurized milk can be affected by large numbers of somatic cells in raw milk. Increased somatic cell numbers are positively correlated with concentrations of plasmin, a heat-stable protease, and of lipoprotein lipase in freshly produced milk. Activities of these enzymes can supplement those of bacterial hydrolases, hence shortening the time to spoilage.

The major determinants of quantities of these enzymes in the milk supply are the initial cell numbers of psychrotrophic bacteria, their generation times, their abilities to produce specific enzymes, and the time and temperature at which the milk is stored before processing. Several conditions must exist for lipolyzed flavour to develop from residual lipases in processed dairy foods, that is, large numbers ($>10^6$ CFU/ml) of lipase producers, stability of the enzyme to the thermal process, long-term storage and favourable conditions of temperature, pH, and water activity.

SPOILAGE OF CHEESES

Factors that determine the rates of spoilage of cheeses are water activity, pH, salt to moisture ratio, temperature, characteristics of the lactic starter culture, types and viability of contaminating microorganisms, and characteristics and quantities of residual enzymes. With so many variables to affect deteriorative reactions, it is no surprise that cheeses vary widely in spoilage characteristics. Soft or unripened cheeses, which generally have the highest pH values, along with the lowest salt to moisture ratios, spoil most quickly.

In contrast, aged, ripened cheeses retain their desirable eating qualities for long periods because of their comparatively low pH, low water activity, and low redox potential. For fresh, raw milk pasta filata cheeses, Melilli determined that low initial salt and higher brining temperature (18%C) allowed for greater growth of coliforms, which caused gas formation in the cheese. Factors affecting the growth of the spoilage microorganisms, *Enterobacter agglomerans* and *Pseudomonas* spp. in cottage cheese, were higher pH and storage temperature of the cheese. Some of the spoilage microorganisms were able to grow at relatively low pH values when incubated at 7°C and were able to grow at pH 3. 6 when grown in media at 20°C. Rate of salt penetration into brined cheeses, types of starter cultures used, initial load of spores in the milk used for production, pH of the cheese, and ripening temperature affect the rate of butyric acid fermentation and gas production by *C. tyrobutyricum*.

Fungal growth in packaged cheeses was found to be most significantly affected by the concentration of CO_2 in the package and the water activity of the cheese. Cheddar cheese exhibiting yeast spoilage had a high moisture level (39.1%) and a low salt in the moisture-phase value (3.95%). Roostita and Fleet determined that the properties of yeasts that affected the spoilage rate of Camembert and blue-veined cheeses were the abilities to ferment/assimilate lactose, produce extracellular lipolytic and proteolytic enzymes, utilize lactic and citric acid, and grow at 10°C.

PREVENTION AND CONTROL MEASURES

PREVENTION OF SPOILAGE IN MILK

In the early days of development of the commercial dairy industry, milk was produced under much less sanitary conditions than are used today, and cooling was slow and inadequate to restrict bacterial growth. Developments during the first half of the twentieth century created significant reductions in the rate of spoilage of raw milk and cream, by making it possible for every-other-day pickup of milk from farms and shipments of raw milk over long distances with minimal increases in bacterial cell numbers.

Rapid cooling and quick use of raw milk are accepted as best practices and can affect the spoilage ability of *Pseudomonas* spp. present in milk. Pseudomonads that had been incubated in raw milk for 3 days at 7°C had greater growth rates and greater proteolytic and lipolytic activity than those isolated directly from the milk shortly after milking. As the quality of raw milk improved, so did that of pasteurized milk. Heating of milk to 62.8°C (145°F) for 30 min or to 71.7°C (161°F) for 15 skills the pathogenic bacteria likely to be of significance in milk as well as most of the spoilage bacteria.

However, processors learned that long shelf life of pasteurized fluid milk products requires a higher temperature treatment as well as prevention of contamination between the pasteurizer and the sealed package. In particular, it is imperative that filling equipment be sanitary and that the air in contact with the filler, the milk, and the containers be practically sterile. Whereas in the early to mid-twentieth century, milk was delivered daily to homes because of its short shelf life, today's fluid milk products are generally expected to remain acceptable for 14–21 days. Pasteurization standards for several countries are listed in Table. A shelf life of 21 days and beyond can be attained with fluid milk products that have been heated sufficiently to kill virtually all of the vegetative bacterial cells and protected from recontamination. Ultra-pasteurized milk products, heated at or above 138°C for at least 2s, that have been packaged aseptically can have several weeks of shelf life when stored refrigerated. Ultra-high-temperature (UHT) treatment destroys most spores in milk, but *B. stearothermophilus* can survive.

Aseptic processing, as defined in the Grade A Pasteurized Milk Ordinance, means that the product has been subjected to sufficient heat processing to render it commercially sterile and that it has been packaged in a hermetically sealed container. These dairy foods are stable at room temperature. The addition of carbon dioxide to milk and milk products reduces the rates of growth of many bacteria. King and Mabbitt demonstrated improved keeping quality of raw milk by the addition of CO_2. Loss and Hotchkiss found lowered survivor rates of both *P. fluorescens* and the spores of *B. cereus* during heating of milk containing up to 36 mM CO_2.

McCarney, Mullen, and Rowe determined that carbonation may be a desirable treatment for cheese milk when on the day of collection populations of psychrotrophic bacteria are approximately 10^5 CFU/ml. Rajagopal, Werner, and Hotchkiss demonstrated that treatment with CO_2 at a pressure of 689 kPa and temperature of 6.1°C produced a substantial decrease in bacterial counts, resulting in milk that was within the grade A raw milk limits for up to 8 days of storage. A disadvantage can be that an acidic flavour note may be produced in a CO_2-treated milk product. When CO_2 is dissolved in milk, the pH decreases and does not return to the original pH value following the removal of CO_2 before pasteurization.

High hydrostatic pressure treatments of milk are effective in killing vegetative bacterial cells, but spores are mostly refractory to this treatment. The phase of growth of the bacteria and the temperature of incubation are significant variables affecting the sensitivities of bacterial cells to high pressures. Cells in the stationary phase are more resistant than those in the exponential phase of growth. Survivor curves have shown resistant tailing populations. Other alternative treatments for the pasteurization of milk, such as ohmic heating, microwave heating, UV radiation, electron beam irradiation, pulsed electric fields, infrared processing, and high voltage arc discharge, may have the potential to be used alone or in combination with other treatments. However, all pasteurization processes need to be validated through the combined use of process authorities, challenge studies, and predictive modeling, and must be verified to ensure that critical processing limits are achieved.

PREVENTION OF SPOILAGE IN CULTURED DAIRY PRODUCTS

Cultured products such as buttermilk and sour cream depend on a combination of lactic acid producers, the lactococci, and the leuconostocs to produce the desired flavour profile. Imbalance of the culture, improper temperature or ripening time, infection of the culture with bacteriophage, presence of inhibitors, and/or microbial contamination can lead to an unsatisfactory product. A buttery flavour note is produced by *Leuconostoc mesenteroides* subsp. *cremoris*. This bacterium converts acetaldehyde to diacetyl, thus reducing the "green" or yogurt-like flavour. A diacetyl to acetaldehyde ratio of 4:1 is desirable, whereas the green flavour is present when the ratio is 3:1 or less. Proteolysis by the lactococci is necessary to afford growth of the *Leuconostoc* culture, and citrate is needed as substrate for diacetyl production Although cooking of the curd destroys virtually all bacteria capable of spoiling cottage cheese, washing and handling of the curd after cooking can introduce substantial numbers of spoilage microorganisms. It is desirable to acidify alkaline waters for washing cottage cheese curd to prevent solubilization of surfaces of the curd.

However, more pseudomonads can be adsorbed onto cottage cheese curd from wash water when adjusted to pH5 (40–45%) rather than adjusted to pH7 (20–30%). Flushing packages of cottage cheese or sour cream with CO_2 or N_2 suppressed the growth of psychrotrophic bacteria, yeasts, and molds for up to 112 days, but a slight bitterness can occur in cottage cheese after 73 days of storage. Cheesemakers can use the addition of high numbers of lactic acid bacteria to raw milk during storage to reduce the rate of growth of psychrotrophic microbes. For fresh, raw milk, brined cheeses, gassing defects can be reduced by presalting the curd prior to brining and reducing the brine temperature to <12°C. Pasteurization will eliminate the risk from most psychrotrophic microbes, coliforms, leuconostocs, and many lactobacilli, so cheeses made from pasteurized milk have a low risk of gassiness produced by these microorganisms.

Most bacterial cells, including spores, can be removed from milk by centrifugation at about 9,000*g*. The process, known as bactofugation, removes about 3% of the milk, called bactofugate. Kosikowski and Mistry invented and patented a process for recovering this bactofugate which is heated at 135°C for 3–4 s, then added back to the cheese milk. The process can reduce the population of butyric acid-producing spores by 98%. Spore-forming bacterial growth and subsequent gas production in aged, ripened cheeses can be minimized with a salt to moisture content of ≥3.0%.

Other potential inhibitors of butyric acid fermentation and gas production in cheese are the addition of nitrate, addition of lysozyme cold storage of cheese prior to ripening, direct salt addition to the cheese curd, addition of hydrogen peroxide, or use of starter cultures that form nisin or other antimicrobials. The most popular mold inhibitors used on cheeses are sorbates and natamycin. Sorbates tend to diffuse into the cheese, thereby modifying flavour and decreasing their concentration, whereas very little natamycin diffuses. Electron beam irradiation, studied by Blank, Shamsuzzaman, and

Sohal for mold decontamination of Cheddar cheese, can reduce initial populations of *Aspergillus ochraceus* and *Penicillium cyclopium* by 90% with average doses of 0.21 and 0.42 kGy, respectively. Since nearly all mold spores are killed by pasteurization practices that limit recontamination and growth, although difficult, are vital in prevention of moldy cheeses. Modified atmosphere packaging (MAP) of cheeses can retard or prevent the growth of molds, and optimum MAP conditions for different types of cheeses were described by Nielsen and Haasum. For processed cheeses containing no active lactic acid starter bacteria, low O_2 and high CO_2 atmospheres were optimum; for cheeses containing active starter cultures, atmospheres containing low O_2 and controlled CO_2 using a permeable film provided the best results. For mold-ripened cheeses requiring the activity of the fungi to maintain good quality, normal O_2 and high, but controlled, CO_2 atmospheres were best.

In Italian soft cheeses such as Stracchino, vacuum packaging decreased the growth of yeasts, resulting in a shelf life extension of >28 days. Processing times and temperatures used in the manufacture of cream cheese and pasteurized process cheese are able to eliminate most spoilage microorganisms from these products. However, the benefit of the presence of competitive microflora is also lost. It is very important to limit the potential for recontamination, as products that do not contain antimycotics can readily support the growth of yeasts and molds. Sorbates can be added; however, their use in cream cheese is limited to amounts that will not affect the delicate flavour.

PREVENTION OF SPOILAGE IN OTHER DAIRY PRODUCTS

The high salt concentration in the serum-in-lipid emulsion of butter limits the growth of contaminating bacteria to the small amount of nutrients trapped within the droplets that contain the microbes. However, psychrotrophic bacteria can grow and produce lipases in refrigerated salted butter if the moisture and salt are not evenly distributed. When used in the bulk form, concentrated (condensed) milk must be kept refrigerated until used.

It can be preserved by addition of about 44% sucrose and/or glucose to lower the water activity below that at which viable spores will germinate (a_w 0.95). Lactose, which constitutes about 53% of the nonfat milk solids, contributes to the lowered water activity. When canned as evaporated milk or sweetened condensed milk, these products are commercially sterilized in the cans, and spoilage seldom occurs. Microbial growth and enzyme activity are prevented by freezing. Therefore, microbial degradation of frozen desserts occurs only in the ingredients used or in the mixes prior to freezing.

METHODS FOR DETECTION AND ISOLATION

It has been a long-standing practice to use microbiological standards for indicator microorganisms as a predictor of the safety and quality of dairy products, and many countries have regulations or guidelines for these microbes. While these tests can be useful as a general indication of the cleanliness of the dairy processing operation, they may not necessarily correlate with the shelf life of the products. Boor, Carey, Murphy, and Zadoks reported results of audits of pasteurized milk quality collected from 23 plants in New York State over a 10-year period. On an annual basis, the percentage of samples that met the Grade A Pasteurized Milk Ordinance Standard Plate Count limit of 20,000 CFU/ml after 14 days of storage at 6.1°C ranged from 12 to 32%.

Tests for coliform bacteria were positive for 5–15% of the samples on initial testing and increased up to 34% after 14 days of storage. Sensory tests on the 14th day of storage revealed that 33–59% of the milks were still acceptable. After about 17 days of storage, the dominant spoilage bacteria belonged to the spore-forming genera *Paenibacillus* (39%) and *Bacillus*(32%) and to heattolerant *Microbacterium lacticum* (14%). As an outgrowth of the efforts in the early twentieth century to improve the safety and quality of milk products, the American Public Health Association standardized the methods for detection of spoilage indicators and published them in the Standard Methods for the Examination of Dairy Products. Recommended methods for various microorganisms.

Common tests in use today for the prediction of shelf life of fluid milk products use a preliminary incubation or keeping quality step followed by standard microbiological testing. These methods are designed to determine low levels of thermoduric Gram-negative bacteria, such as psychrotrophic coliforms and pseudomonads, that have survived pasteurization and are most likely to grow under typical storage conditions.

The recommended methods have the disadvantage of taking several days to complete. There is a vast array of rapid test methods available for use in dairy product testing. The preferred method for assaying for specific spoilage microorganisms can often depend on the product characteristics, such as amount of competing microflora, pH, and water activity. Fungi can be particularly troublesome, because they can adapt to the environment of the food and can be difficult to detect on conventional plating media within the standard incubation times.

In yogurts, yeasts often grow slowly in conventional laboratory plating methods, but as few as 10 CFU/ml were detectable after 16h of incubation by PCR amplification of the conserved region of their 18SrRNA. Several investigators have made comparisons of a number of alternative yeast and mold detection methods in shredded cheese, hard and soft cheeses, cottage cheese, yogurt, and sour cream, and found that, while results for all of the methods were statistically similar, price, speed, and convenience of use are often overarching considerations when users choose a method. Rapid genomic subtyping methods, such as RAPD, RFLP, and AFLP, can be used to determine the sources of fungal contamination in a manufacturing environment. Laleye *et al.* compared four plating media for recovery of spoilage lactococci from gassing cheeses and determined that MRS agar and APT agar gave the best results. For detection of *C. tyrobutyricum* in gassing cheeses, the classical method of most-probable-number testing in RCM-lactate or BBMB-lactate medium followed by confirmation on LATA or DRCM medium, and gas chromatographic analysis of volatile and nonvolatile organic acid by-products was determined to be both lengthy and difficult to perform.

Herman and Lopez-Enriquez, Rodriguez-Lazaro, and Hernandez have developed PCR-based detection methods that are reported to detect less than one spore of *C. tyrobutyricum* per milliliter of milk. Cocolin, Innocente, Biasutti, and Comi developed a PCR-denaturing gradient gel electrophoresis method that could detect 10^4 CFU of *Clostridium* spp. per milliliter in gassing cheeses.

CONCLUSION

While the introduction of pasteurization has helped to ensure the safety of dairy products, progress has been slower in preventing the microbial spoilage of cheese and dairy products. Worldwide standardized pasteurization practices would be an effective first step in eliminating or reducing the levels of many spoilage microorganisms. However, preventing postprocess contamination by spoilage microorganisms and retarding the growth of surviving organisms remain a challenge. Novel technologies and preservatives are needed to prevent the growth of spoilage microorganisms and extend the shelf life of dairy products.

Limited applicability of current approved antimycotics such as sorbic acid and natamycin provides a major opportunity to expand the arsenal of preservatives available for today's dairy processor. In addition, studies to determine the interaction of current preservative technologies against spoilage microorganisms are also needed. Improved methods for detecting spoilage microbes, especially the slow-growing psychrotrophs and fungi, could assist in finding the niche environments in processing facilities that lead to postprocess contamination. The next century will bring many challenges to the dairy processor, but maintaining the quality and shelf life of this highly nutritious food should not be one of them.

5

Stainless Steel in the Dairy Industry

INTRODUCTION

Dairying has been an agricultural practice since people first started domesticating animals. Milk and dairy products are a vital part of the diet for many people. They contain most of the basic elements necessary for children to grow and are an important part of the human diet.

Dairy products constitute one of the five main food groups that together comprise a healthy and balanced diet. Significant amounts of protein are found in dairy products along with most of the micronutrients we need. These include calcium, the B-group of vitamins, vitamin A, iodine, magnesium, phosphorus, potassium and zinc. Milk and dairy foods can also help to improve bone and dental health and may have a role to play in protecting the body against hypertension. The progress in dairy science and technology has increased the level of hygiene required during the manufacture of dairy products in order to preserve their nutrients. The modern dairy industry requires the use of cleanable, corrosion-resistant stainless steel equipment to meet the needs of milk product consumers everywhere.

WHAT MAKES STAINLESS STEEL A SUSTAINABLE MATERIAL

Before we can determine whether stainless steel is a sustainable material, we should first define what we mean by sustainability in relation to what is known as the triple bottomline: People, Planet and Profit.

PEOPLE

The material, in its use or in its production process, respects the human being, especially in terms of health and safety. A sustainable material does not harm the people working to produce it, or the people who handle it during its use, recycling and ultimate disposal. Stainless steel is not harmful to people during either its production or use. A protective layer forms naturally on all stainless steels because of the inclusion of chromium. The passive layer protects the steel from corrosion–ensuring a long life. As long as the correct grade of stainless is selected for an application, the steel remains inert and harmless to the people who handle it and the environment. These characteristics have made stainless steel the primary material in medical, food processing, household and catering applications.

PLANET

The emission footprints of the material, especially those related to carbon, water and air, are minimised. Reuse and recyclability are at high levels. The material has low maintenance costs and a long life, both key indicators that the impact of the material on the planet is at the lowest levels possible. The electric arc furnace (EAF), the main process used to make stainless steels, is extremely efficient. An EAF has a low impact on the environment in terms of both CO_2 and other emissions.

The EAF is also extremely efficient at processing scrap stainless, ensuring that new stainless steel has an average recycled content of more than 60%. Stainless steels are easily recycled to produce more stainless steels and this process can be carried on indefinitely. It is estimated that about 80% of stainless steels are recycled at the end of their life. As stainless steel has a high intrinsic value, it is collected and recycled without any economic incentives from the public purse.

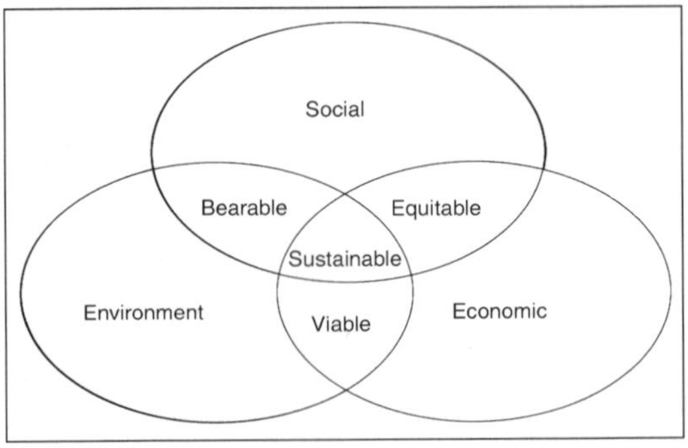

PROFIT

The industries producing the material show long-term sustainability and growth, provide excellent reliability and quality for their customers, and ensure a solid and reliable supply-chain to the end consumer. Choosing stainless steel for an application ensures that it will have low maintenance costs, a long life and be easy to recycle at the end of that life. This makes stainless an economical choice in consumer durables (such as refrigerators and washing machines) and in capital goods applications (such as transportation, chemical and process applications).

Stainless steels also have better mechanical properties than most metals. Its fire and corrosion resistance make stainless a good choice in transportation, building or public works such as railways, subways, tunnels and bridges. These properties, together with stainless steels' mechanical behaviour, are of prime importance in these applications to ensure human beings are protected and maintenance costs are kept low. Stainless also has an aesthetically pleasing appearance, making it the material of choice in demanding architectural and design projects. Taking into account its recyclability, reuse, long life, low maintenance and product safety, the emissions from the production and use of stainless steels are minimal when compared to any other alternative material. A detailed and precise analysis of the sustainability of stainless steel makes the choice of stainless a logical one. This might explain why, as society and governments are becoming more conscious of environmental and economic factors, the growth in the use of stainless steel has been the highest of any material in the world.

STAINLESS STEEL IS THE ESSENTIAL MATERIAL, FROM FARM TO TABLE

DECADES OF EXPERIENCE IN DAIRY

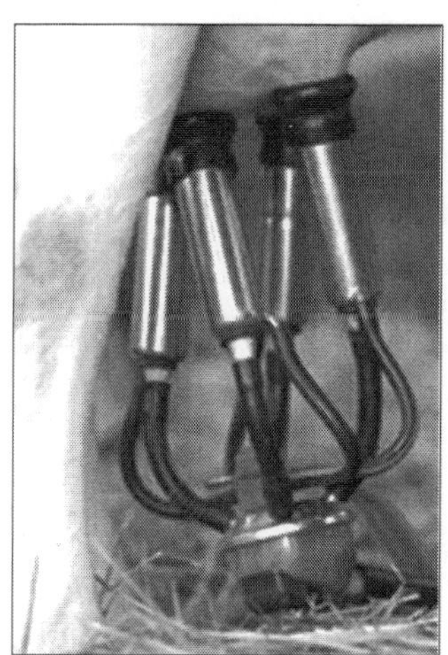

Milk is an emulsion containing about 87% water. The remaining 13% is made up of fatty acids, inorganic compounds, vitamins, and enzymes which do not dissolve in milk. Fresh milk is an ideal culture medium for microbial flora that can spoil the end product. Thus, the manufacture of milk and milk products is subject to very stringent rules. These rules cover the way in which the livestock are kept and milked, preparation methods, additives, processing equipment, and the transport tanks that move the milk from the farm to the processing plant. On its journey from the farm to the consumer, milk comes into contact with the walls of the equipment in which it is being processed or transported.

The final product must reach the consumer meticulously clean and free from all germs. It is for this reason that the dairy industry has employed stainless steel for more than sixty years. The compact and smooth surface of stainless steel prevents bacterial contamination and facilitates cleaning and disinfection.

WHY STAINLESS STEEL

The development of stainless steel in the food industry is explained by the fact that it corresponds exactly to the requirements expected of materials in contact with food.

The requirements fall into one of the following three categories:

1. Chemical, bacteriological and organoleptic neutrality with regard to the food product.
2. Ability to be cleaned so the hygiene and appearance of the product is guaranteed.
3. Durability, including resistance to corrosion and aging.

Other factors also contribute towards making stainless steel the preferred material for the entire food processing industry. These include its mechanical characteristics, expansion coefficient, thermal conductivity and ease of use.

Chemical and Biological Neutrality

People are more aware than ever of the impact of the materials used to manufacture and transport food. Certain materials are widely distrusted because of problems with pollution, allergies and the volume of technical, scientific and medical information available. A number of studies have found that stainless has no adverse affects on human health, despite its wide and lengthy use in fields such as food, health and human hygiene. Stainless steel is a stable homogeneous alloy composed principally of iron, chromium (13 to 30%) and nickel (0 to 25%).

Cleaning and Disinfection

Cleaning involves the elimination of both visible and invisible contamination that adheres to the surface of a material. However, cleaning does not necessarily destroy the micro-organisms that are present on the material. Full bacteriological cleanliness is obtained only after surfaces are disinfected. Disinfection aims to reduce the microbial population on a surface to a level that is compatible with satisfactory hygiene practice and prevents contamination of the food.

Durability and Corrosion Resistance

Chromium, a component of stainless steel, forms a protective oxide compound on the surface of the metal. Known as a passive film, this layer slows and even prevents corrosion. If the surface of the metal is damaged, the passive film reconstitutes spontaneously at room temperature through the reaction of the chromium with water and oxygen.

The stability of the passive layer is the determining factor that ensures stainless steels resist corrosion. Stability can be affected by the nature of the corrosive environment. This includes the oxidising power of the material that comes into contact with the stainless, its acidity level, chloride content and temperature. The corrosion resistance of stainless steel is very important when it is being cleaned or disinfected.

When a piece of stainless steel equipment is being cleaned in place, only products that are highly alkaline or acid should be used to obtain perfect hygienic conditions. Stainless steels' exceptional resistance to corrosion of has enabled the dairy industry to develop widely and rapidly. Stainless behaves quite neutrally and does not alter the taste of fresh milk.

SEGMENTATION OF THE DAIRY MARKET

The market for dairy products can be divided into the following segments:

- Milk (including raw milk, pasteurised milk, sterilised milk, ultra-high temperature (UHT) sterilised milk, and milk powder).
- Ice cream.
- Fresh dairy products (including cream, heavy cream, UHT sterilised cream, fresh cheeses, yoghurt and dairy-free deserts such as flavoured milk, jelly milk, dessert creams, foams, egg custards, crème caramel, and rice pudding).

- Dairy compounds such as casein, caseinates and lactoserum or whey).
- Ripened cheeses (including soft, veined, pressed paste, baked firm, cooked or uncooked).
- Butters (including raw butter, salted butter, reduced-fat butter, cooking butter).

WHICH STAINLESS STEEL

Both the equipment and facilities used in the dairy industry today are made from austenitic stainless steels.

ASTM (%)	EN	Type	Chem. Composition
304	1.4301	Austenitic	18Cr, 9Ni
316	1.4401	Austenitic	17Cr, 10Ni, 2Mo

It is generally accepted that a reduction in the roughness of a surface results in less soiling. The soiling is reduced because a smaller surface are comes into contact with the surrounding environment. This is another reason why cold rolled stainless steel is generally used for stainless steels that come into contact with foods.

EQUIPMENT USED TO MANUFACTURE DAIRY PRODUCTS

The equipment required to manufacture various dairy products includes:

- Farm equipment (including milking equipment, barns and sheds, milk tanks...).
- Road tankers.
- Vats (such as storage tanks, maturation tanks, process tanks with agitators…).
- Heat treatment equipment for pasteurisation or sterilisation (for example, plate exchangers, tubular coolers, evaporators...).
- Specific equipment for making dairy products such as cheese and butter (for example, curd slicer, churns, butyrate machines…).
- Other equipment (such as packaging lines, pumps, valves...).

The table below gives a rough idea of the grades encountered for the different equipment used in the dairy industry.

Equipment	End Use	Grades
Refrigerated storage tank	All dairy products	304
Centrifuge, Pasteurizer	Milk, Yoghurt, Cream, Butter	304, 316
Plate and tubular heat exchangers	Milk, Cheese, Cream, Butter, Yoghurt	316
Packaging machine	Milk, Cream, Yoghurt	316
Ultra filtration equipment	Cheese	316
Maturation tank	Cheese, Ice Cream, Cream, Butter	304, 316
Cheese racks	Cheese	304
Other equipment	All dairy products	304, 316

CRITERIA DETERMINING THE CHOICE OF STAINLESS STEEL

Stainless steel should be utilised in the dairy industry where the following criteria are important:

- Hygiene and food safety
- Improved corrosion
- Waste water treatment
- Cost reduction in cleaning and corrosion resistance to acid
- Sterilisation and pasteurisation at high temperatures

In nearly all equipments needed in the milk and dairy industry (tank, heat treatment equipment, tubular coolers, packaging lines, agitators, etc), stainless steel brings the most effective answer to the multiple requirement for a safe and economical production process.

WHAT THEY ARE SAYING ABOUT STAINLESS STEEL IN THE DAIRY INDUSTRY

The economic advantages and technical merits of stainless steel grades have been appreciated by the milk and dairy industry for a number of years. The following testimonials show that these benefits are becoming more widely understood.

CASE STUDY IN JAPAN

Dairy products go through a diverse range of processes as they are moved from the farms where the milk originates, to the production plants where it is turned into consumer products such as pasteurised milk, cream and yoghurt. Stainless steel is widely used in almost all of the processes the milk passes through on its journey from farm to consumer. In Japan, stainless steel products are used in all phases of the dairy production process.

These phases include:

- Transportation of the raw milk
- Inspection
- Purification
- Homogenisation
- Sterilisation
- Cooling
- Filling
- Final inspection
- Shipment to shops.

Different grades of stainless are used in each phase of dairy production. For example, grade SUS304 is utilised in products used to receive the milk and in all phases up to and including homogenisation. In the sterilisation and cooling processes, either grade SUS316 or SUS316L is used. During these processes, the products can reach temperatures as high as 130°C.

These grades of stainless are also used in the production of cheese and butter, both of which contain salt. SUS316 or SUS316L can withstand both high temperatures and the corrosive properties of salt. Equipment used in ice-cream making is usually made from grade SUS304 as it can withstand the cold temperatures required.

Dairy products are very vulnerable to bacteria and have a short shelf-life.

To prevent deterioration of the product, all dairy machinery and equipment used in the production process should have the following characteristics:

- *Product Integrity*: Equipment must have accurate control and measurement devices and there should be no leaks of oil or other contaminants from the equipment into the product.

- *Cleanliness*: Equipment must have smooth surfaces that do not allow bacteria to breed. They should also be no higher than the reach of an average person's hands to ensure they can be cleaned thoroughly.
- *Disassembly:* Equipment must be easy to take apart so it can be thoroughly cleaned and sterilised.
- *Inspection*: The design of the equipment should enable the visual inspection of the product during the production process.

Fig. Milk Production Plant

In addition to hygiene, the characteristics of equipment used in the dairy industry include: resistance to chemical solutions used in cleaning (such as chloride-based sterilising agents, acids and alkalis); strength and workability.

Stainless steel meets all of these requirements. Other materials are often unsuitable because they cannot withstand the harsh conditions found in many food processing applications.

For example, sterilisers are subject to a lot of pressure. Alternative materials such as aluminium are not strong enough to withstand the pressure required. There is also a danger that aluminium will leach ions during cleaningin-place (CIP). Stainless can withstand high levels of pressure and does not leach during CIP.

TESTIMONIAL FROM SYNLAIT MILK LTD

The dairy industry is very dependent upon the use of stainless steel, for its excellent strength, its excellent corrosion resistance and the hygienic benefits of using a clean and green material.

Also, the ability of the correct grade of stainless steel to be used in many dairy plant application-as long as the stainless steel plant is well fabricated and properly cleaned routinely.

The varied applications of stainless steel in a modern milk processing plant can be demonstrated as follows: Stainless steel is used to manufacture the truck-mounted milk tanker vessels that collect milk from the stainless steel tanks on dairy farms and deliver it to the dairy factory; The milk receiving plant at the dairy factory is made of stainless steel because of strict international sanitary and hygiene requirements; The milk and cream processing tanks at the dairy factory are all made of stainless steel; The large milk powder dryer vessels are made from stainless steel; All processing vessels for milk powder are stainless steels of various grades (usually types 304/316/2205); The milk powder bagging plant, the materials delivery lines are all in stainless steel.

Fig. Chris Peacock, Energy Centre Manager, Synlait Milk Ltd

TESTIMONIAL FROM AVERY CONSULTING ASSOCIATES

One measure of nickel containing stainless steels sustainability is the number of years it has been used for dairy and food processing equipment. Early versions of stainless steel were developed in the early 1900's, but Dr. W. H. Hatfield is credited with inventing in 1924 the nickel containing 18-8 alloy or what is known today as Type 304.

In 1929 it is reported the first stainless steel tanker was used for transporting 3000 gallons of milk. This date coincided with the well publicized use of stainless steel in 1929-1930 for the top seven arches of the Chrysler Building in New York City. The late 1920's was a significant time in the advancement of food sanitation and hygiene by the establishment of 3-A Sanitary Standards in North America.

3-A came about through the cooperative efforts of the International Association of Food Industry Suppliers (IAFIS), the International Association for Food Protection (IAFP) and the Milk Industry Foundation (MIF). One of the main 3-A activities has been the development of 68 Equipment Standards and nine Acceptance Practices. These Standards are recognized and used world-wide by the dairy and food industries. One of the first Standards was Sanitary Standards for Storage Tanks for Milk and Milk Products dated March 13, 1946.

There have been eight up-dated versions, but most of the stainless steel material provisions have seen little change, for example:

- Originally the stainless steel was specified as 18-8, today Type 304 and 316 are standard.
- Originally a carbon content not more than 0.12% was specified and today the limit is 0.08%, but in practice the carbon is usually 0.03% or less.
- The mill finishes allowed and grinding of welds is essentially unchanged.

In essence, the Storage Tanks made to the Standard have passed the test of time for some 64 years.

Examples of long time service life are not easy to obtain but one large dairy and food company furnished a couple of examples of equipment still in service.

- A Type 316 Lay-down cooker installed in 1954 and still in service.
- A Type 304 stainless steel cream cheese former purchased on September 15, 1949 and still in service.

Fig. Lay Down Cooker

The most frequent need for new stainless steel equipment in the dairy process industries is related to manufacturing process changes that in turn may require a different design, size change or other modifications.

When stainless steel equipment is properly maintained, seldom is the replacement related to material failure, corrosion or just old age. Further more when the stainless steel is finally retired, there is a significant reclaim value.

TESTIMONIAL FROM PACKO INOX

Packo Inox began producing milk cooling tanks in 1965. Today, based on its "hygienic competences", the company still produces cooling tanks, along with milk processing equipment, milking machine parts, hygienic centrifugal pumps, pharmaceutical and biotechnology processing equipment and tanks, and food processing equipment.

The use of stainless steel for milk cooling tanks is prescribed by law in Europe. The general public also prefers that products and components used in the agro-food industry are made from stainless steel.

Other materials are no longer accepted. Stainless steel has gained a large segment of the food sector because it:

- Does not leach elements
- Has a surface that bacteria cannot adhere to easily
- Is easy to clean and resistant to aggressive foods (such as fruit juices, spinach, fatty acids).

Despite the ease of cleaning stainless steel, cleaning procedures need to be followed carefully to prevent biological fouling. The smoother the surface, the less bacteria can adhere to it. A fine polished finish is better than a rough one. At Packo Inox we even can electro-polish the stainless so it has a very low surface roughness. Packo also masters the CIP or "Cleaning in Place" technology of stainless steel equipment for a controlled cleaning to the highest hygienic standards.

In the past, milk was collected from the farm on a daily basis. Now it is more and more common for the milk to be collected every three days. This means bigger volumes and more efficient collection (only two farms per pick-up, instead of ten in the past).

In order to preserve the milk for three days, the finish of the milk cooling tank is a very important factor. The quality of the milk is even more important for (special) cheeses. Other benefits of stainless steel that are important to the food industry include its mechanical strength and wear resistance. Our products are an important part of the total investment budget in a dairy. Customers want to be sure that they are stable, hygienic, and long lasting.

The sustainability of stainless is a good sales argument. A milk-cooling tank is used for many years. The life cycle impact of stainless steel on the environment is becoming more and more important. The well designed Packo products therefore have a high second hand value and are found around the globe. Stainless steel has almost completely pushed aside copper in the dairy industry. Aluminium products were available for a while, but in the long term, the price advantage was not enough to counter aluminium's limited sustainability. The price of milk is determined by the market, and a premium is paid for high quality milk.

Fig. Batch Pasteurizer for Hard Cheese

Hygiene and ease of cleaning are very important to achieve that premium. Our milk cooling tanks are used all over the world in all kind of environmental and hygienic conditions. They are cleaned with all types of cleaning agents, so highly resistant grades of stainless, such as the proven 304 or even 316, are used.

Fig. Vertical Milk Cooling Silotank

We manage to engineer a product with minimum raw materials while ensuring that it has a long life span. We tested lower Ni containing alloys, but we have never introduced other materials in this market. We, and most important of all, our customers, are happy with the proven stainless steels we have been using over 45 years.

TESTIMONIAL FROM THE INTERNATIONAL DAIRY FEDERATION

Stainless steel is generally preferred over other metals. In part this is due to its properties which include ease of cleaning and its resistance to corrosion, chemical products and scratches. However, a major reason for using stainless is its surface which gives a clean and shiny look and does not require paint protection.

Therefore there is no risk of contamination and maintenance is reduced:

- Stainless has multiple uses, particularly where the product comes into contact with a metal, or where regular cleaning is required (for example, pumps, packaging machines, or pipelines).
- Due to its corrosion-resistance, stainless steel is stronger and has a longer life span which is vital for our business.
- The dairy sector is a big consumer of water, energy and chemicals. Stainless Steel contributes positively to reduction of waste volumes.

TESTIMONIAL FROM BRAZIL

Stainless steel is seen as one of the sustainable catalyzing agents in the milk production chain in Brazil. The milk production chain in Brazil is of major economic, social and environmental importance. It is estimated that the sector generates four million jobs within the one million small, medium and large dairy producers in Brazil. It is important to make these businesses profitable, in order to keep the workforce in the field and avoid migration to the big cities.

Successful dairy farming requires the integration of agriculture and cattle raising. Producers must efficiently produce the energy and protein demanded by the herd. The milk production chain begins in the agricultural industry and requires equipment, fertilizer, pest control and seed producers. Even in this first phase of the milk production chain, the characteristic properties and attributes of stainless make it an important part of the agricultural process and products.

However, when we talk about the process of producing milk and its derivative products, the role of stainless steel changes from that of supporting actor to leading actor. The machines, equipment and facilities used for milk production use stainless steel intensively.

The vacuum milking machines and cooling tanks on the farm, and the trucks that transport the milk to be processed all use stainless steel solutions. The processing factories which produce UHT milk, powdered milk, cream, cheese, butter, condensed milk, sweets, ice cream and chocolate are intensive users of stainless steel due to its properties, characteristics and attributes. When the products are shipped to the cafeterias, bakeries, supermarkets, and ice cream parlours where they are sold, they are stored and displayed in fridges, freezers and shelves which also intensively utilise stainless steel. The Brazilian dairy industry has a yearly turnover of approximately USD$8 billion. This represents around 8% of the country's entire food industry.

TESTIMONIAL FROM GEA FARM TECHNOLOGIES

GEA Farm Technologies GmbH introduced stainless steel into its products about 50 years ago. Stainless steel is now used for all applications where parts come into contact with milk at a dairy farm. These include the milking claws, pipes, pumps, cooling tanks, and components that are installed in the corrosive environment of the barn (such as parlour frames, stalls, covers, control boxes, and feeding systems).

The reasons for using stainless steel are food safety guidelines and laws, and the dairy farmer's requirements for robust, reliable, long-lasting solutions in a tough environment. Stainless steel is the only material that has been able to combine the durability, stiffness and resistance against corrosion required in the dairy industry.

- The durability of material (limited corrosion compared to carbon steel)
- Longevity of milking, cooling and feeding equipment in a corrosive environment
- Limited maintenance requirements for stainless products
- Its perception as a premium product.

The trend in the dairy industry with regard to food safety regulations is to become stricter. In many countries, dairy farming is becoming more specialised. Farmers look for professional equipment that has the lowest total cost of ownership.

Acceptance of alternative materials is limited. Stainless steel is seen as the guarantor of food safety, milk quality and the highest hygienic standards.

However, cost saving requirements, the weight of equipment, and the additional features provided by new materials are reasons that might make manufacturers turn to solutions other than stainless steel. Farming in general aims to be sustainable.

Any governmental support, especially in Europe, is linked to sustainable production which includes sustainable product solutions. Stainless steel is, to a certain extent, a sales argument. Compared to most modern alternatives, stainless steel can be recycled.

As dairy farming is strongly depending on natural resources, there is a clear trend to save water, energy and chemicals. Government initiatives in many countries force our customers to review their production schemes to ensure they are more environmental friendly and reduce the consumption of scarce resources such as water. GEA is developing more efficient product systems that incorporate pre-cooling or heatrecovery systems to reduce energy costs.

At GEA, we favour stainless steel from the manufacturing and engineering perspective. Supply management in terms of availability and predictable pricing is a challenge. For decades, stainless steel has helped dairy farmers keep the quality of their milk at the highest level. This ensures safety in the food chain and profitability for the dairy farmer.

TESTIMONIAL FROM THE INSTITUTE NATIONAL DE LA RECHERCHE AGRONOMIQUE (INRA)

Today the dairy industry utilises a large amount of stainless steel in all its forms, throughout the milk and dairy-product production chain. Stainless steel was introduced several years ago to solve problems such as cleaning resistance and equipment hygiene. Hence, its resistance to corrosion and ease of cleaning have been developed through the improvement of stainless steel's surface properties which make it neutral to chemicals, bacteria and the product it is in contact with. Since the eighties, laboratories from the Institute National de la Recherche Agronomique (INRA) have worked on the integration of these properties. In the process, INRA and in particular the laboratory from Villeneuve d'Ascq (PIHM) has established close collaborations with industrial equipment manufacturers to develop the properties of stainless.

It is difficult to find alternative products to compete with stainless steel in the food industry. In the dairy industry in particular, processing is often done at high temperature and in harsh conditions. However, in some manufacturing operations alternative materials are employed. Their use is still marginal in processing lines and confined to applications such as seals and diaphragms (made of polymers) or filters and pumps (ceramics).

Stainless steels of type 304 and 316 have proven that they can resist the harsh production conditions mentioned. There is a question as to whether the stainless grades used in the food industry are over-specified. The dairy industry is currently changing its processes to milder conditions preserving the nutritional qualities and integrating hygienically designed systems requiring less tough cleaning conditions. Therefore new 'less-rich' stainless products and compositions could be introduced. Developments in stainless steel are expected in niche areas for specific applications.

At INRA, we think stainless could be developed in two directions:

1. Work on the micro-topography or nano-topography of the surface to reduce organic fouling and microbial fouling (biofilm).
2. Develop the concept of coatings and focus on surface modifications using techniques such as ion bombardment, plasma treatments, or surface nanotechnology. This would enable a lower grade of stainless to be used as a base of these new surfaces and not directly in contact with food products, provided the resistance (wear) of the coating could be maintained over time.

A comprehensive approach to developing gentler processing techniques for dairy products could enable producers to utilise softer cleaning processes. This would reduce the impact of harsh cleaning products, and stainless steel, on the environment.

CONCLUSION

Stainless steels have a smooth, neutral surface which does not pick up tastes or smells. Stainless steels are extremely strong so they can withstand tough industrial environments. Today dairy equipment is made of stainless steels because it is easy to clean, disinfect and does not react with the lactic acids formed by fermenting milk. Strict standards of hygiene are possible at every stage of its use.

6

Cross-flow Membrane Applications in the Food Industry

INTRODUCTION

Over the last two decades, the worldwide market for membrane technology in the food industry increased to a market volume of about € 800–850 million and is now the second biggest industrial market for membranes after water and wastewater treatment including desalination.

The key membrane technologies in the food industry are the pressure-driven membrane processes:

- Microfiltration (MF),
- Ultrafiltration (UF),
- Nanofiltration (NF) and
- Reverse osmosis (RO).

The market share ofUF systems and membranes accounts for the largest share of the membrane market with 35%, followed by MF systems and membranes with a share of 33%, and NF/RO systems and membranes with a share of 30%.

Other membrane processes such as:

- Membrane contactors (MC),
- Electrodialysis (ED) and
- Pervaporation (PV) have only a small market share.

The major applications in this market are in the dairy industry (milk, whey, brine, etc.) followed by other beverage industries (beer, fruit juices, and wine, etc.). The success of membrane technology in the food and beverage market is directly linked to some of the key advantages of membrane processes over conventional separation technologies.

Among these advantages are:

- Gentle product treatment due to moderate temperature changes during
  processing;

- High selectivity based on unique separation mechanisms, for example sieving, solution-diffusion or ion-exchange mechanism;
- Compact and modular design for ease of installation and extension;
- Low energy consumption compared to condensers and evaporators.

The key disadvantage of membrane filtration is the fouling of the membrane causing a reduction in flux and thus a loss in process productivity over time. The effect of fouling can be minimized by regular cleaning intervals. In the food industry it is common to have at least one cleaning cycle per 24-h shift. Other actions to reduce fouling are directly related to plant design and operation.

During the plant design, the selection of a low-fouling membrane, for example hydrophilic membranes to reduce fouling by bacteria, andmembrane modules with appropriate channel heights, for example modules with open channel design to avoid blockage by particles, can reduce the risk of fouling and contamination significantly. Operating the plant below the critical flux–the flux below which a decline of flux over time does not occur, and above which fouling is observed–can extend the time between cleaning intervals significantly but is commonly related to low-pressure/low-flux operation, which translates into low capacities.

Alternatively, operating the process in turbulent flow regime can reduce the effect of fouling, but the generation of turbulence is linked to an increase in pressure drop and therefore higher energy costs.

Other limitations to the application ofmembrane processes might be related to the feed characteristics, for example increase of viscosity with concentration, or to separationmechanismsused in the membrane process, for example osmotic pressure increases with concentration. Successful applications of membrane processes in the food industry will be introduced. The first part of this stage will focus on the dairy industry, the largest and most developed membrane market in the food industry, followed by the fermented food products–beer, wine and vinegar–fruit juices and other established membrane applications. The final section of this stage will give an outlook of potential membrane applications in the food industry focusing especially on the emerging membrane technologies: membrane contactors, pervaporation and electrodialysis.

DAIRY INDUSTRY

DAIRY INDUSTRY OVERVIEW

The dairy industry has used membrane processing since its introduction in the food industry in the late 1960s to clarify, concentrate and fractionate a variety of dairy products. Applying membrane technology to whey processing allowed the production of refined proteins and commercial usage and thus transformed a waste byproduct from cheese production into a valuable product. In addition to whey processing, membrane technology is also used for fluid milk processing with clear advantages. Further, specific milk components can be obtained without causing a phase change to the fluid milk by the addition of heat as in evaporation, or an enzyme, as done in most cheese-making techniques.

The filtered milk can then be directly used in the manufacture of such dairy products as cheese, ice cream and yoghurt. By applying membranes with different pore sizes and molecular weight cut-offs (MWCOs), the milk can be modified by separating, clarifying, or fractionating a selected component in milk from other components. The pressure-driven membrane processes MF, UF, NFand RO are the most common membrane processes in the dairy industry and based on their applicability range it is possible to separate virtually every major component of milk as shown in Figure, thus enabling the manufacturing of products with unique properties and functionalities.

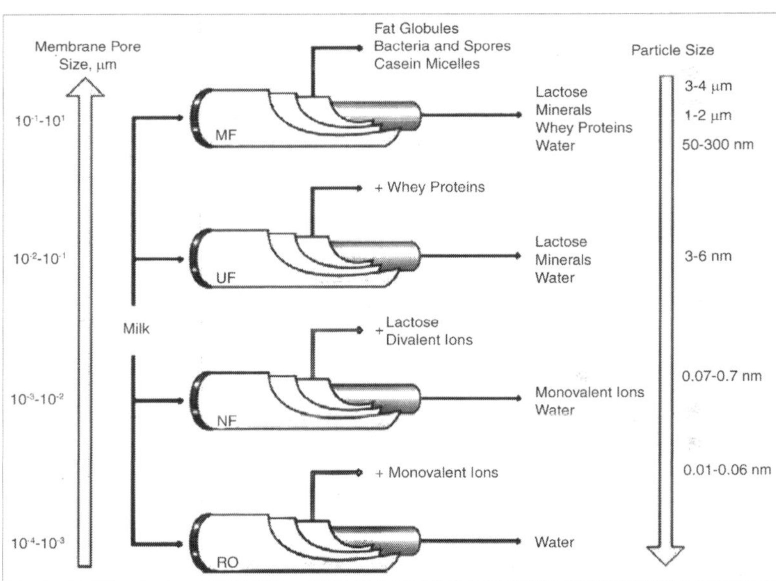

Fig. Milk Processing with Membrane Technology

KEY MEMBRANE APPLICATIONS

The key applications of cross-flow membrane technology in the dairy industry are discussed.

Removal of Bacteria and Spores from Milk, Whey and Cheese Brine

The removal of bacteria and spores from milk to extend its shelf-life by MF is an alternative way to ultrapasteurization. In this approach, the organoleptic and chemical properties of the milk are unaltered. The first commercial system of this so-called Bactocatch was developed by Alfa Laval

[1–3] and marketed by Tetra Pak under the name Tetra Alcross®Bactocatch. In this process, the raw milk is separated into skim milk and cream. The resulting skim milk is microfiltered using ceramic membranes with a pore size of 1.4 μm at constant transmembrane pressure (TMP). Thus, the retentate contains nearly all the bacteria and spores, while the bacterial concentration in the permeate is less than 0.5% of the original value in milk.

The retentate is then mixed with a standardized quantity of cream. Subsequently, this mix is subjected to a conventional high heat treatment at 130°C for 4s and reintroduced into the permeate, and the mixture is then pasteurized. Since less than 10% of the milk is heat treated at the high temperature, the sensory quality of the milk is significantly improved.

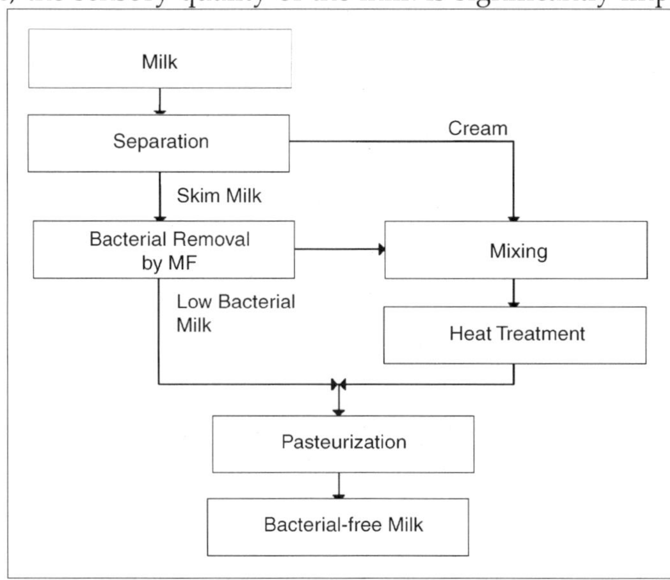

Fig. Bacterial Removal from Milk by MF

MF for the removal of bacteria and spores can be further applied in the production of other dairy products. In the production of cheese, the use of low bacterial milk improves also the keeping quality of cheese due to the removal of spores, thus eliminating the need of additives (*e.g.*, nitrate). While in the production of whey protein concentrates (WPC) and isolates (WPI), this MF concept is used to remove bacteria and spores giving a high quality product. Hence, by applying MF the heat treatment of the WPC/WPI is kept to a minimum, which preserves the functional properties of the whey proteins.

Finally, in the manufacture of cheese the concentrated curd is submerged in a salt solution to improve the cheese preservation and to develop the flavour and other cheese properties. This process is called brining. Efficient sanitation of cheese brine has become a major concern to the dairy industry in recent years. This results from the possibility of post-contamination of cheeses in the brine, especially by pathogenic bacteria. The application of MF for sanitation of cheese brine, using ceramic or spiralwound membranes, results in a superior cheese quality compared to the traditional processes of heat treatment and kieselguhr filtration. MFhas the advantages of being simple to perform, of maintaining the chemical balance of the brine and of eliminating filter aids. In the brine treatment by MF it is normally necessary to make a prefiltration of the brine solution, which is easily done by dead-end filter bag or cartridge with a pore size of 100 μm.

Milk Protein Standardization, Concentration and Fractionation

The protein content of milk is subjected to natural variations during the year. Standardization of milk by UF offers the possibility of increasing or decreasing the protein content in milk without the need of adding milk powders, casein and whey protein concentrates. Skim milk and 1% milk with increased protein content have an improved appearance (whiter milk) and higher viscosity.

The sensory quality of increased protein milk is therefore more similar to that of higher fat milks resulting in an improved consumer appeal. Another application of UFis the standardization of protein and total solids in milk for use in fermented dairy products, such as cream cheeses, yoghurt and cottage cheeses. The resulting dairy products have superior quality and sensory characteristics compared to those produced from milk concentrated by conventional methods. With the quality obtained by membrane filtration, attributes such as consistency, post-processing and extent of syneresis are easier to control. However, the use of membrane-processed milk often requires an adjustment in starter culture selection and fermentation conditions due to the compositional changes in the UF milk.

Concentrationof milk, whichconventionally isdonebyevaporation techniques, can also be achieved by RO. The concentrated milk has its greatest potential in ice-cream manufacturing, since all the solids are retained in the concentrateand 70% of the water is removed. MF and/or UF are used in the production of milk protein concentrates (MPC), which are products containing 50–58% of protein.

These products are used as food additives and it is therefore extremely important to maintain the functionality of the proteins. By using UF membranes in combination with MF and/or diafiltration (DF) with the corrected adjustments of pH, temperature and filtration conditions, it is possible to produce the desirable MPC for a specific food application.

Themost promisingMFapplication in the dairy industry is the fractionation of milk protein. The separation of micellar casein from the whey proteins can be achieved by ceramic membranes with a pore size of 0.2 μm at a constant TMP. The resulting retentate has a high concentration of native calcium phosphocaseinate that can be used for cheese making.

Native casein has an excellent rennet-coagulation ability that will make calcium phosphocaseinate an exceptional enrichment for cheese-milk. The permeate can be further processed byUFto produce high-qualityWPC. These protein concentrates can be further separated into lactoferrin, β-lactoglobulin and α-lactalbumin via ion-exchange chromatography. Both β-lactoglobulin and α-lactalbumin have great potential markets.

β-lactoglobulin can be used as a gelling agent and α-lactalbumin, which is very rich in tryptophan, can be used in the production of peptides with physiological properties. Another application can be the production of infant milk. The fractionation of milk proteins using membrane technology enables the recovery of value-added protein ingredients. Further, the casein and whey proteins are separated without the need of heat or enzymes. The potential applications of membrane separation in milk processing are shown in Figure.

Whey Protein Concentration and Fractionation

Whey is a by-product from the cheese industry. It has low content of solids and high biological oxygen demand (BOD), which creates a major disposal problem for the dairy industry. In the past, all whey was disposed of as sewage, sprayed on fields or used for animal feed. By applying membrane technology whey can be concentrated to produce WPC and WPI, as well as fractionated and purified to obtain purified α-lactalbumin and β-lactoglobulin. Hence, a once wasted product can be converted into high value-added products and at the same time one of the key pollution problems of the dairy industry can be solved. Consequently, the use of UFand RO to concentrate whey was one of the first applications of membranes in the dairy industry. Due to the complexity and diversity of whey, it is necessary to use different membrane processes to produce a specific product.

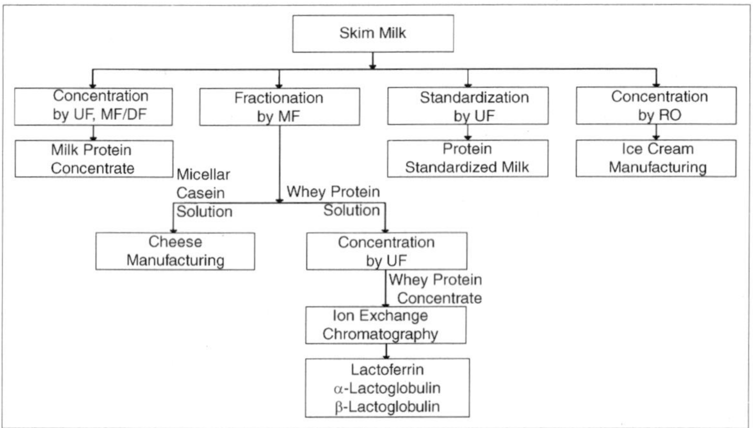

Fig. Applications of Membrane Technology in Milk Processing

The production of WPC with 35–85% protein in the total solids can be achieved by a combination of UF and DF. MF can be used as a pretreatment to remove both bacteria and fat and allows the production of WPI with 90% protein in the total solids. Whey proteins have not only a high nutritional value but also functional properties. They can be used as gelling, emulsifying and foaming agents. Therefore, whey concentrates have farreaching applications not only in dairy foods, but also in confectionary, nutritional foods, beverages and even processed meats.

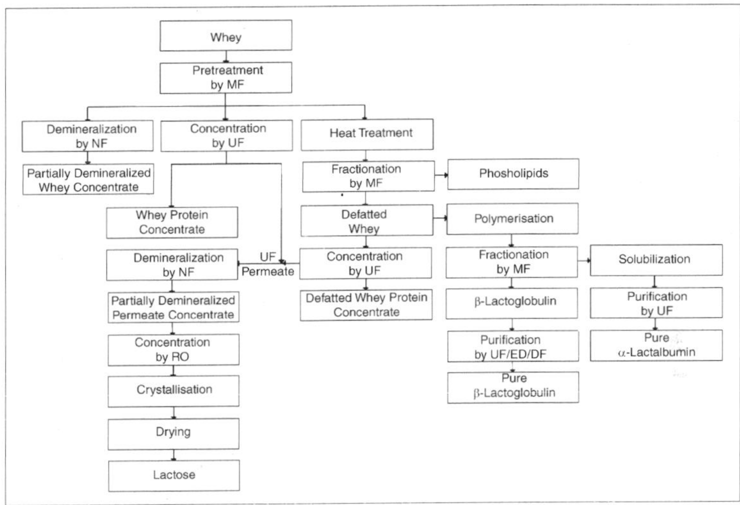

Fig. Applications of Membrane Technology in Whey Processing

The presence of fat in whey leads to decreased functional properties and shorter storage time. Several processes involving membranes have been developed to remove the residual fat from whey. The most common process, developed byMaubois et al. and Fauquant *et al.*, exploits the ability of the phospholipids to aggregate by calcium binding under moderate heat treatment for 8 min at 50°C. This process is called thermocalcic precipitation. Defatted whey is then obtained by MF with a pore size of 0.14 μm to separate the resulting precipitate.

Defatted whey can be further processed by UF, which also improves the performance in the subsequent membrane processes. The defatted WPC has a foaming capacity similar to that of egg white and the same protein content. Its applications can be as raw material in the pastry and icecream production. The MF retentate, which contains a high amount of phospholipids, can be used as an effective emulsifier agent for food and cosmetic applications.

The purified proteins β-lactoglobulin and α-lactalbumin can be obtained from the defatted whey. At low pH (4.0–4.5) and under moderate heat treatment for 30 min at 55°C, α-lactalbumin polymerizes reversibly entrapping most of the residual lipidsand the other whey proteins with the exception of the β-lactoglobulin. The fractionation of β-lactoglobulin from the remaining proteins can then be done by MF with apore size of 0.2 μm or centrifugation.

The resulting soluble phase, rich in β-lactoglobulin, can be further purified by UF coupled with electrodialysis (ED) or DF. Purification of α-lactalbumin from the MF retentate can be achieved by solubilization at a neutral pH and subsequently by UF using a membrane with an MWCO of 50,000 Dalton. It has also been reported that membranes can be applied for the isolation of Kcasein-glycomacropeptid (GMP) from cheese whey. GMP can find several applications in the pharmaceutical industry.

Studies have shown that GMP avoids the adhesion of Escherichia coli cells to the intestine walls, protects against influenza and prevents adhesion of tartar to teeth. It should also be noted that membrane filtration also plays a major role in the lactose manufacture from whey using UF and RO and in the production of lowcarbohydrate beverages with high dairy protein content.

Whey Demineralization

In the dairy industry, the NFprocess is used to concentrate and partially demineralize liquid whey. Due to the selectivity of the membranes most of the monovalent ions, the organic acids, and some of the lactose will pass the membrane. NF is a very interesting alternative to ion exchange and ED if moderate demineralization is required. One advantage of NF compared to the other two processes is that NF is a simple process, which partially demineralizes and concentrates the whey at the same time.

The maximum level of demineralization by NF is about 35% reduction of the ash content with a concentration factor of about 3.5–4. By applying a DF step it is possible to increase the level of demineralization up to 45%. Other applications of NF in whey processing include: concentration and partial demineralization of whey UF permeates prior to the manufacture of lactose and lactose derivatives, converting. salt whey. to normal whey while solving a disposal problem, treating cheese brine solutions to be reused. The potential applications of membrane separation in whey processing are shown in Figure.

Cheese Manufacturing

Another early application of membrane technology in the dairy industry was in cheese manufacturing for production of Feta cheese and brine treatment by UF. Nowadays, membrane-processed milk is also successfully used in the manufacturing of quark and cream cheeses. Together with WPC production, the use of UF milk for the production of cheese is the most widespread application of membranes in the dairy industry.

The advantages of UFconcentrated milk in cheese making compared to traditional methods are the following:

- Increases the total solids, which increases the cheese yield and therefore decreases the production costs in terms of energy and equipment;

- Reduces the rennet and starter culture requirements since UF-milk has a good ability of enzymatic coagulation;
- Reduces the wastewater processing costs of the cheese plant;
- Improves the quality and composition control;
- Increases the nutritional value due to the incorporation of the whey protein in the cheese.

UF in cheese processing can be used in three ways:

(1) *Preconcentration*: The standardized cheese milk is concentrated by a factor of 1.2–2 and it can be used for most cheese types. This allows the capacity of the cheese vats and whey draining equipment to be doubled. However, the cheese yield will not be significantly improved since only 4. 5–5% of the protein content is increased. It is used to produce Cheddar, Cottage Cheese and Mozzarella, and it can be used to standardize cheese milk and manipulate its mineral composition, resulting in a more consistent quality in the final product.

(2) *Partial Concentration*: The standardized cheese milk is concentrated by a factor 2–6. It is used in the manufacture of Cheddar cheese by using for example, the APV-SiroCurd process, in which the milk is concentrated five times with DF in order to standardize the salt balance. It is also used to produce other cheese types like Queso Fresco, structure Feta, Camembert and Brie.

(3) *Total Concentration*: The standardized cheese milk is concentrated to the total solids content in the final cheese. This provides the maximum yield increase and since there is no whey drainage, the cheese can be manufactured without the need for a cheese vat. It is used to produce cast Feta, quark, cream cheese, Ricotta and Mascarpone.

The UF permeate, which contains mainly lactose, can be concentrated by RO. The permeate from the RO process can be polished by another RO unit. After pasteurization orUVlight treatment, the permeate from the polisher can be used at the plant as process water, thus reducing the water costs of the plant. Although UF has advantages in cheese production, the increase of whey content in the cheesedueto the concentration of all milk proteinscan have a negative effectonthe ripening of semihard and hard cheeses. Therefore, UFshould be viewed as a complementary process to cheese manufacturing and not as an alternative process.

FERMENTED FOOD PRODUCTS

In the production of the fermented food products, for example beer, wine and vinegar, membranes have initially established themselves as a clarification step after the fermentation. Initially, dead-end filters were used in the production of fermented food products followed by the first trials of cross-flow filtration for the clarification of beer, wine and vinegar in the 1970s. However, the first industrial application in this segment was the dealcoholization of beer by RO in the 1980s. In the last decade, membrane filtration has established itself for the clarification of wine, beer and vinegar and based on its now proven reliability in other production steps.

BEER

The conventional brewing process starts in the brew house with the stepping of the malt with hot water to produce wort, a thick sweet liquid. The wort is then passed to the wort boiler in which it is brewed/boiled for up to 2 h followed by clarification and cooling. The clarified and cooled wort is combined with yeast and passed on to the fermentation tanks in which the yeast converts the grain sugar to alcohol and as such produces beer. Before being transferred to the bright beer tanks, the beer is commonly clarified. The finished beer might then be fine-filtered and pasteurized before bottling. In the case of beer dealcoholisation, the alcohol removal takes place before the beer clarification. The overall brewing process with potential applications of cross-flow membrane filtration is shown in Figure.

Beer from Tank Bottoms/Recovery of Surplus Yeast

After fermentation, yeast is settling at the bottom of the fermentation vessels. The settled tank bottoms account for 1.5–2% of the total beer volume and, apart from the yeast, contain a high proportion of beer that is lost if not recovered. In order to recover the beer and concentrate the yeast up to 20% DM, a continuous membrane process has been developed, which separates the beer from the yeast by cross-flow MF with plate-and-frame modules or tubular modules. The layout of this process with plateand-frame modules is shown in Figure.

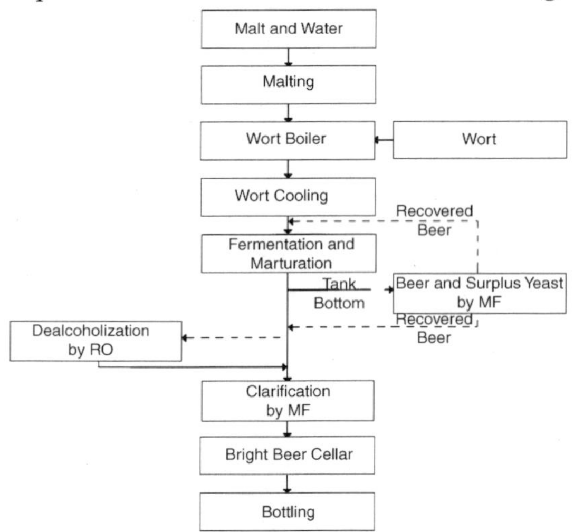

Fig. Beer Production with Membrane Technology

The investment and operating costs of the beer recovery plant are balanced by the beer recovered from the yeast.

For a typical brewery with an annual production of 2 million hl, the recovered beer amounts to 24,000 hl, or about 1% of the annual production. Furthermore, the recovered yeast has an increased dryness that supports further processing.

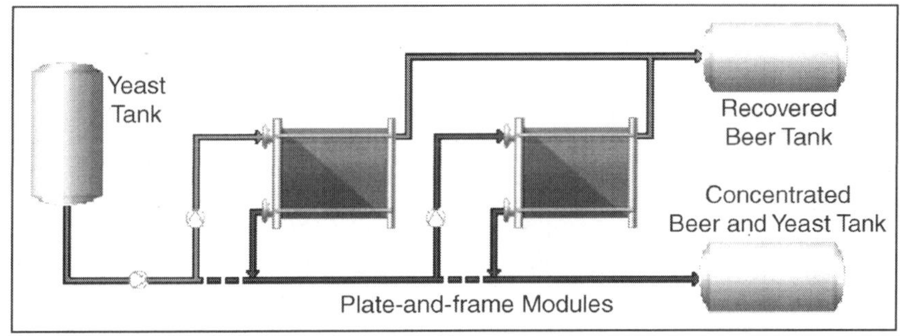

Fig. Recovery of Beer and Surplus Yeast from Tank Bottoms

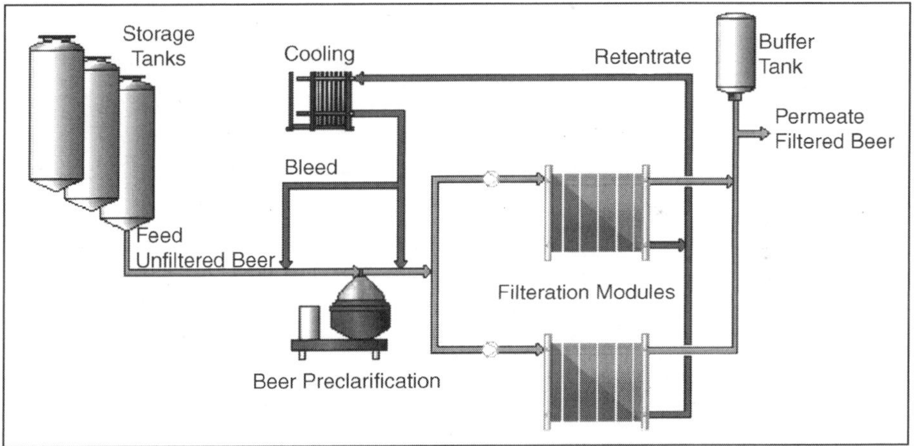

Fig. Concept of Beer Clarification by MF

Beer Clarification

In the traditional brewing process, the clarification of the beer after fermentation and maturation is often achieved by a separator followed by kieselguhr filtration, a process that is associated with handling and disposal of the powder as well as large amounts of effluents.

To overcome these problems, cross-flowMFwith plate-and-frame cassettes has been adopted to remove yeast, micro-organisms and haze without affecting the taste of the beer. The concept of this process is shown in Figure.

Beer Dealcoholization

The demand for low-alcohol and alcohol-free drinks has been constantly growing over the last decade. The market development, for example in Germany shows an increase in the annual consumption of alcohol-free drinks from 130.4 l per person in 1980 to 248.4 l per person in 1999.

While in the same period the consumption of alcoholic drinks decreased from 179.5 to 156.3 l per person. RO can be used to reduce the alcohol concentration 8–10 times, while maintaining the beer flavour.

The dealcoholization of beer by RO is divided into four steps:

1. *Preconcentration*: The beer is separated into a permeate stream containing water and alcohol and a retentate stream consisting of concentrated beer and flavours.
2. *Diafiltration*: Addition of desalted and deoxygenized water to balance the volume removal with the permeate combined with continuous water and alcohol removal with the permeate.
3. *Alcohol Adjustment:* Fine tuning of taste and alcohol content by addition of desalted and deoxygenized water.
4. *Post-treatment*: To balance taste losses due to removal of the taste carrier alcohol, components such as hops and syrups are added to the dealcoholized beer.

All the steps are operated at temperatures of 7–8°C or lower, resulting in a highquality beer, the flavour of which is not affected by a heating process. After dealcoholization, the beer is clarified before bottling.

WINE

The traditional wine-making process starts with the crushing and pressing of the grapes followed by must correction, if required. The grape juice from the pressing is centrifuged and transferred to the fermentation tanks, where the fermentation process starts under the addition of yeast. When the fermentation is completed, the yeast fraction from the wine is removed and the wine is moved into barrels for aging. After the aging, the mature wine is clarified, tartar stabilized, sterile filtered and bottled.

Membrane processes can replace several of the different separation steps involved in the traditional wine production as shown in Figure. When the taste of the wine has been deteriorated or dealcoholization of the wine is desired, then these steps are taken before the sterile filtration.

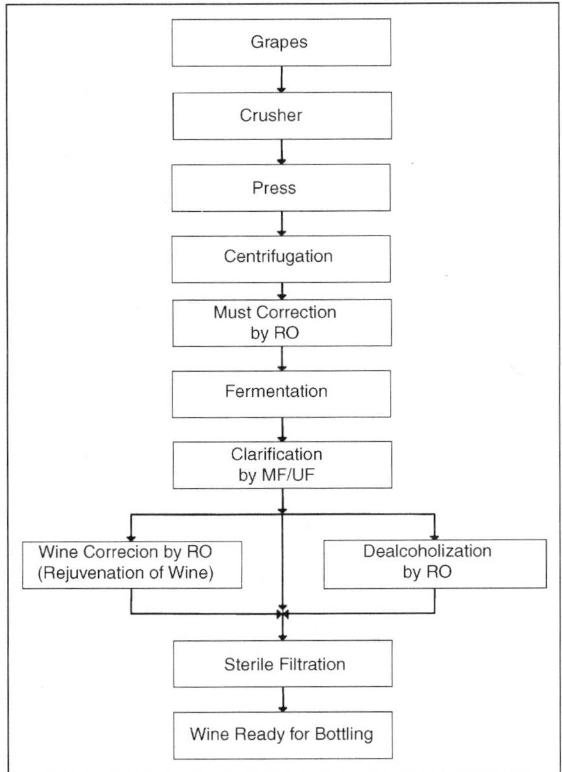

Fig. Membrane Processes in the Wine Production

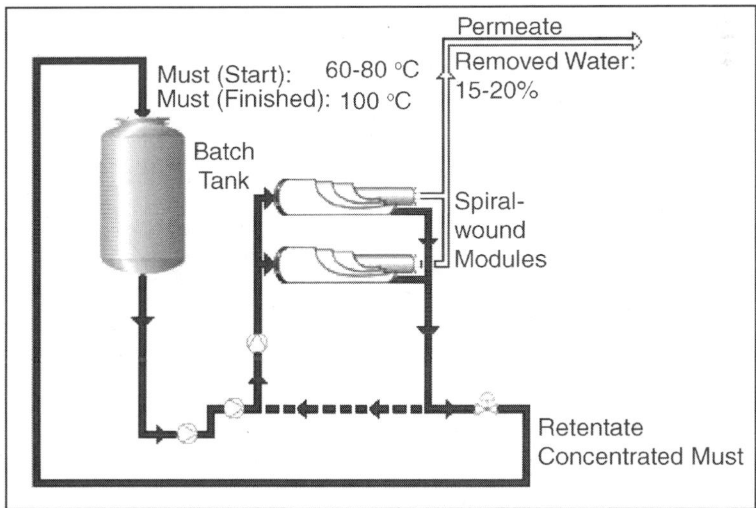

Fig. Batch Plant for must Correction by RO

Must Correction

As an alternative to chaptalization or other treatments, RO can be applied to increase sugar contents in the wine without addition of nongrape components at ambient temperature and to adjustand balance the composition of the must. The use of RO leads to enrichment in tannins and organoleptic components by water reduction between 5 and 20%.

This method is particularly suitable to reverse the dilution of the must quality due to rain during the harvest by the selective removal of excess water. However, applying this method to must from grapes of stalled maturity due to cold weather was found to be less effective, since apart from sugar, acid and green tannins are also concentrated. In general, the use of this method is limited by the legislation in the different countries. The concept for a must correction plant is shown.

Clarification of Wine

The traditional fining after fermentation often involves several steps of centrifu-gation and kieselguhr filtration to obtain the desired quality. The use of MF/UF can reduce the number of steps by combining clarification, stabilization and sterile filtration in one continuous operation and eliminates the use of fining substances and filter material. The key to success in the clarification of wine is the membrane selection with regard to fouling behaviour and pore size. Another important factor is the membrane pore diameter. A selection of critical wine compounds and their sizes is given. Typically, MFmembranes with pore diameters between 0.20 and 0.45 μm are used for white wine and between 0.45 and 0.65 μm for red wine filtration.

Rejuvenation of Old Wine (Lifting)

Aging might deteriorate the taste of wine vinified to be consumed young. A diafiltration process by RO can be applied to lift the wine by removing the negative aroma components causing the stale taste with the permeate. The wine is treated by an RO unit, which concentrates the wine slightly by removing mainly water, little alcohol and the negative aroma components.

Table. Wine Compounds and Sizes

Component	Size
Large suspended solids	50–200 μm
Yeast	1–8 μm
Bacteria	0.5–1.0 μm
Polysaccharides	50,000–200,000D
Proteins, tannins, polymerized anthocyanins	10,000–100,000D
Simple phenols, anthocyanics	500–2000D
Ethanol, volatiles	20–60D

The volume lost by the permeate may be replaced by continuously adding demineralized water to avoid remineralization of the wine. The diafiltration process slightly decreases the alcohol content of the wine but improves the quality of the old wine so that it can be sold at a higher price or blended with younger wine. The advantage of this lifting process is that it does not change the structure and composition of the wine, while the effect of the alcohol reduction is minor.

Alcohol Removal

Similar to the beer market, the demand for low alcohol wine has increased in recent years. Initial trials in the production of alcohol-free wine can be dated back to 1908 when Jung took out a patenton the thermal dealcoholization of wine. Presently, RO is used to remove ethanol and water, which have a relatively low molecular weight in comparison to the other compounds in wine, which passes through the membrane, while the larger compounds of the wine matrix are rejected.

The process is similar to the dealcoholization of beer, and can be similarly subdivided in preconcentration, diafiltration and alcohol adjustment. Apart from producing alcohol-free wines, this technique can be used to adjust the alcohol level in wine. Wine makers often allow their grapes to ripen until an optimum rich flavour is achieved. At this stage, the grape juice often contains high sugar levels, which result in high alcohol content after fermentation. The alcoholic aroma, however, suppresses other flavours in the wine. By use of RO, the wine can be slightly concentrated by removing water and part of the alcohol. This allows wine makers to harvest grapes depending on the grape flavour ripeness and independent of their sugar contents.

VINEGAR

The production of vinegar is an old process, referred to in the history as far back as Babylon 5000 BC. Over the years, the product has been developed according to nationality and tradition, resulting in widely different methods of production.

Vinegar is produced by an aerobe fermentation of bacteria (genus acetobacter) reacting on dilute solutions of ethyl alcohol such as cider, wine, fermented fruit juice or dilute distilled alcohol. The different raw materials (apples, grapes, malt, rice, etc.) each contribute to giving the vinegar its special aroma and flavour.

In the traditional production process, vinegar requires a reaction time between 3 and 6 months for formation and sedimentation. For some vinegar types, fining agents are also necessary, which are added to the vinegar after fermentation. The final filtration takes place after storage in order to remove the colloids formed. In Figure, the production process of vinegar including membrane technology is shown.

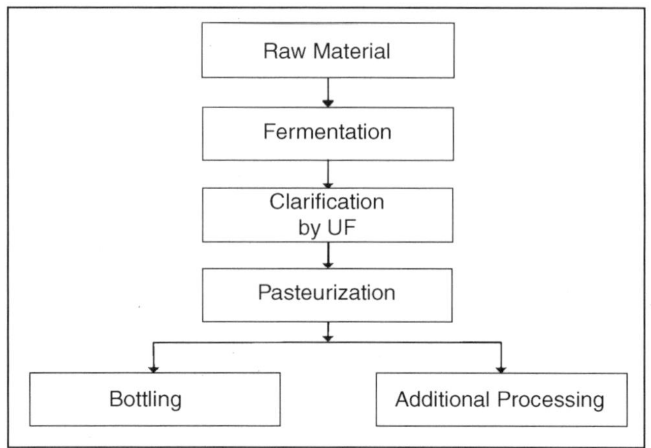

Fig. Membrane Technology in Vinegar Production

Clarification of Vinegar

The clarification of vinegar by UF is positioned directly after the fermentation step and can substitute many steps in the traditional production. The vinegar fining byUF can be applied for a wide range of vinegar types and results in a vinegar product on the permeate side, that has similar colour and organoleptic qualities to the original vinegar but no turbidity. Additionally, proteins, pectins, yeast, fungi, bacteria and colloids are removed and thus the filtration/sedimentation and the clarification are substituted and the storage time reduced. Hence, the permeate from the UF step can be directly pasteurized before bottling or additional processing. However, UF cannot give the vinegar the aroma, which is normally obtained during storage. This aroma is secured by the storage time in the wholesale and retail stages instead.

FRUIT JUICES

The general production flow in the fruit juice industry starts with grinding or crushing of the fruits into an optimal and uniform size of particles and then pressing out the fruit mash. The traditional fining process consists of long retention time in tanks followed by kieselguhr filtration and requires large amounts of enzymes, gelatin and other chemicals. After clarification/fining, the fruit juice is concentrated to reduce costs for transportation and storage.

The common approach to concentrate fruit juice is by using an evaporator combined with an aroma-recovery unit concentrating the apple juice from originally 11–12 Brix to over 70 Brix. The concentrated fruit juice can then be optionally pasteurized before transportation. The general fruit juice production process including membrane processes is shown in Figure.

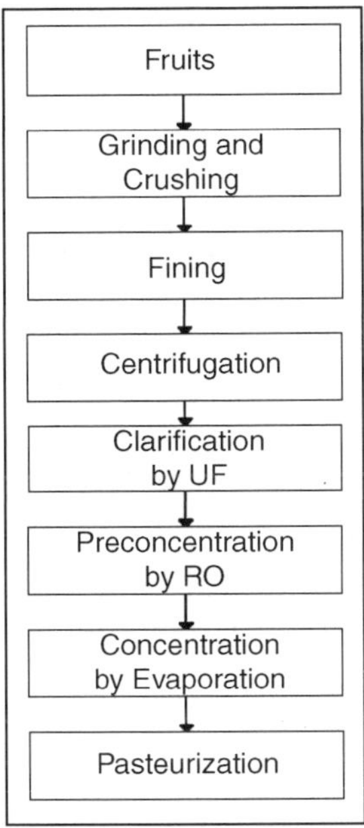

Fig. Membrane Processes in Fruit Juice Production

FRUIT-JUICE CLARIFICATION

The clarification of fruit juice, mainly apple but also grape, pineapple and orange juice by UF has proven to be an attractive substitute for the traditional fining and filtering process from an economic and qualitative point of view since the 1970s.

The UF process removes the suspended solids and other high molecular solids and the filtered juice obtains a clarity and excellent quality, which has not previously been obtainable. Thus, the UF process substitutes the fining step in the traditional process. In order to achieve high yield, high capacity and excellent quality, an enzyme treatment and proper prefiltration must be carried out before the UF system is utilized.

Until now, the industrial standard is to use polymeric and ceramic tubular modules for the clarification of the juice. However, this module type is associated with low packing density and high membrane replacement costs. Furthermore, this process is commonly run in batch mode and diafiltration water has to be added in the final stage of the clarification to maximize the process yield.

More recently, a new concept has been developed, which combines a high-speed separator with spiral-wound UF modules to overcome these limitations.

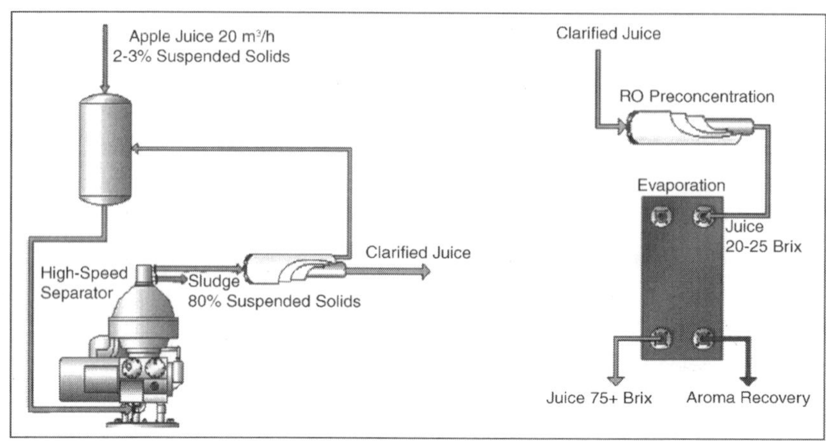

Fig. Juice Clarification (Left) and Juice oncentration (Right)

FRUIT-JUICE CONCENTRATION

For the concentration of apple juice, the combination of RO and evaporation can provide an interesting process combination. RO as initial step can remove more than 50% of the water content prior to evaporation, while maintaining 98–99% of sugar and acid as well as 80–90% of volatile flavours in the concentrate.

By applying RO, concentration levels of 20–25 Brix can be achieved, while the subsequent evaporation can boost these levels to above 75 Brix. By applying this concept, only 7–9kWhperm3 fruit juice are required, which represents an energy saving of 60–75% compared to direct evaporation. Furthermore, the permeate from the RO unit can be recycled as process water.

THER MEMBRANE APPLICATIONS IN THE FOOD INDUSTRY

Apart from the production processes, there are many other applications of membrane processes in the food industry. The first part of this section provides an overview of other key membrane applications in the food industry directly related to the product stream. The aim is not to give a complete listing of all possible applications but to document the diverse applicability of membranes in the food production. The second part of this section focuses on the membrane applications in the food industry related to process water and wastewater.

MEMBRANE PROCESSES AS PRODUCTION STEP

The continuous improvement and proven use of membranes in the industry has established membrane technology as a molecular separation unit in a wide range of applications in the food industry. A selection of other established membrane applications in the food industry from the continuously growing list of applications is presented.

MEMBRANE PROCESSES FOR WATER AND WASTEWATER

The food industry is one of the largest water-using industries. In the industry, water is used as an ingredient, for initial and intermediate cleaning of the product, and as a key agent in the sanitation of the plant. Depending on the purpose, the requirements for the water vary significantly.

The water used in the food industry can be generally classified into three types:

(1) *Process Water*: Potable water used as an ingredient, is part of or in direct contact with the food.

(2) *Boiler and Cooling Water:* Soft water to avoid scaling and fouling of the cooling and heating equipment.

(3) *General Purpose Water*: Potable, often chlorinated water to rinse raw materials, prepared products, and equipment.

After usage, the different water streams have to be treated as for recycling or for discharge. Membrane processes play an important role in both the pretreatment of the water before usage and post-treatment of the water before recycling or discharge. Some applications of membranes in the pretreatment and posttreatment of water are summarized.

FUTURE TRENDS

It is predicted that membrane processes will continue to grow at average annual growth rates of 5–8% in the foreseeable future. Apart from the worldwide acceptance and use of membrane processes, the key drivers for this development can be related to three key areas.

NEW APPLICATIONS OF MEMBRANE PROCESSES

The development of new applications of the established membrane processes MF, UF, NF and RO will be driven by economical and environmental targets.

An additional driver for membrane processes is the high growth rate of the market for functional foods, a segment in which membranes has a high potential. Some of the most recent research trends on membrane applications for MF, UF, NF and RO in the food industry are summarized.

NEW MEMBRANE PROCESSES

In recent years, three new membrane processes have been developed for applications in the food industry. The processes and their potential in the food industry are shown in the following.

Table. New Applications of MF, UF, NF and RO in the Food Iindustry

Application Processes	Membrane
Dairy	
Concentration of whole and skim milk	RO
Partly demineralized WPC (baby food, special WPC products)	NF
Production of whey protein concentrates and isolates	UF
Defatting of whey for high protein WPC	MF
Standardization of the protein content in cheese milk	MF
Wine	
Preclarification of grape juice	MF/UF
Fruit juices	
Clarification of pulpy tropical fruit juices	MF
Concentration of tomato juice	MF and RO
Other applications	
Concentration of chicken blood plasma	
Filtration of extra virgin olive oil	MF/UF
Dry degumming of vegetable oil	UF/NF

Pervaporation

While the use of pervaporation for the dehydration of organic compounds is stateof-the-art in the industry, the use of pervaporation for the recovery of organic compounds from aqueous solutions is still limited. The key features of pervaporation are the mass transfer of components through a commonly non-porous polymeric or zeolite membrane combined with a phase change from liquid to vapour.

The driving force of pervaporation is an activity difference between the feed and permeate side, while the mass transfer can be described based on the solution diffusion model.

For the food industry, three potential applications have been under investigation:

(1) *Removal of Alcohol from Wine*: A concept has been patented by Lee et al. by using hydrophilic membranes and is carried out similarly to alcohol removal by RO.

(2) *Aroma Recovery from Raw Material (Fruit Juices, Beer, Herbal and Flowery Extracts)*: A commercial process has been developed and successfully tested at a fruitjuice concentrate company.

(3) *Recovery of Aroma Components during Fermentation*: Pilot-scale experiments during the fermentation of wine demonstrated the feasibility to recover the complex wine aroma.

Pervaporation is, however, despite its successes and potentials, so far not established in the food industry.

Electrodialysis

Electrodialysis is used to separate uncharged molecules from charged molecules and is therefore used for, for example, the separation of salts, acids, and bases from aqueous solutions. The key advantage over other membrane processes is the selectivity of electrodialysis towards charged molecules without affecting uncharged molecules. The driving force of the process is based on a gradient of the electrical potential and the separation is achieved based on the Donnan exclusion mechanism using ion-exchange membranes. This mechanism enables electrodialysis to enrich and concentrate electrically charged ions from aqueous solutions.

Potential applications in the food industry are, for example:

- *Tartaric Stabilization of Wine by Removing Potassium, Calcium Cations and Tartrate Anions*: Has been commercialized and is recognized by the International Wine office as. good practices.
- *Lactic-acid Recovery from Fermentation Broth*: Realised on a commercial scale to improve productivity.
- *Whey Demineralization*: Effective demineralization after concentration by NF, used in the dairy industry.

The use of electrodialysis in some applications is well established in the food industry but the market share of electrodialysis is small compared to MF, UF, NFand RO.

Membrane Contactors: Osmotic Distillation

The concept of membrane contactors was developed during the 1970s, however, the commercialization of the Celgard Liqui-Cel® hollow-fibre module in 1993 led to the breakthrough of this technology. Membrane contactors are devices that achieve a gas/liquid or liquid/liquid mass transfer of one phase to another without dispersion by passing phases on both sides of a microporous membrane.

Controlling the pressure difference between the two phases carefully, one of the phases can be immobilized in the pores of the membranes and an interface between the two phases can be established at the mouth of each pore. The driving force of the process is the concentration and/or pressure difference between the feed and the permeate side and mass transfer is based on distribution coefficients.

Selected applications in the food industry are:

- *Bubble-free Carbonation of Soft-drinks*: Realised in the Pepsi bottling plant in West Virginia to carbonize about 424 l of beverage per minute.
- *CO2 Removal Followed by Nitrogenatation*: Used in the beer production to preserve the beer and to obtain a dense foam head.
- *Deoxygenized Water*: Water for the dilution of high-gravity brewed beer.

- *Alcohol Removal by Osmotic Distillation:* Has been tested for wine but not commercialized.
- *Concentration of Fruit Juices by Osmotic Distillation*: Achieves concentrations greater than 60 Brix.

Membrane contactors are currently one of the most active fields of membrane process and application development with many interesting spin-offs for the food industry.

INTEGRATED PROCESS SOLUTIONS: SYNERGIES AND HYBRID PROCESSES

The development of integrated process solutions such as synergies and hybrid processes is one relatively unexplored area of process development. Until now, commonly only one unit of operation is considered to achieve a predefined separation. Combinations of conventional processes such as centrifugation, evaporation, liquid–liquid extraction and adsorption with membrane processes are rarely used, even though they might offer economical benefits to the end user.

However, by integrating membrane processes in their product range, more and more system builders combine the conventional processes with membrane technology. Hence, it seems reasonable to assume that the economic benefits of such process combinations and a wider understanding within the industry of their potentials will support the long-term growth of membrane technology. Overall, cross-flow membrane processes have established themselves in the food industry and many exciting developments will ensure their importance for the future.

7

Concentrated and Dried Milk Products

DEFINITIONS

Concentrated and dried milk is produced for direct sale to the consumer, but are particularly important as food ingredients, providing a source of milk solids in a variety of other products. The removal of water from fresh milk gives advantages in terms of reduced storage and transport costs, convenience in use, and, in some cases, a useful extension to shelf life. Concentrated milk is intended to be reconstituted by the consumer, by dilution with water, to give a similar composition to that of fresh milk. It is generally produced as a 3:1 concentrate containing approximately 10-12% milk fat and 36% total milk solids. It gives little benefit in terms of keeping quality or convenience, and has not become an important product.

Bulk condensed milk is an important source of milk solids in confectionery, bakery products, ice cream, concentrated yoghurt and other products, and is manufactured in large quantities for this purpose. It may be made from whole, skimmed, or reduced fat milks, depending on the end use. Most bulk condensed milk is made by evaporation, and the degree of concentration is usually within the range 2.5:1 to 4:1, depending on usage. The keeping quality is limited because it is not sterilised during or after processing.

Sweetened condensed milk may be made from whole or skimmed milk either in bulk as a food ingredient, or in small cans or tubes for direct sale to the consumer. When made from whole milk, it should contain at least 8% fat and 28% total milk solids; when made from skim milk it contains at least 0.5% fat and 24% milk solids. After evaporation, sufficient sugar is added, usually as sucrose or glucose, to prevent most microbial growth.

The sugar concentration in the aqueous phase of retail products is usually in the range of 63.5-64.5, giving a water activity of about 0.86, but is often much lower in bulk material. For bulk, whole milk products the sugar index is about 42; this is because the product is stored refrigerated for fairly short periods. The product is packed in hermetically sealed metal containers for retail trade, and milk cans, barrels, steel drums or bulk tanks for industrial purposes. Significant quantities of bulk sweetened condensed milk are used in the confectionery, bakery and prepared food industries. Evaporated milk is similar in composition to bulk condensed whole milk, but is usually heat processed and canned to give a 'commercially sterile' product. Evaporated milk is produced by the removal of about 60% water from whole milk, which results in the lactose content being about 11. 5%.

It normally contains at least 7.5% fat and 25-26% total milk solids, and is also permitted to contain stabilising salts to maintain optimum viscosity after sterilisation. Some products are made from skimmed milk, and some are 'filled milk' where other fats are used to replace milk fats. Most evaporated milk is sold directly to consumers for use in home cooking. Dried milks are manufactured as food ingredients in large quantities, and with widely varying compositions, depending on their end use. Both dried whole milk and skimmed milk powders are produced, but there is also a range of products with specific characteristics for particular applications in food processing *e.g.* lipase-free, calcium-reduced. Dried milks are now mostly produced by spraydrying, or occasionally by drum or roller-drying, and usually have a moisture content of less than 5% to give microbiological stability.

INITIAL MICROFLORA

The initial microflora of concentrated milk is that of the raw milk from which it is produced. Sugar used in sweetened condensed milk may be an additional source of yeasts and moulds and bacterial spores, including thermophilic spores.

PROCESSING AND ITS EFFECTS ON THE MICROFLORA

Examples of processes used to produce condensed, evaporated and dried milk products are shown in Figures. In each case, the initial steps of milk storage, transport, separation and standardisation are the same as those used for fresh milk. The first key stage is therefore the pasteurisation or pre-heating process. The time and temperature applied depends on the intended use of the product, but, as a minimum, will correspond to milk pasteurisation. Much higher processes are used in some instances. For example, in large-scale continuous production of evaporated milks, temperatures as high as 121°C may be applied for several minutes to stabilise milk proteins.

Condensed milk is also subjected to processes more severe than milk pasteurisation, with the exact process being determined by the nature of the product required. This preheating helps to increase viscosity and improve other characteristics. These processes may be less controlled than conventional pasteurisation, but it is important that a safe minimum process is always applied. As with fresh milk, most vegetative bacteria will be destroyed during heating, but some thermoduric types and bacterial endospores are likely to survive all but the most severe processes. The second common process in the manufacture of all types of concentrated milk products is the removal of water, usually by evaporation. The most common type of evaporator used in the dairy industry is the falling film evaporator, which is both energy-efficient and readily controllable. It is common to link several evaporators together in series to form what is known as a 'multiple effect evaporator', with a common condenser and vacuum source. The vapour produced in the first effect heats the second, and so on, producing a stepwise decrease in temperature from 70-80°C in the first effect, to about 40°C in the last. The vacuum, however, is greater in the lowest temperature effect, so that the milk flows from high to low temperature.

This process is very efficient and produces milk at the required concentration without a second pass. The temperatures within the lower temperature effects of the evaporator are low enough to permit the growth of thermophilic and some mesophilic spores, and quite high numbers may develop in the effects during prolonged production runs. Growth of certain thermophilic species has even been reported in milk at temperatures as high as 70°C. The growth of thermophiles must be controlled, by limiting the length of production runs, effective plant cleaning and sanitation, and ensuring that adequate standards of plant hygiene are applied.

CONCENTRATED MILK

Raw milk is given a heat treatment approximating that of pasteurisation. It is then concentrated at a low temperature, followed by standarisation, homogenisation and pasteurisation before packaging. Pasteurisation is usually done at 79.4°C for 25 sec; the product is stored at 10°C to prevent growth of thermoduric bacteria and any post-pasteurisation contaminants.

BULK CONDENSED MILK

In the manufacture of bulk condensed milk, the milk is first separated, if necessary, and standardisation of fat content is often carried out after concentration. Unless skimmed milk is used, homogenisation is also usually carried out at this stage. A pre-heating process is then applied, using a continuous heater or a 'hot well'. Temperatures of 65.6–76.7°C are often used, but higher temperatures of 82.2-93.3°C for as much as 15 minutes may be applied to obtain a higher viscosity product and to impart other desirable characteristics.

These processes will greatly reduce the number of vegetative bacterial cells in the milk, but they are not under the same degree of control as conventional pasteurisation. The heater or 'hot wells' can act as incubators for thermophilic bacteria, especially if the product is held in the lower temperature range, allowing bacterial numbers to build up; it is also possible that pathogens may survive some lower pre-heat temperatures. Therefore, a further HTST pasteurisation step should be applied to eliminate this hazard.

The preheated milk is then concentrated in a vacuum-pan or in a multiple-effect evaporator at a temperature range of 54.4-57.2°C After evaporation, the product is not sterile and will support rapid microbial growth. It is also likely that post-process contamination could occur during standardisation or packaging.

Therefore, effective post-process hygiene procedures, and rapid cooling to <5°C are necessary to achieve the required shelf life. The process is depicted in Figure.

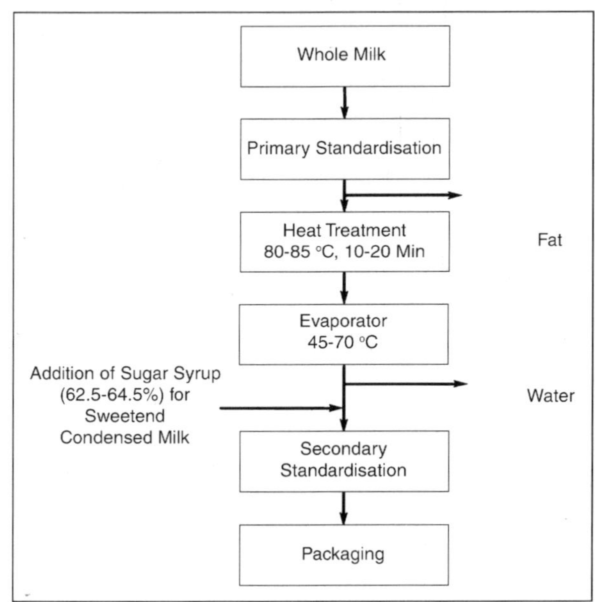

Fig. Production of Condensed Milk

SWEETENED CONDENSED MILK

In the manufacture of sweetened condensed milk, the milk is pre-heated, and may also undergo superheating. Temperatures within the range 82-100°C for 10-30 minutes are used, and these processes are sufficient to destroy vegetative cells.

For bulk, sweetened condensed milk, sugar can be added before concentration at varying levels depending on the end use. This material is not usually microbiologically stable and has a limited shelf life. In the production of sweetened condensed milk for retail sale, sugar is added during the later stages of evaporation.

The sugar is normally added as a 65% solution, and the finished product then contains a high enough solute concentration to give an aw of 0.83-0.86. It is this reduced aw, rather than a heat process, that confers microbiological stability, and a long shelf life when packed in pre-sterilised cans or tubes.

However, some osmophilic yeasts and moulds are able to grow in the product, and may cause spoilage. Evaporation is carried out at a temperature of around 57.2°C, but can drop to 48-9°C late in the cycle. Partially cooled milk is seeded with very fine lactose crystals to force crystallisation. A high standard of hygiene during the later handling and filling stages is necessary to prevent contamination. A particular problem with sweetened condensed milk is its high viscosity, and 'sticky' nature, which makes cleaning processing equipment difficult.

This high viscosity means that positivedisplacement, plunger-type fillers are needed to fill the product. These are complex and difficult to clean and may become heavily contaminated with micrococci and yeasts if not properly maintained.

EVAPORATED MILK

The manufacture of canned evaporated milk is very similar to that of bulk condensed milk, but the product is given a long shelf life by applying a heat process designed to give commercial sterility. Because of this, the milk has to be stabilised to prevent coagulation during processing and to minimise 'age thickening' during storage.

Stabilisation is achieved by the addition of permitted salts, including phosphates, citrates and bicarbonates, which are used to maintain the pH of the milk at 6.6-6.7. Pre-heating is also important, and temperatures of 120-122 °C for several minutes are used to denature whey proteins. Only a few bacterial spores are likely to survive such a process.

Condensation is usually performed at a temperature lower than 54.5°C. After evaporation, the milk is homogenised, cooled and stored. It is then standardised, and further stabilising salts may also be added at this point. It is important to ensure that cooling is rapid and sufficient to minimise any microbial growth during this procedure.

The milk is then filled into cans, hermetically sealed, and sterilised using batch retorts or continuous sterilisers. Processing at 115°C for 15-20 minutes, or 120°C for 10 minutes, has been traditionally applied, but recently there has been a move towards UHT processing followed by aseptic filling into pre-sterilised cans or cartons.

Processing at 130°C for 30 seconds, to 150°C for less than one second may be used. Retorted canned milk is commercially sterile, and only extremely heat-resistant spores of organisms such as *Bacillus stearothermophilus* are likely to survive. These spores do not germinate unless the cans are then stored at high ambient temperatures. Aseptically filled evaporated milk may become recontaminated during filling, unless stringent hygiene procedures equivalent to those used in filling other UHT milk products are used. The process is depicted in Figure.

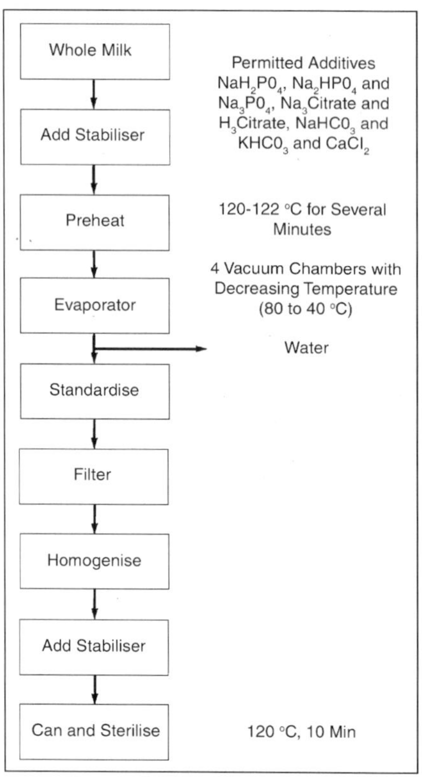

Fig. Production of Evaporated Milk

DRIED MILK

Drying is used, after evaporation, to produce a stable, powdered product with a residual moisture content of 2-5%. Most dried milk powders are now spraydried, and drum and roller dryers are little used. Spray drying is a more energy-efficient process and causes less heat damage to the product. Therefore, only spray drying will be considered further. Before evaporation and drying, the milk is standardised, if required, and heattreated.

Vegetative bacteria, including Enterobacteriaceae and *Listeria monocytogenes* have been shown to survive the drying process, and therefore all raw milk should receive a process at least equivalent to pasteurisation. Skimmed milk may also be subjected to low, medium and high heat processes to give varying degrees of protein denaturation as required. Typically, a low heat process will be 74°C for 30 seconds, a medium heat process 80-100°C for 1-2 minutes, and a high heat process may be equivalent to an ultra high temperature treatment. Milk for dried whole milk powders is heated at 85-95°C for several minutes. UHT heating units result in products that have excellent microbiological quality, which is important when dried milk is to be used as an ingredient in baby food. The heat-treated milk is then evaporated to about 50% total solids before drying. As the drying process does not kill all vegetative bacterial cells, effective cleaning and hygiene procedures are required to ensure that the heat-treated milk does not become recontaminated. The current practice is to link the evaporation plant and dryer as a single integrated unit. Two systems of spray drying are used: jet or nozzle dryers, and rotary atomiser dryers.

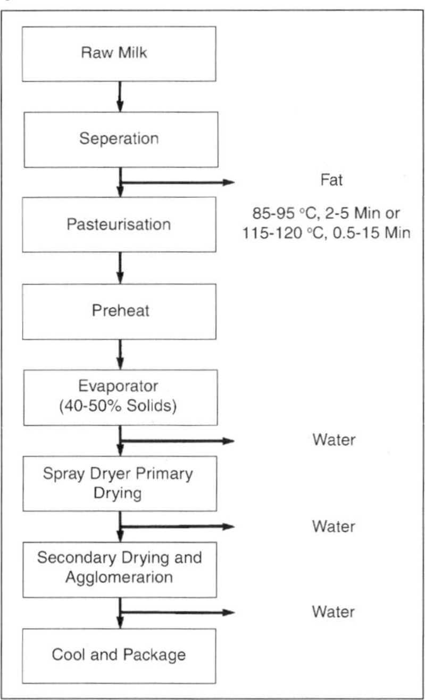

Fig. Production of Skimmed Milk Powder

Each dryer produces powders with specific characteristics. In the case of jet dryer systems, milk is fed to a high-pressure pump, then pumped under pressure to a series of jets or nozzles within the drying chamber. The impact of hot air on the milk causes the liquid to break up into fine droplets that form milk powder. In the rotary atomiser, the milk enters the drying chamber through slots or holes located at the periphery of a circular disc fixed to a rotating shaft.

Modern spray dryers usually consist of several stages, and incorporate a final drying stage using a fluidised bed dryer. Spray dryers operate by mixing pre-heated atomised milk droplets with heated air at an inlet temperature of 180-220°C. The air is cooled to an exit temperature of 70-95°C, and moisture is removed from the milk. This gives very rapid drying at a vaporisation temperature of about 50°C, and the temperature of the dried particles remains below that of the cooled air. The dried particles are then removed, cooled, and packaged. The aw of the finished milk powder is too low to allow any microbial growth. The full process is depicted in Figure.

SPOILAGE

CONDENSED MILK

Unsweetened condensed milks are not commercially sterile, and so, are favourable media for microbial growth. Spoilage can be caused by heat-resistant organisms from raw milk, for example *Bacillus* spp. and enterococci, or by postprocess contaminants, such as pseudomonads and members of the Enterobacteriaceae. As long as the product is handled and stored correctly only thermoduric and thermophilic organisms will grow slowly. Shelf life varies from a few days to weeks, depending on the degree of contamination, the severity of the heat treatment applied, and the effectiveness of temperature control during cooling and storage. The pattern of spoilage is very similar to that described for pasteurised fresh milk, although organisms adapted to slightly lower aw values may have an advantage.

SWEETENED CONDENSED MILK

The low aw of sweetened condensed milks ensures that only osmophilic and osmotolerant organisms are able to grow. Canned products may be spoiled by slow growth of osmophilic yeasts, particularly *Torulopsis* spp., which enter the product after heating and may produce sufficient gas to cause blown cans. If sufficient oxygen is present in the headspace, or the can has a small pinhole leak, moulds such as *Aspergillus* and *Penicillium* spp. may grow as 'buttons' on the surface of the product. This problem is associated with poor plant hygiene.

Bulk products with lower sugar concentrations are more susceptible to spoilage. Mould growth may occur on the surface of stored milk. Again, *Penicillium* and *Aspergillus* are the main genera involved. Occasionally, bacterial spoilage by osmotolerant micrococci and *Bacillus* spp. may occur in these products, causing thickening, and eventually, lipolysis and proteolysis.

EVAPORATED MILK

Spoilage of commercially sterile canned evaporated milk is uncommon, but is a result of either under-processing, or post-process contamination. Species of bacilli such as *B. stearothermophilus*, *Bacillus coagulans*, and *Bacillus licheniformis* may survive the heat process and cause acid coagulation, a slight cheesy odour and flavour, and 'flat sour' spoilage of the milk. However, many strains are obligately thermophilic and are only a problem at elevated storage temperatures, or if cooling is too slow.

Non-acid curd is caused by *Bacillus subtilis*; this can then be digested to a brownish liquid with a bitter taste. *Bacillus megaterium* is responsible for the formation of coagulum, which is accompanied by cheesy odour and gas. Blown cans associated with putrefactive spoilage by *Clostridium* spp. occur very occasionally. Spoilage caused by under-processing is very rare in recent times, mainly as a result of improvements in process technology and control. Post-process spoilage can be caused by a wide range of species, and the spoilage characteristics are therefore varied. The situation is very similar to that described for other sterilised, and UHT milk products. Bacteria may enter the product as a result of faulty can seaming, or subsequent seam damage, corrosion, and in aseptically filled products, following a breakdown in the integrity of the aseptic filling process.

DRIED MILKS

Relatively low numbers of microorganisms survive processing. Heat resistant organisms and mould are responsible for deterioration of milk powders, if the product is allowed to absorb moisture during prolonged storage. The aw of dried milks is otherwise much too low to support microbial growth, and a general decrease in microbial counts occurs during storage.

PATHOGENS: GROWTH AND SURVIVAL

Concentrated milks are not normally regarded as high-risk products, principally because of the relatively severe heat treatments used in their manufacture. As with other pasteurised and UHT processed milks, the main concern for condensed and evaporated milk is post heat-treatment contamination by pathogens. Dried milks, however, are the subject of considerable concern, particularly in view of their widespread use in infant foods. There have been a number of outbreaks of foodborne disease associated with dried milk powders.

CONDENSED/EVAPORATED MILK

Listeria Spp.

The fate of *L. monocytogenes* has been studied in these products. The organism declined during storage in sweetened condensed milk at 21°C, but the population remained stable at 7°C. In evaporated milk, growth was recorded at both temperatures.

Clostridium Spp

A study of the incidence of clostridia in sweetened condensed milk showed that about 40% of the samples contained >100 cfu/100 g. These contaminants were identified mainly as *Clostidium butyricum* and *Clostridium perfringens*. However, the aw of these products is too low to allow the germination of spores and vegetative cell growth.

Staphylococcus Aureus

Although there are no reported cases of foodborne disease associated with canned sweetened condensed milk, its aw of 0.85 is very close to the minimum value that would allow *Staph. aureus* to grow, although toxin production would be inhibited. However, bulk products with much lower sugar contents might be at risk if they become contaminated. Therefore, adequate hygiene is an important control.

DRIED MILK

Although dried milk products have been implicated in a number of foodborne disease outbreaks, these have usually been the result of post-pasteurisation contamination by pathogens. Foodborne pathogenic bacteria are unable to grow in dried milk powders, but may survive for long periods.

Salmonella Spp.

There have been several significant salmonellosis outbreaks associated with dried milk powders, and *Salmonella* contamination has come to be regarded as a serious potential hazard in these products. In 1964 to 1965, a nationwide outbreak occurred in the USA associated with non-fat milk powder produced at one plant, but then agglomerated at a number of other locations. This outbreak produced reports of infection throughout the USA and led to a major United States Department of Agriculture (USDA) investigation of the incidence of *Salmonella* contamination in milk drying plants. It was found that contamination was widespread in both product and environmental samples, and this finding gave rise to a number of improvements in hygiene, sanitation and process control. Despite this, another smaller outbreak occurred in Oregon in 1979, associated with non-fat dried milk contaminated with *Salmonella typhimurium* and *Salmonella agona*. Surveillance results have also continued to show persistent low-level *Salmonella* contamination in the US. In 1986, a major outbreak of salmonellosis was reported in the UK associated with dried milk powder-based infant formula, contaminated with *Salmonella ealing*. The organism is thought to have originated in raw milk and then spread through the plant. It seems to have entered the insulation material of the dryer through small cracks in the dryer wall, and this then acted as a reservoir from which *S. ealing* could repeatedly contaminate the finished product. In 2005, powdered infant formula contaminated with *S. agona* was implicated in an outbreak involving 104 infants in France. Despite the introduction of HACCP and further recommendations for the prevention of contamination, dried milk-associated outbreaks continue to be reported around the world. Such outbreaks are often linked to contamination in equipment that is poorly designed and difficult to clean effectively, and the *Salmonella* strains involved are often found to be lactose-positive.

Staphylococcus Aureus

Contamination of dried milk powders with staphylococcal enterotoxins was a significant problem in the 1950s, and several outbreaks were recorded, often caused by growth and toxin production in the concentrated milk prior to drying. Improvements in temperature control and hygiene prior to drying have largely eliminated this problem. However, in 1986, several outbreaks were reported in Egypt associated with imported non-fat dried milk. Analysis of samples showed no viable pathogens, but staphylococcal enterotoxins A and B were found at concentrations high enough to cause illness.

More recently, in 2000, a very large outbreak of staphylococcal food poisoning was reported in Japan, which affected over 13,420 people. This outbreak was associated with consumption of semi-skimmed liquid milk, which was manufactured using dried skimmed milk powder. It was thought that some temperature abuse could have occurred during production of the dried milk, allowing *Staph. aureus* to grow and produce heat-stable toxin, which then persisted through to the finished product and cause intoxication, even though the thermal processes had destroyed the organism.

Listeria Monocytogenes

No cases of listeriosis associated with dried milk products have been reported. However, the ubiquity of *Listeria* spp. in dairy plants and other wet processing areas, and the cases of listeriosis linked to other dairy products suggest that contamination of dried products is likely. The survival of *L. monocytogenes* during spray drying and storage of product has been investigated. Spray drying was found to give a small reduction in numbers, and the viable count continued to decline during storage, but viable *L. monocytogenes* could still be isolated from some samples after 12 weeks.

Bacillus Spp.

Bacillus cereus has been found to be a common contaminant in dried milk. In the US, 62.5% of samples of milk powder were found to be positive, and, in Brazil, the organism was isolated from 80% of samples examined. Although there have been many reports of *B. cereus* food poisoning associated directly with dried milk consumption, in 2005, milk powder contaminated with *B. licheniformis* and *B. subtilis* was the cause of an outbreak in Croatia involving 12 children. Reconstituted milk that was held for 2 hours prior to consumption, without boiling, was identified as the cause. *B. cereus* spores can survive for many months in dried milk powders, and rapid growth has been shown in reconstituted powders at ambient temperature. Dried milk is thought to have been the source of *B. cereus* in an outbreak affecting eight people, associated with macaroni cheese, which was found to contain *B. cereus* at levels of 108-109 cfu/g.

Cronobacter and Enterobacter Spp.

Cronobacter and *Enterobacter* spp. are not normally regarded as foodborne pathogens, but there have been a number of sporadic outbreaks of neonatal meningitis caused by *Cronobacter sakazakii* associated with dried milk consumption, with fatality rates as high as 30–80%. Powdered infant formulae contaminated with *C. sakazakii* was responsible for outbreaks among infants: one involving nine infections and two deaths in 2004, in France, and the other caused five infections and one death in 2005, in New Zealand.

These outbreaks are thought to have been due to growth of the organism in the reconstituted powder. The presence of any members of the Enterobacteriaceae in infant formulae may therefore be a cause for concern. Studies have shown that *C. sakazakii* can survive spray-dying when inoculated into skimmed milk powder. *Enterobacter agglomerans* has also been isolated from milk powder.

Toxins

The mycotoxin aflatoxin Ml has occasionally been found in dried milk. The drying process has been found to reduce the concentration, but a significant amount is able to survive processing and storage of finished product for long periods.

8

Characteristics, Costs, and Issues for Organic Dairy Farming

INTRODUCTION

Organic milk production has been one of the fastest growing segments of organic agriculture in the United States. Between 2000 and 2005, the number of certified organic milk cows on U.S. farms increased by an annual average of about 25 per cent, from 38,000 to more than 86,000. Many of these cows were on small dairy operations that had switched to organic production to improve farm profitability.

While organic milk cows accounted for about 1 per cent of all U.S. milk cows in 2005, the sector continues to grow. USDA estimates indicate that organic milk increased from 2 per cent of U.S. fluid milk product sales in 2006 to 3 per cent in 2008. Certified organic milk production systems rely on ecologically based standards that prohibit the use of antibiotics and hormones in the cow herd and the use of synthetic chemicals in dairy feed production. Certified organic milk production systems also attempt to accommodate the animals' natural nutritional and behavioural requirements, such as ensuring that cows have access to pasture.

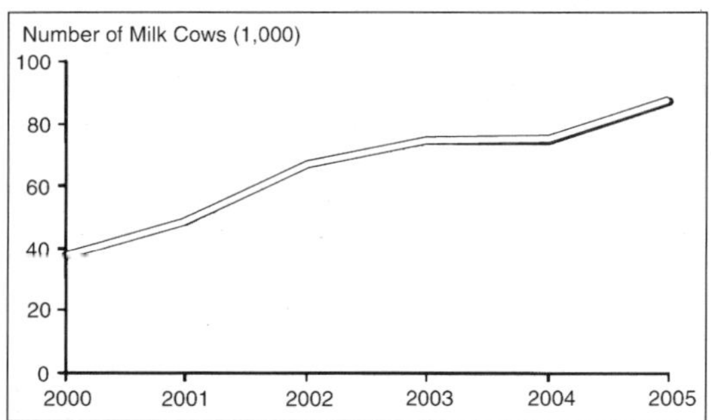

Fig. Number of Organic Milk Cows on U.S. Farms

Notes: Between 2000 and 2005, the number of organic milk cows increased by an annual average of about 25 per cent

These requirements add to production costs and create challenges for widespread adoption, such as higher managerial costs and risks of shifting to a new way of farming, and significant time and costs associated with the transition to organic production. This report describes organic dairy farms in the United States, including information about farm size, location, production costs, and the types of technologies used, and discusses the challenges of organic milk production. Although the analysis focuses on organic dairy farms, a comparison with conventional dairy farms adds value to the discussion.

BACKGROUND

Organic milk producers usually begin as conventional dairy operators who then go through what can be a challenging and costly transition process. During the transition, organic dairies must change their animal husbandry, land, and crop management, source new and different inputs, and initiate the certification process. To become a certified organic dairy under current standards of USDA's National Organic Programme, the pasture and cropland providing feed for organic dairies must be managed organically for a minimum of 36 months.

Current standards also require the dairy herd to be fed 100 per cent organic feed and to receive organic health care for 12 months before being certified. Organic dairy animals may not be given hormones, such as rBST, or antibiotics for any reason. Grazing is required for all animals over 6 months of age. These requirements mean that products and feeds that meet organic standards must be found, and organic feeds can be priced significantly higher than conventional feeds.

Also, the approach to management must be adjusted on most farms as many conventional inputs, such as antibiotics, are no longer available. The certification process can also be time consuming and tedious as farmers must develop an organic systems plan that describes practices and substances used in production. In addition, detailed production records must be kept for 5 years post-certification for a farm to be in compliance with the regulations, and access to these records must be provided to USDA and its certifying agents.

USDA's *National Organic Programme* (NOP) rules state that access to pasture must be provided for ruminant animals, but do not indicate how much pasture should be allocated or how much dairy feed should be provided by pasture. The most common technology used on conventional dairy operations confines milk cows in large barns and limits access to pasture. Therefore, interpretation of the pasture rule, largely left to individual certifiers, has important implications for land requirements and costs of organic milk production for farmers considering the transition. Partly in response to comments, complaints, and noncompliance regarding pasture use on organic dairy operations, USDA proposed a rule in October 2008 to clarify and strengthen the NOP pasture requirement. This proposed rule would amend livestock and related provisions of the NOP, providing better consumer assurances that the USDA organic label on dairy products means that cattle graze on pasture during the pasturegrowing season. Milk prices paid to U.S. producers are determined by a complex system.

A minimum, or base price, is determined by a combination of the dairy price support programme and Federal milk marketing orders. Quality adjustments are made to the minimum price based on the content of fats and other milk solids and the volume of milk sold, among other factors. Organic milk pricing is subject to the same minimum as all other milk, but processors pay a premium for the value added by the organic brand. Also, organic producers with cows using pasture as their primary forage may receive higher prices because the milk tends to have higher fat and other solids content.

Organic milk producers are paid a fixed price per hundredweight (cwt) for organic milk, according to annual contracts with organic creameries that purchase the milk. In contrast, conventional milk producers are paid a blend price determined by spot markets for butter, cheese, nonfat dry milk, and whey, which may vary dramatically each month. The relative price stability of organic milk, compared with conventional milk, is a benefit for producers who transition to organic.

DAIRY FARM DATA

Dairy farm data used in this study came from USDA's 2005 Agricultural Resource Management Survey (ARMS) of U.S. milk producers. The ARMS, conducted annually by the National Agricultural Statistics Service (NASS) and Economic Research Service (ERS), provides detailed farm information on income, expenses, assets, and debt, as well as farm and operator characteristics.

The 2005 ARMS included a version that highlights milk production practices and costs. This version targets dairy operations in 24 States that accounted for more than 90 per cent of national milk production and covered all major production areas. The surveyed dairy farms were chosen from a list of farm operations maintained by USDA's National Agricultural Statistics Service (NASS). The target population of the dairy version included farms that were in the dairy business for all 12 months of 2005 and milked at least 10 cows at any time during the year.

The dairy survey collected information to estimate average milk production costs. Screening out farms that milked fewer than 10 cows excluded farms with dairy cows for onfarm consumption and other noncommercial activities, such as youth projects. A subsample that targeted organic operations was also part of the 2005 ARMS dairy version. Of the total 2,987 dairy farms sampled, 737 samples were targeted at organic operations in 19 States as identified by the major organic milk processors and certifiers.

After accounting for nonresponse and missing data, information on 1,787 farms, including 352 certified organic milk operations in 14 States, were available from the ARMS. Among the organic dairies, 325 sold more than 90 per cent of milk production as certified organic, 18 were transitioning to organic production, and 9 were mixed operations. Each surveyed farm represented a number of similar farms in the population as indicated by the surveyed farm's expansion factor. The expansion factor, or survey weight, was determined from the farm's selection probability, expanding the sample to represent the target population. Farm survey weights ensured that the sample expanded to represent dairy operations in the 24 States and that organic operations represented an appropriate share of the population despite a disproportionate representation in the sample. Organic farms accounted for 18 per cent of the sample, but only 2 per cent of the weighted number of farms.

ECONOMIES OF SIZE IN ORGANIC MILK PRODUCTION

The emergence of large conventional dairy farms and the continued shift of production towards such farms suggest that economies of size play a major role in the structure of dairy farming. Economies of size and the role it takes in the structural changes observed in conventional milk production were documented by MacDonald *et al.* This section reports on the relationship between operation size and production costs in organic milk production, including what size and costs might mean for the structure of the industry. To evaluate the relationship between organic milk production costs and operation size, surveyed producers were divided into groups by size, and differences in farm characteristics and practices, production costs and net returns, and labour use were compared among the groups.

The size groups were defined by the largest number of cows milked on the operation during 2005:

- Fewer than 50 cows;
- 50-99 cows;
- 100-199 cows; and
- 200 cows or more.

CHARACTERISTICS AND PRACTICES BY SIZE

Data for 2005 indicated that about 45 per cent of organic dairies milked fewer than 50 cows, while 87 per cent had fewer than 100 cows. These small operations accounted for a disproportionately small share of organic milk cows and production. In contrast, about 13 per cent of organic dairies had 100 cows or more, but they accounted for 44 per cent of milk cows and nearly half of production. The largest organic dairies—those with 200 cows or more—had an average herd size of almost 500 cows per farm and included nearly a third of organic milk cows. These large dairies had a higher average milk yield per cow than smaller dairies and produced 37 per cent of organic milk. The most striking difference among organic dairies in each size group was their location. Northeast and Upper Midwest farms accounted for 96 per cent of dairies with fewer than 50 cows. Farms in the West accounted for 80 per cent of dairies with 200 cows or more. Within each region, 97 per cent of organic dairies in the Northeast, 88 per cent of organic dairies in the Upper Midwest, and 85 per cent of organic dairies in the Corn Belt had fewer than 100 cows. In contrast, 83 per cent of organic dairies in the West had 100 cows or more and 63 per cent had 200 cows or more. The use of several milk production technologies and practices tended to increase with size of organic operation, but most of the differences were between the smallest and other organic farms. For example, use of a milking parlor increased from 22 per cent for the smallest dairies to nearly all dairies with 100 cows or more. Thirty-eight per cent of the smallest farms and over 50 per cent of other farms participated in the Dairy Herd Improvement programme.

PRODUCTION COSTS AND NET RETURNS BY SIZE

Average feed costs differed little among the dairies in each size group, but average operating costs for organic dairies increased from the smallest to largest size group due to the additional costs of hired labour on the largest farms. Total operating costs were about $2 per cwt higher on the largest organic dairies than on the smallest. Once capital costs were added, cost differences among the size groups were negligible, as lower capital costs on the larger operations offset the additional hired labour costs. The smallest farms, however, used significantly more unpaid labour, mainly from farm operators and other family members, than did larger farms. After adding an opportunity cost for this unpaid labour, total economic costs for organic dairies declined with size and were nearly $14 per cwt less on the largest farms than on the smallest. The relationship between average production costs and operation size for organic dairies was similar to that for conventional dairies among the size groups that characterize the organic industry.

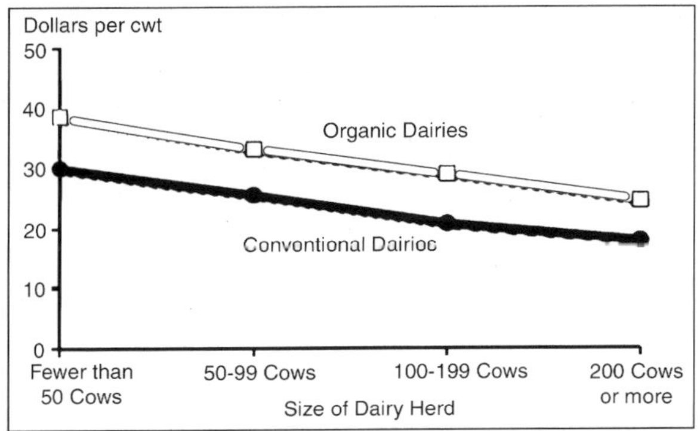

Fig. Total Economic Costs for each Type of Dairy Producers, by Farm Size

Notes: The relationship between production costs and operation size for organic dairies was similar to conventional diaries, only at higher costs. Costs shown for conventional dairies of 200 cows or more are reported for 200-499 cows by MacDonald *et al.*, with an average size of 295 cows. The average size of organic dairies in the 200 cows or more group is 490 cows.

Average production costs for conventional milk production declined from about $30 per cwt on operations with fewer than 50 cows to about $18 per cwt on operations with 200-499 cows. Average costs dropped to less than $14 per cwt on conventional operations with more than 1,000 cows. Lower costs among the largest conventional producers suggest that similar economies of size may be available to organic producers if they increase the size of their operation above the industry norm.

However, the additional costs of complying with pasture requirements and securing organic inputs in large volume may limit the cost advantages for larger organic operations. Net returns to the organic dairy enterprise were computed as the difference between the gross value of production and total economic costs.

Average net returns in 2005 were negative for all organic dairy size groups (from-$12.93 per cwt among dairies with fewer than 50 cows to-$1.26 per cwt among dairies with 200 cows or more). These averages, however, mask the variation in net returns among dairies. Some operations may be more productive because they are well managed, while others may pay less than average for inputs or receive above-average milk prices, and thus these farms may be profitable while their group, on average, is not. For example, 10 per cent of organic dairies with fewer than 50 cows and almost half of those with 200 cows or more generated positive returns above total economic costs.

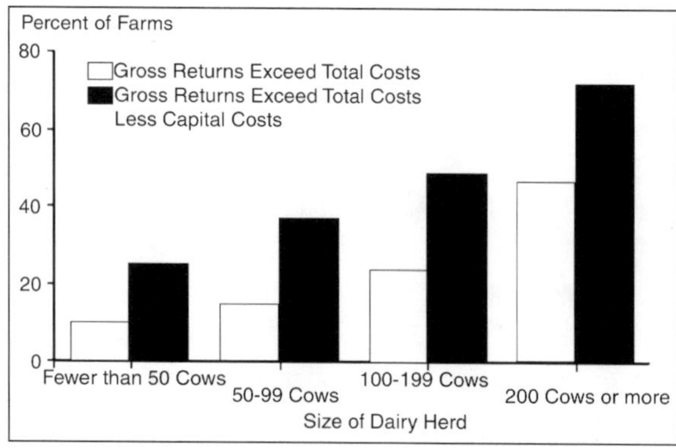

Fig. Organic Dairy Operations with Positive Returns, by Size of Operation

Notes: Ten Per cent of the smallest and 47 per cent of the largest organic dairies have positive returns above total costs, but many more have positive returns when capital costs are excluded.

Farmers are unlikely to start or expand a dairy operation if they are unable to recover their investment in capital and labour. Farmers who have already made substantial capital investments in dairy facilities and equipment, however, with little or no opportunity for use outside the dairy operation. These costs, therefore, have no bearing on the decision to operate in the short term, only becoming important when these capital assets must be replaced. To better measure costs relevant to shortterm operating decisions, the share of farms with gross returns exceeding all costs except for capital costs was computed. About a fourth of organic dairies with fewer than 50 cows covered these costs, compared with almost threefourths of those with 200 cows or more. Some small organic dairy farms appeared to be earning enough to keep operating, but on average, farms in the smaller size groups were not covering the opportunity costs of their investments in capital and the operator's time.

In contrast, larger organic dairies were much more likely to generate returns above capital and labour costs. These conditions suggest that organic milk production may migrate towards larger operations, as has conventional production. This production change will likely occur over an extended period as existing smaller operations use up their production facilities and equipment, ultimately facing decisions about replacing capital assets or exiting the industry. Also, in the short term, some small operators may continue producing organic milk as a lifestyle choice despite returns that fail to cover the opportunity cost of their time.

LABOUR USE BY SIZE

Small organic dairies are at a cost disadvantage relative to larger dairies due to the opportunity cost assigned to the unpaid labour provided by operators, partners, and family members. Unpaid labour costs for organic dairies with fewer than 50 cows were $13.42 per cwt, compared with only $1.15 per cwt on dairies with 200 cows or more. If this opportunity cost is ignored, the net returns to organic milk production were more similar among the size groups. The largest dairies used substantially more hired labour than the smallest (11,530 hours versus 557 hours), but the hired labour hours per unit of production differed little among the size groups because of much higher production on the largest dairies.

The difference in unpaid labour use among the farm size groups was much less. Organic dairy operations with 200 cows or more used about 700 more hours of unpaid labour, about 20 per cent more than those with fewer than 50 cows. The largest dairies, however, produced about 1,700 per cent more milk as a result of having more cows and an average productivity per cow that was 36 per cent higher than the smallest dairies. Enhanced productivity for these larger dairies means that unpaid labour hours per unit of production fell dramatically across the size groups from 0.82 hour per cwt on the smallest organic dairies to only 0.05 hour on the largest.

Table. Labour Use, by Size of Organic Dairy Operation, 2005

Item	Size of Organic Dairy			
	Fewer than 50 Cows	50-99 Cows	100-199 Cows	200 Cows or More
Per farm				
Hired labour hours	557	1,648	3,051	11,530
Unpaid labour hours	3,612	3,759	4,265	4,322
Total labour hours	4,169	5,407	7,316	15,852
Milk production (cwt)	4,367	8,748	15,825	78,977
Per cwt				
Hired labour hours	0.13	0.19	0.19	0.15
Unpaid labour hours	0.82	0.43	0.27	0.05
Total labour hours	0.95	0.62	0.46	0.20

Unpaid labour is an opportunity cost defined as the time spent working on a dairy operation charged at a wage rate that represents what unpaid workers could earn in off-farm employment. Opportunity costs of labour may vary significantly among producers, and some producers may be willing to accept returns lower than they could earn in nonfarm employment because of lifestyle preferences and costs of switching occupations, among other reasons. The incentive to earn a competitive return for the time spent on the dairy operation, however, may be a motivating force for increasingly larger organic dairies.

REGIONAL DIFFERENCES IN ORGANIC MILK PRODUCTION

Conventional milk production has historically been concentrated in the Upper Midwest and Northeast, mostly in Wisconsin, Minnesota, New York, and Pennsylvania. In the past three decades, however, milk production has expanded rapidly on large operations located in nontraditional areas of the South and West. Most prominently, California surpassed Wisconsin during the early 1990s as the number one milk-producing State.

The continued growth of dairies in these nontraditional areas is the result of a favourable climate, an abundance of alternative crops that can be used for dairy feed, their relative geographic isolation, and population growth. Although more recent in nature, regional development of organic milk production has followed a path similar to that of conventional milk production. Small organic dairy farmers and milk cooperatives in the Northeast and Upper Midwest, along with a major organic milk processor with its own large dairy farm in the West, pioneered organic milk production during the 1990s. Organic milk production was a good fit for the small, pasture-oriented operations in the Northeast, in Wisconsin, and in other parts of the Midwest. Expansion in the West, where California and Oregon have become leading organic milkproducing States, was motivated by many of the same factors that spurred expansion of conventional milk production in this area.

Figure illustrates the dramatic growth of organic milk production in the West, where the number of organic milk cows more than tripled between 2000 and 2005.

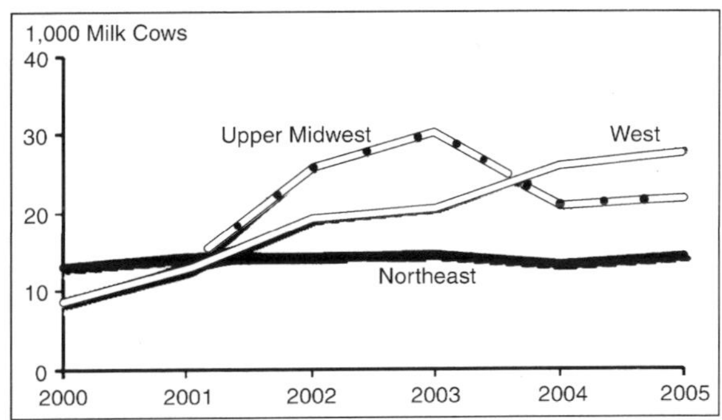

Fig. Number of Organic Milk Cows, by Region

Notes: Between 2000 and 2005, the Number of Organic Milk Cows are more than Tripled in the West.

CHARACTERISTICS AND PRACTICES BY REGION

More than 40 per cent of organic dairies were located in both the Northeast and Upper Midwest, but these operations were small and less productive than those in the West. The Northeast includes organic dairies surveyed in New York, Pennsylvania, Maine, and Vermont; the Upper Midwest includes dairies in Wisconsin, Minnesota, and Michigan; and the West includes those in California, Oregon, Washington, and Idaho.

Despite their large number, Northeast and Upper Midwest dairies accounted for a disproportionately small share of organic milk cows, 29 and 33 per cent, respectively. Operations in the Northeast averaged 53 cows; the Upper Midwest, 64 cows; and the West, 381 cows. Organic dairy cows in the West averaged nearly 16,000 pounds of annual milk production per cow, 2,700 pounds more than in the Upper Midwest and 4,000 pounds more than in the Northeast.

Organic dairies in the Northeast and Upper Midwest were more likely than dairies in the West to produce crops used for dairy cattle feed. Nearly all farms in these regions produced hay for cattle feed, and nearly 80 per cent of farms in the Upper Midwest produced corn. Only 16 per cent of operations in the West grew corn, and just over half produced hay. As a result, the large organic dairies in the West purchased more dairy feed items than those in other regions. The percentage of farms using pasture-based feeding for dairy cattle varied little among the regions.

Table. Characteristics and Production Practices of Organic Dairies, by Region, 2005

Item	Northeast	Upper Midwest	West
% of farms	44	42	7
% of milk cows	29	33	31
% of milk production	25	32	37
Milk cows *(number per farm)*	53	64	381
Milk production *(pounds per cow)*	11,831	13,195	15,902
% of farms			
Feed crops produced:			
Corn (grain and silage)	27	79	16
Hay (alfalfa and other)	96	93	55
Operator education:			
Less than high school	37	14	5
Completed high school	43	69	48
Some college	20	17	47
Production practices:			
DHI programme participation[1]	40	60	66
Pasture-based feeding[2]	71	57	65
Artificial insemination	67	77	82
Embryo transplants or sexed semen	3	2	2
Controlled breeding/calving season	31	39	19
Regular veterinary services	36	38	46
Nutritionist services	42	44	54
Computerized milking system	2	2	6
Computerized feeding system	3	1	27
Milking parlor	28	39	100
Kept individual cow records	59	65	63
Johne's disease programme participation	14	32	35
Onfarm computer records	18	24	34
Dairy information from Internet	30	48	72
Forward-purchased inputs	9	7	21
Negotiate input price discounts	30	13	31

Notes:

[1]Dairy Herd Improvement.

[2]Pasture-based feeding is defined as providing at least half of the forage fed to milk cows during the grazing months from pasture. Organic dairies reported an average grazing period for milk cows of 6.5 months in 2005.

Operators of organic dairies in the West were, on average, more educated than those in other regions. Nearly half of farm operators in the West attended college, compared with 20 per cent or less in the other regions. More education may explain why the use of some production practices was more common on dairies in the West. Operators of organic dairies in the West were more likely to participate in the Dairy Herd Improvement programme, use artificial insemination, use regular veterinary and nutritionist services, use computerized milking and feeding systems, access dairy information from the Internet, and forward-purchase inputs. Higher education may contribute to a greater awareness of these practices and ease the adoption process. Also, the larger dairies in the West were able to spread the fixed costs of the investments required by some of these practices over more units of production.

PRODUCTION COSTS AND NET RETURNS BY REGION

Average operating costs were lowest for dairies in the Upper Midwest by more than $1 per cwt than in the other regions. Lower operating costs in the Upper Midwest resulted from feed costs that were about $1 per cwt less than in the Northeast and hired labour costs that were nearly $1.70 per cwt less than in the West. Once capital costs are added, the cost difference between the Upper Midwest and West were minimal due to the impact of size economies for the larger operations in the West. Size economies were the predominant factor in the difference between total economic costs in each region, ranging from $37.59 per cwt on the small Northeast operations to $25.13 per cwt on the large operations in the West. Most of the difference in total economic costs in the West came from unpaid labour charges that were more than $9 per cwt less than in the Northeast and about $5 per cwt less than in the Upper Midwest.

Table. Production Costs and Returns of Organic Dairies, by Region, 2005

Item	Northeast	Upper Midwest	West
Dollars per cwt sold			
Feed:	13.48	12.52	12.80
Purchased feed	6.66	3.36	9.69
Homegrown harvested feed	5.92	8.62	2.47
Grazed feed	0.90	0.55	0.64
Hired labour	1.60	1.61	3.28
Capital costs	6.31	5.44	3.67
Opportunity cost of unpaid labour	10.75	6.76	1.64
Cost summary:			
Operating costs	19.03	17.92	19.46
Operating and capital costs	25.34	23.36	23.13
Total economic costs	37.59	31.47	25.13
Gross value of production	26.83	23.56	23.47
Returns above total economic costs	-10.76	-7.91	-1.66

Notes: Costs are defined in Appendix A: Measuring Milk Production Costs. The gross value of production includes milk sales, cull and breeding animal sales, revenue from leasing dairy animals or space to other operations, co-op patronage dividends, dairy assessment rebates or refunds, and the value of manure. The value of milk sales was determined from prices reported by the survey respondents.

A breakdown of annual feed costs per cow in each region reveals costs that were significantly less in the Northeast ($400 per cow less) and Upper Midwest ($500 per cow less) than in the West. More than half of total feed costs on organic dairies in the Northeast stemmed from homegrown feed and grazed forages, while these sources accounted for more than 70 per cent of feed costs in the Upper Midwest.

Organic dairies in these regions may have incurred lower feed costs than those shown here if their production costs were lower than the market prices charged for these inputs. In contrast, more than three-fourths of the total feed cost on organic dairies in the West was from purchased feed items. Despite higher feed costs per cow on organic dairies in the West, feed costs per cwt were competitive with organic dairies in other regions.

Total labour and capital usage were also much higher on dairies in the West, but total costs per cwt were significantly less. The cost advantage of organic dairies in the West resulted from economies of size on larger dairies and higher productivity. Almost 50 per cent of organic dairies in the West had an average milk production per cow of 15,000 pounds or more, and only 12 per cent of organic dairies were producing less than 10,000 pounds.

In the Northeast and Upper Midwest, only a quarter of producers were producing 15,000 pounds or more, and 25 per cent of Upper Midwest producers and more than a third of producers in the Northeast had average production less than 10,000 pounds. This difference in milk yield may be due to productivity-enhancing technologies and practices more common on organic dairies in the West. Due to this cost advantage, net returns for dairies in the West were significantly greater than in the other regions.

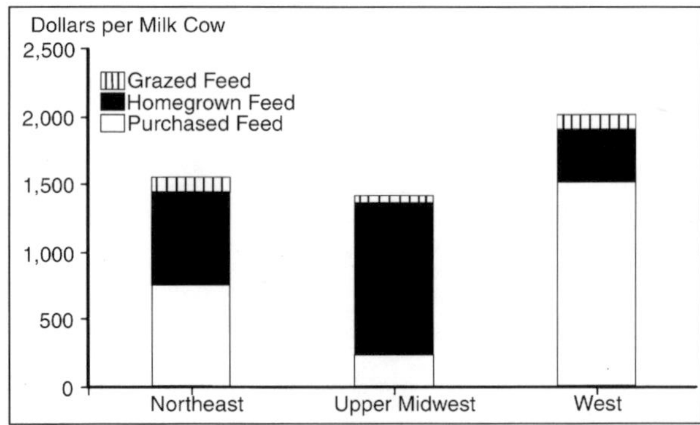

Fig. Organic Dairy Feed Costs per Cow, by Region

Notes: Total feed costs per cow were highest for organic dairies in the West, where a much higher proportion of dairy feed was purchased than in the other regions

LABOUR USE BY REGION

Charges for unpaid labour accounted for most of the differences in total costs for organic dairies in each region. Unpaid labour costs were nearly $11 per cwt in the Northeast, nearly $7 per cwt in the Upper Midwest, but only about $2 per cwt in the West. Without these charges, the difference in total economic costs among the regions would be less than $3.50 per cwt. Total labour use for organic milk production was significantly higher in the West due to the larger operations, but labour use per cwt was much less.

Table. Labour use of Organic Dairies, by Region, 2005

Item	Northeast	Upper Midwest	West
Per cow			
Hired labour hours	24	17	26
Unpaid labour hours	76	53	12
Total labour hours	100	70	38
Per cwt			
Hired labour hours	0.20	0.13	0.16
Unpaid labour hours	0.64	0.40	0.07
Total labour hours	0.84	0.53	0.23

Total labour use per cwt in the West (0.23 hour) was less than half that in the Upper Midwest (0.53 hour) and less than a third of that in the Northeast (0.84 hour). Part of this difference in labour use per cwt was due to higher productivity in the West, but labour use per cow was also significantly less. Organic dairies in the West used 38 hours of labour per cow, compared with 100 hours in the Northeast and 70 hours in the Upper Midwest. Less labour use per cow was due, in part, to the labour-saving practices more often used on dairies in the West and to economies of size.

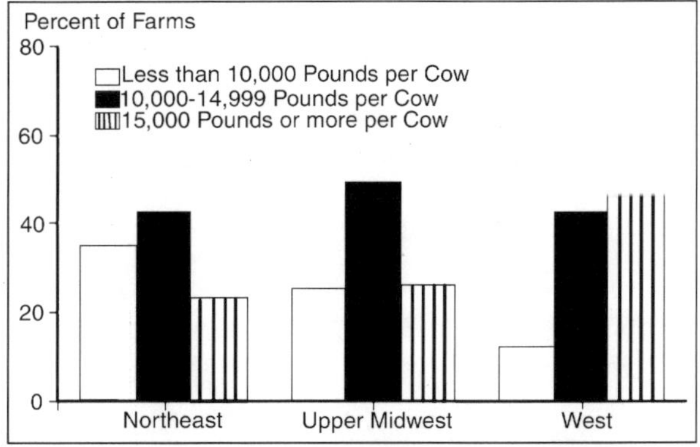

Fig. Milk Production, by Region

Notes: Nearly half of organic dairies in the West had milk cows that produced more than 15,000 pounds per year, compared with less than 30 per cent in the other regions

PASTURE USE IN ORGANIC MILK PRODUCTION

The most common technology used on conventional dairy operations confines milk cows in large barns and limits access to pasture. This means that forage from grazing comprises very little of the forage fed to dairy cows on most conventional dairies. Access to pasture is a requirement for the organic certification of dairy operations. Forage from grazing is also an important element of the feeding programme on many organic dairies.

Milk producers may find it easier and less expensive to maintain organic pastures for grazing dairy cows than to either purchase or produce and harvest organic crops and forage for dairy feed. Also, grazing systems may be less stressful for dairy cattle and contribute to lower veterinary expenses. Pasture-based production may also have environmental benefits, such as improved soil quality and reduced soil erosion. Pasture use for dairy feed on organic dairies, relative to conventional dairies.

More than 60 per cent of organic milk producers reported that at least half of their total forage ration came from pasture during the grazing months (an average of 6.5 months per year), compared with 18 per cent of conventional dairies. Nearly 90 per cent of organic dairies sourced at least 25 per cent of their total forage ration from pasture. In contrast, 70 per cent of conventional dairies reported that less than 25 per cent of their total forage ration fed to dairy cows came from pasture, while 40 per cent obtained none from pasture.

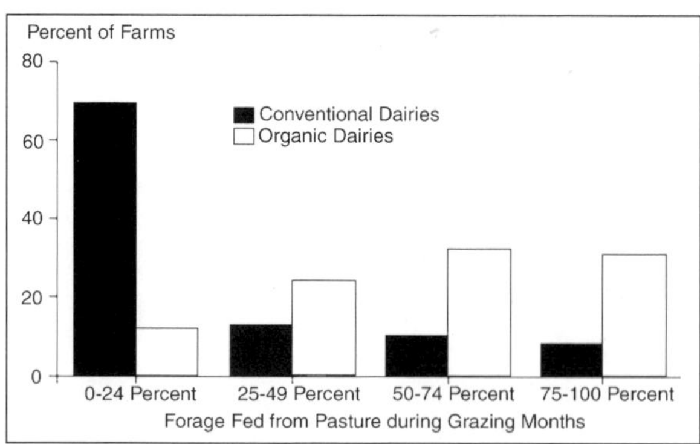

Fig. Producer Type, by Share of Dairies Forage Fed from Pasture

Notes: More than 60 per cent of organic dairies obtained at least 50 per cent of the forage fed to dairy cows from pasture, while nearly 70 per cent of conventional dairies obtained less than 25 per cent

To evaluate the role of pasture grazing in organic milk production, surveyed producers were divided into groups that indicate the level of pasture grazing as a source of dairy cow forage during the grazing months:

- 0-24 per cent;
- 25-49 per cent;
- 50-74 per cent; and
- 75-100 per cent.

CHARACTERISTICS AND PRACTICES BY LEVEL OF PASTURE USE

Almost two-thirds of organic milk producers reported that at least 50 per cent of the forage fed to dairy cattle during the grazing months came from pasture, and a third reported that 75 per cent or more came from pasture. Only 12 per cent of organic milk producers reported that less than 25 per cent of forage fed came from pasture. Differences between organic dairies where pasture use was highest (75-100 per cent of forage fed) and lowest (0-24 per cent of forage fed) were significant and are emphasized in this section.

Farm characteristics among organic dairies in the middle groups (25-49 per cent and 50-74 per cent of forage fed from pasture) showed little difference. Operations that relied on pasture use the most were the smallest in size and produced the least milk per cow. Organic dairies with 75-100 per cent of forage fed from pasture had an average of 64 milk cows that averaged 11,289 pounds of milk per cow.

Table. Characteristics and Production Practices, by Level of Pasture use on Organic Dairy Operations, 2005

	Forage Fed from Pasture During Grazing Months			
Item	**0-24**	**25-49**	**50-74**	**75-100**
	%	%	%	%
% of farms	12	24	32	31
%of milk cows	21	23	31	25
% of milk production	25	23	31	21
Milk cows *(number per farm)*	135	79	78	64
Milk production *(pounds per cow)*	16,560	13,594	13,319	11,289
Region: *% of farms*				
Northeast (ME, NY, PA, VT)	21	42	43	55
Upper Midwest (MI, MN, WI)	58	44	40	35
Corn Belt (IL, IN, IA, MO, OH)	13	8	5	9
West (CA, ID, OR, WA)	8	6	12	2
Region: *%of cows*				
Northeast (ME, NY, PA, VT)	9	29	28	45
Upper Midwest (MI, MN, WI)	30	46	28	29
Corn Belt (IL, IN, IA, MO, OH)	10	9	4	8
West (CA, ID, OR, WA)	51	16	40	18

In dairy business: *% of farms*				
Less than 10 years	11	18	19	27
10 years or more	89	82	81	73
Pasture rotation:				
At least once a day	39	48	58	72
Every 2-7 days	30	33	38	26
Less than weekly	4	1	id	1
Never	24	18	3	1
Pasture not used for feed	4	0	0	0

Notes: id=Insufficient data for disclosure.

In contrast, dairies with 0-24 per cent of forage from pasture averaged more than twice the number of milk cows (135) and more than 5,000 pounds more milk production per cow (16,560 pounds). Thus, operations that relied less on pasture use (12 per cent) had a disproportionately large share of milk cows (21 per cent) and milk production (25 per cent), while a third of operations that relied most on pasture use accounted for only 25 per cent of milk cows and 21 per cent of production.

Organic dairies with the highest pasture use for feed were located in the Northeast. More than half of these farms were in the Northeast and operated with 45 per cent of the organic milk cows in this group. Operations in the Upper Midwest accounted for the majority of farms using the least pasture (0-24 per cent) and 35 per cent of farms using the most (75-100 per cent). Organic dairies in the West accounted for only 8 per cent of the farms using the least pasture, but these large operations held 51 per cent of the milk cows in this group.

Large operations relied less on pasture as a forage source because of the significant land requirements necessary to supply pasture for large herds. However, some large operations in the West used pasture as an important dairy feed source. Among the farms with the highest pasture use, the West (at 2 per cent) included 18 per cent of the milk cows. Organic dairies that relied the most on pasture use were in business relatively less time than other organic dairies.

Twenty-seven per cent of dairies that relied on pasture for 75-100 per cent of their forage feed had been in business less than 10 years, compared with only 11 per cent that relied on pasture for 0-24 per cent of their forage feed. Also, farm operators who relied the most on pasture forage were younger than other farm operators.

Sixteen per cent of these farm operators were younger than 35 and only 4 per cent were older than 65, compared with 6 and 10 per cent, respectively, of the operators who used the least pasture. Younger farm operators on relatively new dairies were more likely to use pasture-based feeding for organic milk production.

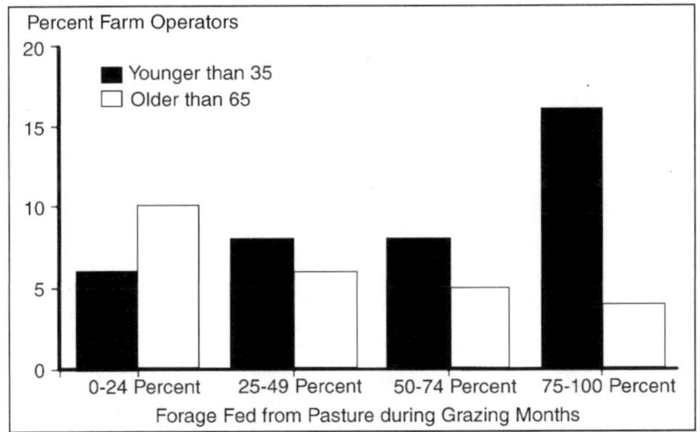

Fig. Farm Operator Age, by the Share of Dairy Forage Fed from Pasture

Notes: Among organic farm operators that used the most pasture for dairy feed, 16 per cent were younger than 35 and only 4 per cent were older than 65

Pasture as a source of forage on organic dairies was closely related to the intensity of pasture management. Rotating pastures is a management strategy that can increase the total volume and quality of dry matter produced on pastures by allowing cows to graze for specified periods before moving them to new pastures.

Seventy-two per cent of organic dairies that reported the highest use of pasture forage rotated pastures at least once a day, compared with less than 40 per cent of dairies that used pasture forage the least. Among dairies that used pasture the least, 24 per cent reported that pastures were never rotated and 4 per cent indicated that pasture was not a source of dairy feed.

PRODUCTION COSTS AND NET RETURNS BY LEVEL OF PASTURE USE

Substituting pasture for more expensive feed sources may appear to be an efficient way to lower dairy feed costs. Average feed costs per cwt of milk, however, were lowest on the organic operations using the least pasture for dairy forage (0-24 per cent), between $1 and $2 per cwt less than on the operations using more pasture.

Table. Production Costs and Net Returns on Organic Dairy Operations, by Level of Pasture use, 2005

	Forage Fed from Pasture During Grazing Months			
Item	**0-24** %	**25-49** %	**50-74** %	**75-100** %
	Dollars per cwt sold			
Feed:	11.61	13.14	13.42	12.90
Purchased feed	7.43	5.15	7.19	6.09

Homegrown harvested feed	3.89	7.51	5.41	5.69
Grazed feed	0.29	0.48	0.82	1.13
Hired labour	2.44	1.85	2.17	2.27
Capital costs	4.11	5.36	4.48	6.70
Opportunity cost of unpaid labour	2.82	6.47	6.24	8.36
Cost summary				
Operating costs	17.74	18.55	18.99	19.44
Operating and capital costs	21.85	23.91	23.47	26.14
Total economic costs	25.33	31.53	30.64	35.99
Gross value of production	24.10	24.49	23.59	25.63
Returns above total economic costs	-1.22	-7.04	-7.05	-10.36

Notes: Measuring Milk Production Costs. The gross value of production includes milk sales, cull and breeding animal sales, revenue from leasing dairy animals or space to other operations, co-op patronage dividends, dairy assessment rebates or refunds, and the value of manure. The value of milk sales was determined from prices reported by the survey respondents.

This relationship changes little even if charges for pasture resources are excluded from the feed costs. Average feed costs per cow declined as pasture use for dairy forage increased. Total feed costs were $1,902 per cow on organic dairies that relied on pasture for 0-24 per cent of forage fed, compared with only $1,409 on organic dairies that relied on pasture for 75-100 per cent of forage fed, a savings of about 25 per cent. As shown previously, however, average production per cow was more than 30 per cent lower on the organic dairies that used the most pasture, thus total costs per cwt were higher.

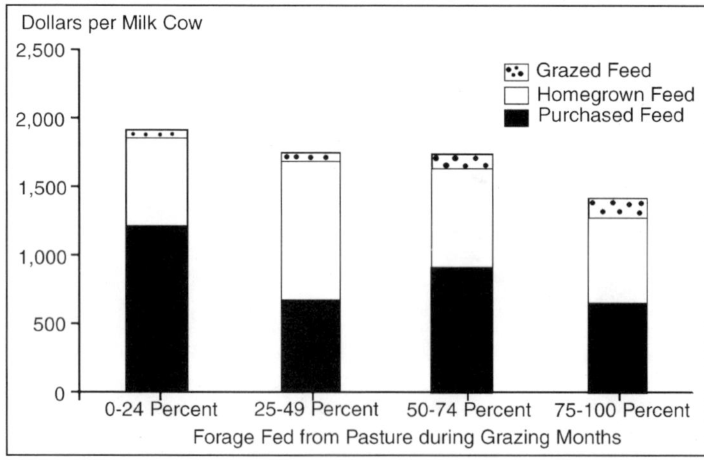

Fig. Feed Costs, by Share of Dairy Forage Fed from Pasture

Notes: Average feed cost per cow on organic dairies were about 25 per cent less on operations using the most pasture.

Breaking down the distribution of milk production per cow for each group provides an indication of how milk yields declined as pasture was substituted for higher energy feed in the dairy ration. Nearly half of organic dairies feeding 0-24 per cent of forage from pasture had annual milk yields at 15,000 pounds per cow or more, compared with just 10 per cent of dairies feeding 75-100 per cent.

In contrast, more than 40 per cent of dairies using the most pasture had an annual milk yield of less than 10,000 pounds per cow, compared with 19 per cent of those using the least pasture. This suggests that improving pasture quality to achieve higher milk production can contribute to the success of organic dairies using pasture-based feeding.

The relationship between pasture use and total production costs follows much the same pattern as seen for size and production costs on organic dairies. That is, the operations using less pasture were much larger and had lower average costs per cwt than the smaller operations using more pasture.

Capital costs were more than $2 per cwt higher and the charge for unpaid labour was more than $5 per cwt higher on the operations where pasture forage accounted for 75-100 per cent of forage fed than on those where pasture forage accounted for 0-24 per cent of forage fed.

Larger operations were able to spread the fixed costs for capital and labour over production from more cows, and each cow was more productive on the larger operations using the least pasture for dairy forage.

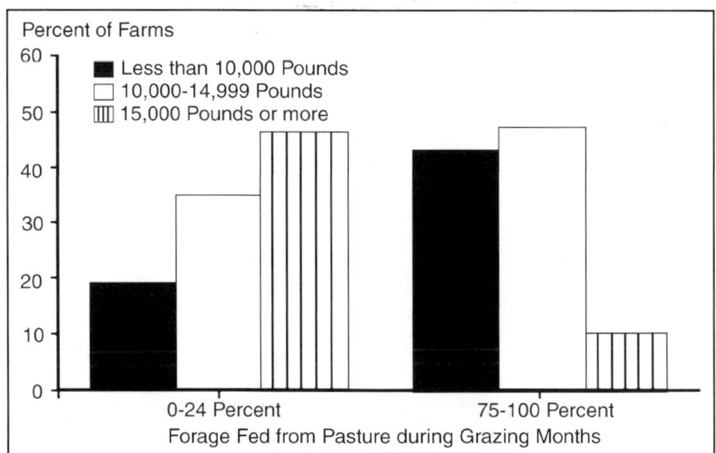

Fig. Milk Production, by Share of Dairy Forage Fed from Pasture

Notes: Nearly half of organic dairies feeding the least pasture forage had milk yields above 15,000 pounds per cow, compared with only 10 per cent of those feeding the most pasture.

Average returns net of total economic costs were negative for dairies in each of the pasture use groups, but were significantly higher among the dairies using the least pasture. This disparity suggests that organic operations using conventional dairy feeding methods, such as confining cows and feeding higher energy feed, were more likely to generate higher returns to capital and labour resources than those relying more on pasture-based feeding.

Thus, the technologies and production methods used on organic dairies could become more like those used on conventional dairies. Changing technologies and production methods may depend on the extent to which pasture requirements for organic dairies must include pasture as part of the dairy feeding programme.

LABOUR USE BY LEVEL OF PASTURE USE

The biggest difference in organic dairy costs between those using the most and the least pasture for dairy forage was the unpaid labour charge. The labour charge on organic dairies feeding 75-100 per cent of forage from pasture was more than $8 per cwt, compared with less than $3 per cwt on dairies feeding 0-24 per cent of forage from pasture. The labour charge contributed about half the difference in total costs that were more than $10 per cwt higher for dairies using the most pasture. Table includes labour use per cow and per cwt for each level of pasture feeding.

Unpaid labour use per cwt on organic dairies feeding 75-100 per cent of forage from pasture was about three times that for those feeding 0-24 per cent of forage from pasture. Part of this difference came from fixed amounts of labour being spread over more output on the larger operations that used the least amount of pasture. Some of the labour difference, however, may be due to the pasture feeding system's being more labour intensive than handling dairy cows in confinement.

Among farms with fewer than 100 cows, the unpaid labour use on dairies feeding the least forage from pasture was still about a third less than on those feeding the most forage from pasture (0.45 hour versus 0.65 hour). In addition, total labour use among these small dairies increased steadily as more pasture was used for dairy feed. This increase suggests that pasture-based feeding systems are inherently more labour intensive than the conventional practice of handling dairy cows in confinement, possibly due to the labour required for moving cows to, from, and between pastures.

Table. Organic Dairy Labour Use, by Level of Pasture Use, 2005

	Forage Fed from Pasture During Grazing Months			
Item	**0-24** %	**25-49** %	**50-74** %	**75-100** %
Per cow				
Hired labour hours	30	20	22	17
Unpaid labour hours	27	52	48	56
Total labour hours	57	72	70	73

Per cwt				
Hired labour hours	0.18	0.15	0.17	0.15
Unpaid labour hours	0.16	0.39	0.36	0.49
Total labour hours	0.34	0.53	0.52	0.65
Per cwt—dairies with fewer than 100 cows				
Hired labour hours	0.15	0.18	0.17	0.16
Unpaid labour hours	0.45	0.52	0.59	0.65
Total labour hours	0.60	0.70	0.76	0.81

Note: Totals may not equal the sum of items due to rounding

COMPARING ORGANIC AND CONVENTIONAL DAIRIES

Organic dairy operations usually begin as conventional dairies that undergo the transition to become certified organic operations. Differences in farm and operator characteristics and production practices of organic and conventional dairies were identified and used to measure differences in milk production costs. These cost differences, along with estimates of organic transition costs, indicate milk price premiums that organic dairies need to be competitive with conventional milk production.

Research models were specified to describe farms that use organic production and the difference in costs between organic and conventional farms. The models accounted for the myriad of factors that influence milk production costs, such as size of operation, region, and production practices, to isolate the cost difference attributed to an organic operation. The models also accounted for the fact that organic producers are not randomly assigned among the dairy population, but instead self-select.

Self-selection could bias the cost comparison if unmeasured factors, such as the level or type of management, were correlated with both organic participation and milk production costs. This research was also designed to examine whether organic systems are more or less competitive in different segments of the U.S. dairy sector.

The models were used to evaluate the competitiveness of organic and conventional milk production for farms located in the Northeast and Upper Midwest, those using pasture-based feeding, and among small dairies, segments of the U.S. dairy sector where organic production is most common. The results provide an indication of when organic milk production was most economical compared with conventional production.

CHARACTERISTICS AND PRACTICES OF ORGANIC AND CONVENTIONAL DAIRIES

Organic dairies were smaller than conventional dairies, averaging 82 cows per organic farm compared with 156 cows per conventional farm. The average milk production per cow was also lower on organic operations, nearly 30 per cent less. Organic operations averaged about 13,600 pounds of milk per cow, compared with nearly 19,000 pounds per cow on conventional operations. More than 80 per cent of organic dairy operations were located in the Northeast or Upper Midwest, compared with 65 per cent of conventional operations.

These regions also included 62 per cent of all organic milk cows, compared with 42 per cent of conventional milk cows. In contrast, only 7 per cent of organic dairies were located in the West, but these operations held about a third of total U.S. organic milk cows, the same as conventional operations. Organic dairies in the West (381 cows) were much larger than those in other regions and similar in average size to conventional operations (431 cows).

The average size of organic dairies in the Northeast was half that of conventional dairies (52 cows versus 104 cows), and those in the Upper Midwest were about two-thirds the size of conven tional dairies (64 cows versus 98 cows). The ARMS includes no data for organic dairy operations in the Southeast or Southwest.

Table. Characteristics of Organic and Conventional Dairy Operations, 2005

	Type of Dairy	
Item	**Conventional**	**Organic**
Milk cows (number per farm)	156	82
Milk production (pounds per cow)	18,983	13,601
% of farms/cows		
Region:		
Northeast (ME, NY, PA, VT)	26/17	44/29
Upper Midwest (MI, MN, WI)	39/25	42/33
Corn Belt (IL, IN, IA, MO, OH)	15/10	7/7
Southeast (FL, GA, KY, TN, VA)[1]	6/6	0/0
Southwest (AZ, NM, TX)[1]	2/10	0/0
West (CA, ID, OR, WA)	11/32	7/31
Milk cows per farm		
Region:		
Northeast (ME, NY, PA, VT)	104	52
Upper Midwest (MI, MN, WI)	98	64
Corn Belt (IL, IN, IA, MO, OH)	108	75
Southeast (FL, GA, KY, TN, VA)[1]	152	0
Southwest (AZ, NM, TX)[1]	781	0
West (CA, ID, OR, WA)	431	381
% of farms		
Farm operator:		
Off-farm occupation	2	4
Education:		
Less than high school	18	26

Completed high school/some college	66	54
Graduated from college	16	20
Age (years)	51	49
In dairy business (years)	23	21
Selling certified organic milk (years)	na	5
Exit dairy business:		
5 years or less	25	16
10 years or less	51	33
20 or more years	30	47

Notes: na=Not applicable. [1]Organic dairies were not surveyed in the Southeast and Southwest regions.

Most farm operator characteristics were similar among conventional and organic dairies. Nearly all farm operators in both groups reported farming as their primary occupation, common for dairy operations due to their substantial onfarm labour requirements. The distribution of operator education suggests that those in the organic group were neither more nor less educated than operators of conventional dairies.

The average age of farm operators on conventional and organic dairies was similar. Most organic operations converted to organic production after years of conventional production. Of the 21 years that organic operators reported being in business, organic milk was produced for only 5 years. Organic producers were more optimistic about their future, as significantly fewer planned to exit in the next 10 years and significantly more planned to be in business for 20 or more years.

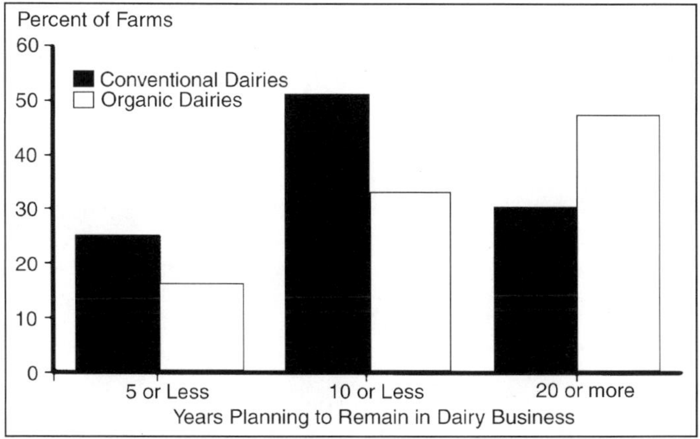

Fig. Plans to Exit the Dairy Business, by Type of Producer

Notes: Operators of organic dairies were more optimistic about their future.

The primary difference in the production practices used by organic and conventional dairies was found in their feeding systems. More then 60 per cent of organic operations reported using pasture-based feeding that provided more than 50 per cent of seasonal forage from pasture (during the grazing months), compared with just 18 per cent of other operations. Although not available to organic producers, rBST was used by 17 per cent of conventional operations that were also more likely to utilize regular veterinary services and a nutritionist to formulate dairy rations. Differences in production practices may have contributed to the higher production per cow on conventional versus organic operations. Labour use also distinguished conventional from organic dairies.

Organic operations used nearly twice the hours of total labour per cwt, on average, than did conventional operations (0.50 hour versus 0.26 hour). Most of the labour difference came from significantly more unpaid labour hours worked on organic dairies and was influenced by the smaller average size and lower productivity of organic dairies. Fixed labour inputs were spread over fewer units of production on the smaller organic dairies.

FACTORS AFFECTING THE USE OF ORGANIC MILK PRODUCTION

Several operator and farm characteristics were statistically associated with the organic approach to milk production. Among operator characteristics, education and planning horizon were important. Dairy farmers graduating from college were more likely to be organic producers.

Table. Production Practices and Labour Use on Organic and Conventional Dairy Operations, 2005

Item	Type of Dairy Conventional	Organic
% of farms		
Production practices		
DHI programme participation[1]	45	46
Pasture-based feeding[2]	18	63
Milking three times or more daily	7	1
rBST (recombinant bovine somatotropin)	17	0
Artificial insemination	82	73
Embryo transplants or sexed semen	10	3
Controlled breeding/calving season	25	35
Regular veterinary services	69	38
Nutritionist services	72	45
Computerized milking system	5	2
Computerized feeding system	7	3
Milking parlor	50	41
Keep individual cow records	61	62
Johne's disease programme participation	20	26
Onfarm computer records	26	21
Dairy information from Internet	38	41

Forward-purchased inputs	20	8
Negotiate input price discounts	35	21
Hours per cwt		
Labour use:		
Paid labour	0.12	0.16
Unpaid labour	0.13	0.34
Total labour	0.26	0.50

Notes:

[1]Dairy Herd Improvement.

[2]Pasture-based feeding is defined as providing at least half of the forage fed to milk cows during the grazing months from pasture. Organic dairies reported an average grazing period for milk cows of 6.5 months in 2005.

Dairy operations planning to exit the industry in the next 10 years were less likely to be organic, indicating that operations with a longer planning horizon were more likely to use the organic approach. More educated dairy farmers with long-term plans to remain in business are probably more willing and able to make the necessary investments or take the additional risks associated with organic production.

Size and location of dairy operations were also important factors influencing operators to go organic. The likelihood of being organic decreased as the number of milk cows on a farm increased. Larger operations had less incentive to go organic because of economies of size in milk production, pasture requirements for organic certification, and possible difficulties sourcing large quantities of organic inputs.

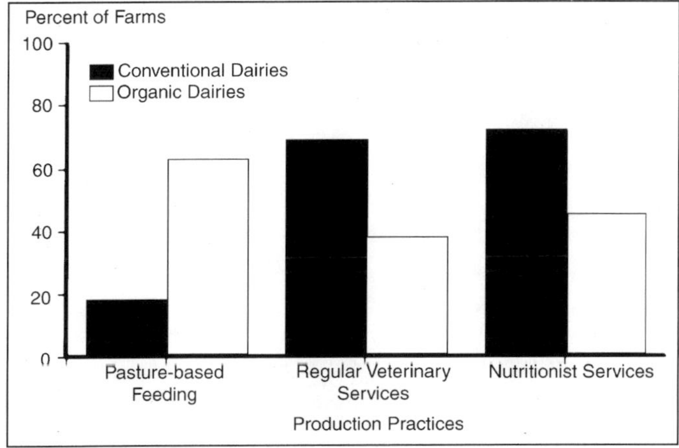

Fig. Production Practices, by Type of Producer

Notes: Organic operations used pasture-based feeding more often, while conventional operations used regular veterinary and nutritionist services more often.

The proximity and accessibility of grazing land to the operation may also have been important because barriers, such as highways and streams, may limit available pasture. Location in the Northeast or Upper Midwest was also associated with a higher probability of being organic. The organic dairy industry began in these areas and may offer a more developed infrastructure for handling organic milk. Operations with a pasture-based feeding programme were more likely to be organic, possibly because the land base enabled them to meet organic pasture requirements and pasture was more easily managed organically than field crops. Results suggest that using pasture as a significant source of dairy feed was one of the best predictors of being an organic dairy. Location in counties with a greater concentration of farms with milk cows included more organic production, potentially as a result of organic processors who chose to locate and recruit in areas with a large concentration of producers in order to reduce milk transportation and other transaction costs.

FACTORS AFFECTING MILK PRODUCTION COSTS

This section of the report examines the relationship between farm and operator characteristics and three levels of production costs—operating costs, operating and capital costs, and total economic costs. Older farm operators had higher costs than younger operators. Operating, operating and capital, and total economic costs all declined as farm size increased, consistent with economies of size. Costs declined as size increased, at a decreasing rate, as fixed capital and labour costs were spread over more units of output.

Significant economies of size with respect to capital and labour were expected, but operating costs also declined with size, possibly due to greater feed efficiency or lower prices paid for feed items on larger farms. Farm location influenced production costs as dairies in most other regions had lower costs than those in the Northeast. Technology use was also an important determinant of production costs. Farms using more technology had lower per unit capital and labour costs, possibly by increasing their productivity.

Pasture-based feeding had a negative, but insignificant, effect on operating costs. Feed costs were lower for organic dairies that substituted pasture for other feed items, but lower production from pasture-fed cows offset the cost savings. Pasture-based feeding was associated with higher total economic costs due to higher labour requirements.

After accounting for factors that influence production costs, operating costs for organic production were $4. 78 per cwt higher, operating and capital costs were $5.65 per cwt higher, and total economic costs were $6.79 per cwt higher than for conventional production among all U.S. dairies. Results were similar for dairies in the Northeast and Upper Midwest and among small farms (less than 150 cows). The estimated difference in production costs between pasture-based organic and pasture-based conventional farms, however, was much less than among all dairies ($2.87 per cwt for operating costs, $3.00 per cwt for operating and capital costs, and $3.57 per cwt for total economic costs). Therefore, it is not surprising that many pasture-based dairies use organic production.

ORGANIC TRANSITION COSTS

The estimated cost differences indicate the additional costs incurred by operations producing organic milk relative to conventional operations but do not include the costs associated with the transition period. Data from the ARMS did not indicate the actual costs incurred during transition, so the estimated cost differences between organic and conventional milk production were approximated for the transition period. Before an operation is certified to sell organic milk, pasture and cropland for dairy feed must be managed organically for a minimum of 36 months, and the dairy herd must be fed and managed organically during the last 12 months of that period. As a result, organic operations must undergo 3 years of higher costs before the higher organic milk prices are received.

Table. Estimated Additional Costs Incurred by Organic Dairy Farms Compared with Conventional Dairy Farms, 2005

	Operating Costs	Operating and Capital Costs	Total Economic Costs
Dollars per cwt sold			
All farms:			
Producing organic	4.78	5.65	6.79
Transitioning to organic	na	0.72	0.86
Total additional costs	4.78	6.37	7.65
Northeast and Upper Midwest farms:			
Producing organic	4.51	5.43	6.77
Transitioning to organic	na	0.69	0.86
Total additional costs	4.51	6.12	7.63
Pasture-based farms:			
Producing organic	2.87	3.00	3.57
Transitioning to organic	na	0.38	0.45
Total additional costs	2.87	3.38	4.02
Small farms (fewer than 150 cows):			
Producing organic	4.67	5.78	7.82
Transitioning to organic	na	0.73	0.99
Total additional costs	4.67	6.51	8.81

Notes:

na=Not applicable.

Transition costs were treated as a capital investment necessary to return the higher organic milk price over the expected life of the operation and thus were not part of annual operating costs.

Higher costs for 3 years are a necessary investment to return higher milk prices over the expected life of the operation. This initial investment is determined by the estimated additional costs incurred by organic operations over the 3-year transition period. During year 3, when both the land and dairy herd must be managed organically, the total additional costs were charged. During years 1 and 2, when only the land is managed organically, 50 per cent of the additional costs were charged.

This corresponds with about half of the feed cost on organic dairies from homegrown supplies, which would be managed organically during the full 3 years. The annualized cost of this investment was computed by spreading it over an expected operating life of 20 years. The estimated transition costs and total additional costs on organic operations are shown in table.

Transition costs were $0.72 per cwt for operating and capital costs and $0.86 per cwt for total economic costs. Thus, the total estimated additional costs among U.S. dairy farms for producing organic relative to conventional milk were estimated at $4.78 per cwt for operating costs, $6.37 per cwt for operating and capital costs, and $7.65 per cwt for total economic costs. Among pasture-based dairies, the cost differences were much lower at an estimated $2.87 per cwt for operating costs, $3.38 per cwt for operating and capital costs, and $4.02 per cwt for total economic costs.

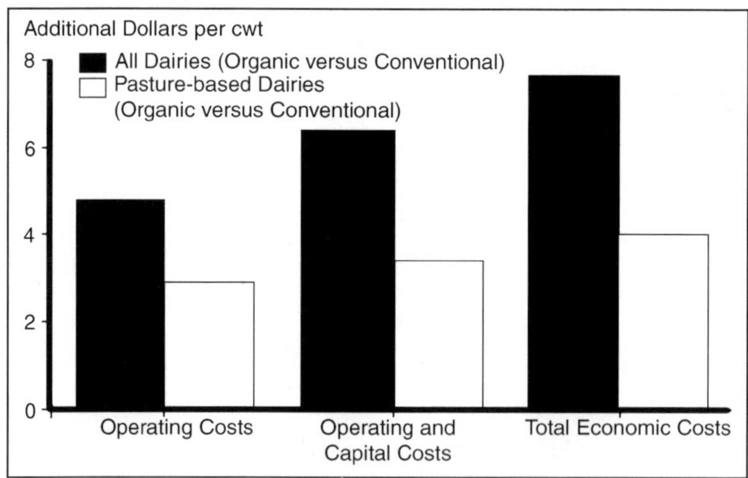

Fig. Additional Costs of Organic versus Conventional Milk Production

Notes: The additional costs of organic compared with conventional milk production were much lower among pasture-based dairies than for all dairies.

CHALLENGES OF ORGANIC MILK PRODUCTION

Organic milk producers were asked in the ARMS what they considered the most difficult aspect of organic milk production. Forty per cent of producers reported that certification paperwork and compliance cost were the most challenging. Sourcing organic inputs, including grains and forages, feed supplements, and replacement heifers, was the most difficult aspect reported by 23 per cent of organic producers. High costs of production and maintaining animal health were challenging aspects reported by 17 and 13 per cent of producers, respectively.

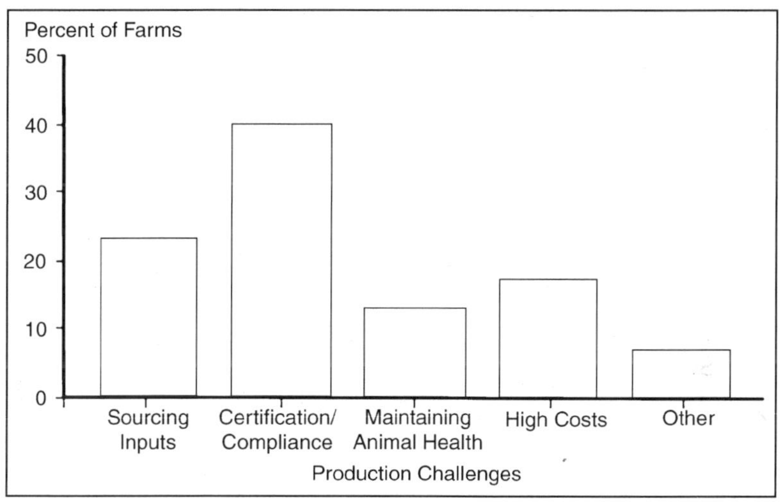

Fig. Challenges of Organic Milk Production

Notes: 40 per cent of organic dairies cited certification paperwork and compliance costs as the most difficult aspect of organic production.

In this section, the challenges of organic milk production are explored by examining how reported challenges to organic milk production varied across the sector. Producer reports were summarized by operation size, region, level of pasture use, and operator characteristics to see what factors may constrain the adoption and growth of organic milk production.

FARM CHARACTERISTICS AND ORGANIC PRODUCTION CHALLENGES

The challenges reported for organic production varied little among dairy size groups, except for the largest dairies. About a third of the largest organic dairies, those with 200 cows or more and an average size of nearly 500 cows, reported sourcing inputs as the most difficult aspect, compared with 20-25 per cent of smaller dairies.

This indicates that sourcing organic inputs in volume may be difficult for some large organic producers and may be a factor constraining the size of organic operations. Smaller dairies reported certification/compliance as the most difficult aspect, and the smallest dairies, those with fewer than 50 cows, were the least likely to report animal health and production costs as most challenging.

Table. Most Difficult Aspect of Organic Milk Production, by Farm and Operator Characteristics, 2005

	Most Difficult Aspect				
Item	Sourcing Inputs	Certification/ Compliance	Maintaining Animal Health	High Costs of Production	Other
% of farms reporting aspect					
Size:					
Fewer than 50 cows	25	44	10	13	8
50-99 cows	20	36	15	21	8
100-199 cows	20	41	19	20	0
200 cows or more	34	30	17	17	2
Region:					
Northeast	19	32	13	30	6
Upper Midwest	24	51	10	6	9
West	51	id	14	20	id
Pasture use:					
0-24 %	13	43	15	16	13
25-49 %	22	47	id	17	id
50-74 %	26	42	14	13	5
75-100 %	24	31	13	21	11
Operator age:					
Younger than 50 years	20	43	16	14	8
50 years or older	26	37	10	21	6
Operator education:					
Less than high school	17	54	4	18	8
Completed high school	22	40	17	15	7
Some college	33	22	16	21	8
Organic experience:[1]					
1 year	26	33	25	11	5
2-4 years	26	43	12	13	7
5 or more years	19	39	12	22	8

Notes: id = Insufficient data for disclosure.

[1]Number of years an operator has produced organic milk.

Organic milk production challenges were different in each region. The most difficult aspect for organic dairies in the Northeast was split between certification/compliance and production costs at a third each. Dairies in the Northeast were the least likely to report sourcing inputs as most challenging, possibly because these small dairies often produce organic dairy feed or can buy it locally. Half of Upper Midwest dairies reported certification/compliance, while half of organic dairies in the West indicated sourcing inputs as the most difficult aspect of organic milk production. The volume of organic inputs needed on large farms in the West may account for the level of concern with sourcing inputs. The most difficult aspect of organic milk production did not differ much among the pasture use groups, except for those using the most pasture.

Dairies that relied on pasture for 75-100 per cent of forage during the grazing months were less likely to report certification/compliance as the most difficult aspect of organic production. Certification/compliance may be less difficult for these dairies because the feeding programme satisfies the pasture requirement for organic certification. More than 40 per cent of the dairies in each of the other pasture use groups reported certification/compliance as the most difficult aspect of organic milk production.

OPERATOR CHARACTERISTICS AND ORGANIC PRODUCTION CHALLENGES

Responses based on operator age varied by 6-7 percentage points. Operators younger than 50 years of age were more concerned with certification/compliance and maintaining animal health. Those older than 50 years of age reported sourcing inputs and production costs as the most difficult aspects of organic milk production. Certification/compliance was reported as the most difficult aspect of organic milk production by more than half of farm operators with less than a high school education. As operator education increased, certification/compliance was less of a concern.

Forty per cent of operators with a high school education, compared with only 22 per cent of those with some college, reported certification/compliance as the most difficult aspect. Results suggest that education may ease the certification process. In contrast, sourcing inputs was reported as most challenging with more frequency as operator education increased. The relationship between organic experience and the challenge of organic production was examined by grouping farm operators by the number of years they had produced organic milk. Dairy farm operators in their first year of organic production were more likely to indicate that maintaining animal health was most challenging, reported by 25 per cent of operators.

Organic milk producers may have learned quickly to manage animal health as these concerns fell to 12 per cent by year 2 and beyond. High production costs were an increasing concern as organic operators became more experienced, but certification/compliance issues were still the primary concern for organic dairy operators regardless of their experience.

CONCLUSIONS

Unique and detailed data from a 2005 survey of U.S. dairy operations were used to characterize organic dairies and to compare them with conventional dairies. The dataset is unique in that it includes a targeted sample of organic producers at a much higher rate than their occurrence in the population of all dairy farms. This targeted sample allows for an examination of the structure and costs associated with organic milk production and an analysis of differences between the conventional and organic sectors. Operation size was a primary determining factor for a dairy operation being organic.

Small farms may view the organic approach as an alternative by which to reorganize current resources to improve farm returns and the odds of economic survival. Small-scale production may also be more conducive to sourcing organic inputs, which may be limited in some areas. Large dairies have more invested in production technologies that typically confine milk cows to large barns and limit access to pasture and are able to take advantage of economies of size. Thus, large farms may have less incentive to consider production alternatives.

Further, large farms may have greater difficultly sourcing sufficient quantities of organic inputs, and transitioning to organic production may require more adjustments due to pasture certification requirements. Large organic dairies more often reported sourcing inputs and organic certification/ compliance requirements as the most challenging aspects of organic milk production. Dairies were more likely to produce milk organically if they were located in the Northeast or Upper Midwest. These areas have a long history of small dairies and thus a successful infrastructure to provide inputs and manage output from several small operations.

The largest U.S. organic milk cooperative pioneered organic milk production in the Northeast and Upper Midwest during the mid-1990s. Proximity to markets with highly affluent consumers also made these regions attractive to organic milk operations. Access to pasture for dairy feed also had a strong influence on whether a dairy becomes organic. Operations using pasture-based feeding satisfy the pasture requirements for organic certification, and organic pasture management is generally easier than organic crop management and less costly than purchasing organic dairy feed.

Fewer small, pasture-based organic dairies were as concerned about certification/compliance requirements as other organic dairies. Results from a statistical model comparing conventional and organic milk production costs indicated that average operating costs for organic dairies were $4.78 per cwt higher, and operating and capital costs were $5.65 per cwt higher after accounting for other factors that influence production costs. Including an estimate of the additional costs incurred during transition, average organic milk production costs were $4.78 and $6.37 per cwt higher, respectively.

With an average price premium of $6.69 per cwt for organic milk, organic milk producers, on average, covered the additional operating and capital costs of organic production in 2005. Most organic dairies were small operations that used primarily unpaid operator and family labour. Returns above operating and capital costs on these small organic operations compared favourably with those of small conventional operations, suggesting that there may be economic incentives for some small existing dairies that have already committed much of the fixed investment to consider the transition to organic milk production.

Additional economic costs for organic production averaged nearly $1 per cwt more than the organic milk price premium in 2005. Thus, low returns to unpaid labour and management may limit startup organic dairies unless they can enter the industry at a much larger scale of production than the current norm. Even though most organic dairies were much smaller than conventional dairies, economic forces suggest that similar economies of size were available to organic producers. Some small organic dairies were earning enough to operate, but many were not able to cover the opportunity costs of investments in capital and the operator's time compared with larger operations.

These economic conditions suggest that organic milk production may migrate towards larger operations, as has conventional production. This production shift will likely occur over an extended period as many existing small organic operations either choose to replace their capital assets with larger production units or exit the industry. In the short term, some small operators may continue producing organic milk as a lifestyle choice, despite generating returns that do not cover the opportunity cost of their time.

Organic milk farms able to use pasture resources for a significant portion of dairy feed were very competitive with pasture-based conventional producers. Average operating costs for pasture-based organic milk production were estimated to be about $3 per cwt higher than those for pasture-based conventional production, and total economic costs for organic pasture-based milk production were about $4 per cwt higher than for pasture-based conventional production, significantly less than the average organic milk price premium in 2005.

Economic incentives appear to favour pasture-based dairies transitioning to organic production, and possibly startup organic dairies that can take advantage of pasture resources suitable for organic dairy feed. While the economics of pasture-based organic milk production compared favourably with that of pasture-based conventional production, pasture-based organic dairies had lower average milk production per cow and higher per unit costs than other organic dairies.

This suggests that organic operations using conventional dairy feeding methods, such as confining cows and feeding harvested forages, are more likely to generate higher returns to capital and labour than those using pasture-based feeding. Thus, the technologies and production methods used on organic dairies may become more like those used on conventional dairies. Interpretation and implementation of revised organic pasture rules may shape the future structure of the organic industry. If pasture rules become more stringent, the challenges of certification/compliance could have a major impact on the sizes and types of farms able to produce certified organic milk. This report attempts to shed light on the structure of organic milk production, factors affecting whether a dairy becomes organic, and the relative costs and returns of conventional and organic milk production.

Based on these findings, implications for the structure of organic milk production were developed. However, conclusions derived from the analysis were based on 2005 organic and conventional milk and feed price relationships and could change with adjustments in relative milk prices, markets for conventional and organic inputs, technological improvements in dairy farming, and new organic pasture regulations.

9

Dairy Market and Policy Issues

INTRODUCTION

Indian dairy producers are caught in a classic "price-cost squeeze," with farm milk prices declining sharply from record highs while feed costs remain high. From January through September 2009, the all-milk price received by farmers was 36% below a year earlier.

Meanwhile feed costs, as measured by alfalfa prices, were down only 20% from a year earlier. The deteriorating economic picture has prompted calls for policymakers to consider how well current dairy policies are assisting dairy producers and what other options might be available.

MARKET SITUATION

The dairy market since 2007 illustrates how an agricultural boom can turn into a bust. Dairy farmers enjoyed excellent returns in 2007 and most of 2008 as strong demand pushed up the price of dairy products and the farm price of milk. In November 2007, the all-milk price hit a record $21.90 per hundredweight.

In 2008, milk prices remained high, but feed prices rose rapidly, creating concern for dairy farmers. The financial danger was a further escalation of feed prices or a price reversal in dairy product prices. Product prices have, in fact, dropped. Feed costs have declined some, but not enough to offset the drop in milk prices.

One simple measure of today's price-cost squeeze affecting dairy farmers is the milk-feed price index, as reported by the Indian Department of Agriculture. The ratio averaged 2.01 in 2008, the lowest since at least 1985 and down from 2.81 in 2007, a year with record-high milk prices. Thus far in 2009, the ratio has averaged 1.56, down from the 10-year average of 2.90. A ratio near 3 or higher is considered positive for milk production. milk price to average between $12.05 per cwt. and $12.25 per cwt., down from $18.29 per cwt. in 2008 and 17%-19% below the 10-year average of $14.83.

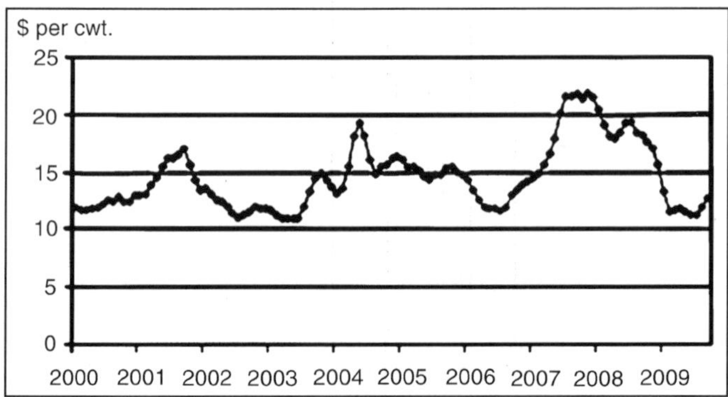

Fig. Monthly All-Milk Farm Prices

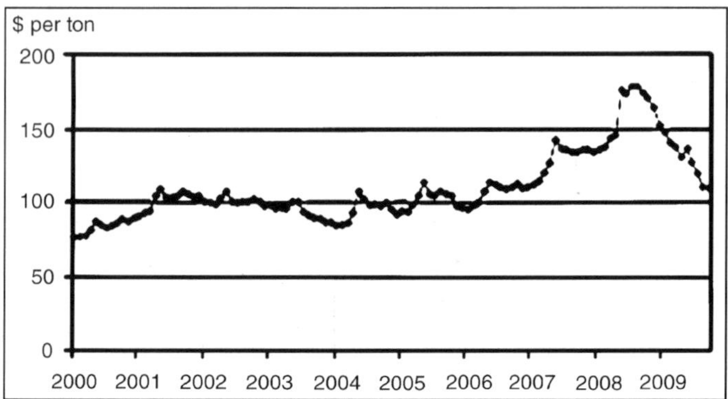

Fig. Monthly Alfalfa Prices

MILK PRODUCTION GROWS

Productivity growth is a hallmark of Indian agriculture, and dairy is no exception. Over the years, improved dairy cattle genetics and better feed management practices have increased output per cow. Dairy farmers continued the advancement last year: milk per cow in 2009 at a record high of 20,493 pounds, up from 20,396 in 2008. Normally, higher productivity is partially offset by a decline in cow numbers, resulting in more modest gains in total milk production.

However, in 2008, dairy farmers increased herds in response to attractive returns, particularly in 2007. As a result, Indian milk production rose 2.3% in 2008, compared with the increase in milk per cow of only 1.0%. Milk supplies expanded at about the same time that demand started to weaken.

In 2009, lower returns have encouraged farmers to cull dairy cows, with the national herd declining 123,000 head or 1.3%. Productivity gains, though, are expected to offset some of the reduction in cow numbers, leaving Indian milk production down just 0.8%. In 2009, the decline in production has been less than the drop-off in demand, resulting in sharply lower prices than a year ago.

DEMAND SLOWS

Dairy exports account for a relatively small but important share of Indian dairy product sales. On a fat basis, exports were estimated at 3% of total use in 2007 and 4% in 2008. Growth in Indian dairy exports stemmed from lower product availability from New Zealand and Australia and the lower-valued dollar. Indian cheese exports saw particularly strong gains. Export prospects have weakened in 2009, with forecast exports dropping below 2007 levels. Among the factors cites for the decline in export demand are the global recession, lower incomes, higher dairy production abroad, and a stronger dollar.

The drop-off in export demand means that more products must be sold on the domestic market, which has driven down dairy product prices and farm milk prices. Domestic demand has also reportedly slowed, given reduced restaurant sales and sales of premium food products, including some dairy items, as consumers reduce overall spending. However, increased purchases of food for home consumption are likely supporting the market to some degree in 2009.

FEED COSTS CLIMB

Feed costs rose sharply in mid-2008. Expanding corn demand for ethanol use, strong global demand for grain, and heightened investment in commodity markets collided with uncertain prospects for Indian corn and soybean yields. In spring/summer 2008, massive flooding in the Midwest led to fears that the Indian corn and soybean supplies would be sharply curtailed at a time when demand seemed limitless. In July 2008, the farm price of corn peaked at $5.47 per bushel, up nearly $2 per bushel from a year earlier. Alfalfa prices followed suit, with farm prices reaching $180 per ton in August compared with $135 a year earlier.

The commodity price boom of 2008 began to collapse in September when financial and commodity markets faltered. Large amounts of investment money began to leave the market, and crop yield prospects for both corn and soybeans firmed up. Supply fears essentially evaporated. As 2008 came to a close, prices for dairy feedstuffs had dropped substantially from highs earlier in the year but remained well above year-earlier levels.

Corn prices in December averaged $4.10 per bushel compared with $3.77 in December 2007. The price of alfalfa was $155 per ton in December 2008, compared with $135 in December 2007. In contrast, soybean prices, which had seen a faster rise the year before, averaged $9.24 per bushel, down from $10.00 in December 2007. Thus far in 2009, average prices for dairy feed have moderated from 2008 highs but remain well above 2007 levels. In recent months has revised its forecasts of 2009 corn and soybean prices downward based on prospects for larger crops this fall.

OUTLOOK FOR 2009 AND 2010

Given the downturn in dairy farm income, dairy economists expect producers in 2009 to send more cows to slaughter and adjust feed rations to save money, which together would result in a slight decline in total milk production in 2009. On the demand side, dairy exports in 2009 have declined as global economic weakness slows foreign demand.

Based on forecasts, the expected supply adjustments and higher support prices announced on July 31 will lift milk prices in the last quarter of 2009. Average farm-level milk prices are expected to rise from $11.60 per cwt. in the April-June quarter to $12.90 per cwt. in October-December 2009. The October-December 2008 prices averaged nearly $17 per cwt. In 2010, production to decline further as farmers cull more cows following low returns in 2009.

Also, exports are expected to pick up slightly as the global economy improves, although expects export prospects will be limited by higher domestic prices and larger exportable supplies in competitor countries. With less milk and somewhat higher demand, the all-milk price is forecast to increase from $12.15 per cwt. in 2009 to $15.05 per cwt in 2010.

CURRENT DAIRY POLICIES TO ASSIST PRODUCERS

Indian dairy policy has been developed over the last seven decades.

The early policies addressed three main problems:

1. Producers lacked bargaining power with milk buyers;
2. Producers suffered from volatile or low prices; and
3. Market participants encountered severe shortages/gluts resulting from marketing a highly perishable commodity.

The policy response resulted in the development of two major government activities that still function today: federal milk marketing orders and the Dairy Product Price Support Programme. While both FMMOs and the DPPSP have their roots in the 1930s and 1940s, the programmes have changed modestly over the years as the industry structure and markets changed. Two other components of Indian dairy policy are relatively new programmes. First, the 1985 farm bill established the Dairy Export Incentive Programme to counter foreign competitor subsidies.

Second, the Milk Income Loss Contract programme was established in the 2002 farm bill as a government payment for dairy farmers in times of low milk prices. Like Indian crop programmes, the MILC programme pays dairy producers when prices decline below a specified level. The following sections describe each of these four components and how they relate to the current market situation. Lower milk and dairy product prices since late 2008 have generated new programme activity. Purchasing dairy products last fall under the DPPSP; MILC payments were triggered beginning in February.

MILK INCOME LOSS CONTRACT PROGRAMME

The Milk Income Loss Contract (MILC) programme pays dairy farmers when farm milk prices fall below an established target price. Section 1506 of the 2008 farm bill extends authority for the MILC programme until September 30, 2012. This programme is similar to long-time subsidy programmes for crops that pay farmers when farm prices drop below certain levels. Farm Service Agency implements the MILC programme. Under MILC, participating dairy farmers nationwide are eligible for a federal payment whenever the minimum monthly market price for farm milk used for fluid consumption in Boston falls below $16.94 per cwt.

Eligible farmers then receive a payment equal to 45% of the difference between the $16.94 target price and the lower monthly market price. The payment quantity is limited to 2.985 million pounds of annual production. Since the inception of the MILC programme, large dairy farm operators have expressed concern that the payment limit has negatively affected their income. For larger farm operations, their annual production is well in excess of the limit, and any production in excess of that receives no federal payments.

To address the issue of rising feed costs, the 2008 farm bill includes a provision that adjusts upward the $16.94 target price in any month when feed prices are above a certain threshold. The law requires calculating monthly a National Average Dairy Feed Ration Cost based on a formula that currently uses to calculate feed costs. In any month that the average feed cost is above $7.35 per cwt., the $16.94 target price will be increased by 45% of the difference between the monthly feed cost and $7.35. For the latter half of 2007 and all of 2008, farm milk prices remained well above the MILC trigger price, precluding the need for any MILC payments.

However, milk prices have since declined below the trigger for MILC payments. The Class I Boston farm milk price for February 2009 was $13.97 per cwt. With the adjustment for feed costs raising the trigger to $17.33 per cwt., MILC payments were activated for the first time in two years at a payment rate of $1.51. The payment rate rose to $2.01 per cwt. in March. Given current prospects in the futures markets for milk, corn, and soybeans, payments are expected to continue during 2009, but at smaller rates.

Individual producers must select which month to begin receiving payments, based on their projection of potential payment rates and the possibility of hitting the production payment limit. As of October 26, 2009, total MILC payments distributed to date were $775 million. The timing of the payments has caused some concern for producers this spring. While milk price data become available during the payment month, data needed for the feed cost adjustor are not available until publishes monthly average feed prices in

Agricultural Prices at the end of the next month. Consequently, MILC payments for a particular month are not processed until two months later.

DAIRY PRODUCT PRICE SUPPORT PROGRAMME (DPPSP)

The Agricultural Act of 1949 first established a dairy price support programme by permanently requiring supporting the farm price of milk. Since 1949, Congress has regularly amended the programme, usually in the context of multiyear omnibus farm acts and budget reconciliation acts. Historically, the supported farm price for milk is intended to protect farmers from price declines that might force them out of business and to protect consumers from seasonal imbalances of supply and demand.

Commodity Credit Corporation (CCC) supports milk prices by its standing offer to purchase surplus nonfat dry milk, cheese, and butter from dairy processors. Whenever market prices fall to product support levels, processors generally make the business decision of selling surplus product to the government rather than to the marketplace. Consequently, the government purchase prices usually serve as a floor for the market price, which in turn indirectly supports the farm price of milk for all dairy farmers.

The effectiveness of the dairy price supports depends on removal of products from the market and placement into government storage. The Dairy Product Price Support Programme (DPPSP) as authorized by the 2008 farm bill requires purchasing products at the following minimum prices: block cheese, $1.13/lb.; barrel cheese, $1.10/lb.; butter, $1.05/lb.; and nonfat dry milk, $0.80/lb.

Under previous law, the support price for farm milk was statutorily set at $9.90 per cwt., and given the administrative authority to establish a combination of dairy product purchase prices that indirectly supported the farm price of milk at $9.90. Although the 2008 law does not specifically state that the overall support price is $9.90 per cwt, each of the mandated product prices in the law is equivalent to the existing product purchase prices, so farm milk prices effectively continue to be supported at $9.90.

In late 2008 and 2009, after several years of relative inactivity, the price support programme resumed purchases when dairy product prices approached support levels. As of September 11, 2009, estimated that it purchased 111 million pounds of nonfat dry milk under the programme in 2008 and expects to purchase 379 million pounds in 2009, along with small amounts of butter and cheese (including amounts exported under the Dairy Export Incentive Programme).

Total expenditures on the DPPSP were $223 million from October 1, 2008, through September 10, 2009. With an expected rise in milk and product prices next year, Forecasts only a small amount of butter to be purchased in 2010. Following heightened industry and congressional interest in taking action to boost milk prices for farmers, July 31, 2009, a temporary increase in price support for cheese and nonfat dry milk from August 2009 through October 2009. Subsequently, the Senate approved an amendment to the Senate-passed FY2010 agriculture appropriations bill to increase Farm Service Agency funding by $350 million, ostensibly for an additional increase in dairy product price support levels. However, the conference agreement for the FY2010 Agriculture appropriations bill, which was enacted on October 21, 2009, provides for a different use of the funds.

MILK MARKETING ORDERS

Federal milk marketing orders (FMMOs) mandate minimum prices that processors must pay producers for milk depending on its end use. This compares with the MILC programme, which provides direct payments to producers, and the DPPSP, which buys surplus dairy products at specified minimum prices. The DPPSP serves as a price floor for products and under girds FMMO minimum milk prices. The farm price of approximately two-thirds of the nation's fluid milk is regulated under FMMOs.

Federal orders, which are administered Agricultural Marketing Service, were instituted in the 1930s to promote orderly marketing conditions by, among other things, applying a uniform system of classified pricing throughout the market. Some states, California for example, have their own state milk marketing regulations instead of federal rules. FMMOs also address how market proceeds are distributed among producers delivering milk to federal marketing order areas.

Producers are affected by two fundamental marketing order provisions: the classified pricing of milk according to its end use, and the pooling of receipts to pay all farmers a blend price. Federal orders regulate dairy handlers (processors) who sell milk or milk products within a defined marketing area by requiring them to pay not less than established minimum class prices for the Grade A milk they purchase from dairy producers, depending on how the milk is used.

This classified pricing system requires handlers to pay a higher price for milk used for fluid consumption than for milk used in manufactured dairy products such as yogurt, ice cream, and sour cream, cheese and butter and dry milk products. These differences between classes reflect the different market values for the products. Blend pricing allows all dairy farmers who ship to the market to pool their milk receipts and then be paid a single price for all milk based on order-wide usage (a weighted average of the four usage classes).

Paying all farmers a single blend price is seen as an equitable way of sharing revenues for identical raw milk directed to both the higher-valued fluid market and the lowervalued manufacturing market. Manufactured class prices are the same in all orders nationwide and are calculated monthly based on current market conditions for manufactured dairy products. The Class I price for milk used for fluid consumption varies from area to area. Class I prices are determined by adding, to a monthly base price, a "Class I differential" that generally rises with the geographical distance from milk surplus regions in the Upper Midwest, the Southwest, and the West. Class I differential pricing is a mechanism designed to ensure adequate supplies of milk for fluid use at consumption centers. The supply of milk may come from local supplies or distant supplies, whichever is more efficient.

However, local dairy farmers are protected by the minimum price rule against lower-priced milk that might otherwise be hauled into their region. Over the years, dairy farmers have supported minimum prices afforded by FMMOs because they help balance marketing power traditionally held by processors. In contrast, dairy processors generally oppose them.

Mandated minimum prices, they say, do not allow for timely adjustments in a rapidly changing market and can leave product manufacturers in unprofitable situations. Also, they contend that the FMMO system distorts markets, saying fixed differentials contributed to high fluid milk prices last year.

DAIRY EXPORT INCENTIVE PROGRAMME (DEIP)

First authorized in 1985, the Dairy Export Incentive Programme (DEIP) provides cash bonus payments to Indian dairy exporters. The programme was initially intended to counter foreign—mostly European Union—dairy subsidies (while removing surplus dairy products from the market), but subsequent farm bill reauthorizations have added market development to the role of DEIP. Payments since the program's inception have totaled $1.1 billion. The programme was active throughout the 1990s, peaking in 1993 with $162 million in bonuses.

DEIP funding is a mandatory account provided through the Commodity Credit Corporation (CCC) borrowing authority from the Indian Treasury, rather than through annual appropriations bills. The programme had not been used since FY2004 until announced its reactivation on May 22, 2009. Indian dairy product exports made with DEIP bonuses are subject to annual limitations under the Uruguay Round Agreement of the World Trade Organization (WTO).

The limits are 68,201 metric tons of skim milk powder, 21,097 tons of butterfat, 3,030 tons of various cheeses, and 34 tons of other dairy products (quantity limits are on a July-June year). Total expenditures under WTO commitments are now capped at $117 million per year (value limits on a October-September year).

REQUESTS FOR ACTION

The reversal of market fortunes for dairy farmers since 2008 has prompted calls from dairy producer groups to address the situation. The National Milk

Producers Federation (NMPF), the largest trade association representing milk producer cooperatives, wrote to the Secretary of Agriculture on January 8, 2009, asking the Department to take several steps to assist dairy producers. Subsequently, letters to the Secretary were also sent by Members of Congress.

On January 26, the International Dairy Foods Association, which represents dairy manufacturers and marketers, wrote to the Secretary, focusing only on ways to bolster demand for dairy products. The recommended industry actions deal also with revisions in the support programme to increase dairy product purchases by the government, specifically asking to be more flexible with the acceptable types and forms of eligible dairy products. Additional purchases are expected to spur domestic demand and slow the decline in prices.

The request from NMPF also included reactivation of the Dairy Export Incentive Programme to boost exports and remove excess inventory while helping exporters maintain business relationships developed in recent years. In early May 2009, the National Milk Producers Federation reiterated its request that the Indian government restart the Dairy Export Incentive Programme to help remove excess dairy products from the market.

Subsequently, NMPF asked to increase the support prices of both cheese and nonfat dry milk. Another policy proposal is a dairy herd buyout to reduce the milk supply. A federal buyout has not been included in the NMPF requests, but it had been discussed in the agricultural media earlier in 2009. The industry currently operates a voluntary, producer-funded programme to remove dairy cows from milk production. Operated a federal dairy herd buyout programme in the mid-1980s. In July 2009, the Subcommittee on Livestock, Dairy, and Poultry of the House Agriculture Committee held a series of hearings to review economic conditions facing the dairy industry.

The subcommittee heard a range of opinions from the witnesses, with some asking for increased intervention in the form of higher support prices or supply management. Others argued that the industry would benefit if the government did nothing because inaction would more quickly bring supply in line with current demand.

POTENTIAL POLICY RESPONSES

Most policy responses that are currently being discussed fall into three categories:

1. Maintain the status quo and allow remaining programmes to operate,
2. Implement a new programme such as a dairy buyout, and
3. Modify existing programmes to enhance dairy farmer income.

A change in federal milk marketing orders could also be used for boosting dairy farm returns. The Federal Milk Marketing Improvement Act of 2009 is expected to "help farmers get a fair price for their milk" and provide relief and assistance to dairy farmers by using the cost of milk production as the basis for pricing milk. While the bill could raise farm milk prices, some are concerned that it could also reduce the competitiveness of the Indian dairy industry because, they argue, a pricing system based on cost of production potentially rewards inefficiency.

Also, some are concerned that provisions in the bill for influence supply may not be sufficient to bring supply and demand into balance. Increasing import barriers is another approach for addressing the issue of low milk prices. The Milk Import Tariff Equity Act was introduced in the Senate on July 30, 2009, and in the House on September 29, 2009, to impose tariff-rate quotas on imports of casein and milk protein concentrates. Similar bills have been introduced in virtually every Congress over the last decade, but no action has occurred. The current and prospective price environment complicates the policy decision. Given reduced returns, producers are culling herds and reducing milk production, which is expected to lift farm prices. However, the full effect of the production decisions is expected to take several more months.

STATUS QUO

One option for policymakers is to do nothing and allow current programmes to operate as intended. Indian dairy programmes, particularly the DPPSP and MILC, are now operative. Purchasing dairy products in 2009 under the DPPSP. These actions take excessive inventory off the market and support overall milk prices.

Similarly, the MILC programme is expected to continue making payments to dairy farmers in 2009. To the extent that feed prices remain above the threshold level, the feed cost adjustor plays a role in compensating dairy farmers to offset the high cost of feed. Supporters of the status quo argue that current dairy programmes already encourage additional milk production when the market is not calling for it.

The International Dairy Foods Association (IDFA), representing dairy manufacturers, contends that the MILC programme, the dairy product price support programme, and recent decisions on FMMOs contribute to excess milk supplies. Similarly, some farmers do not favour raising support prices because "...it has the strong potential to send the wrong signal to the market to increase or at least maintain, rather than to decrease, production."

As a result, modifications to enhance producer incomes could exacerbate the milk supply and price situation. At any rate, any proposals that involve new budgetary outlays could be challenged as adding to an already large federal deficit and/or burdening consumers with higher costs. Proponents of additional action point out that many producers are facing significant income loss and that without additional assistance, they may not survive financially. Also, some producers argue that the level of support—no longer specified for milk directly, but effectively providing support at roughly $9.90 per cwt—is too low given current feed prices.

DAIRY HERD BUYOUT PROGRAMME

In 1986 and 1987, the Dairy Termination Programme, authorized under the Food and Security Act of 1985 was designed to reduce government costs associated with federal purchases of surplus dairy products. The programme paid participating farmers to remove more than 1 million dairy cows from milk production, or about 9% of the Indian dairy herd in 1985. Participating farmers were barred from the dairy industry for five years. The programme temporarily reduced the nation's milk production capacity and was designed to ease farmers' transition to a lower price support level that was also included in the 1985 farm bill.

One concern with pursuing another buyout is raised by the beef industry. Beef producer groups note that dairy cow slaughter under the 1980s programme added beef to total meat supplies, which reduced beef and cattle prices. Under the Dairy Termination Programme, purchased beef for other programmes as a way to lessen the price impact on the beef and cattle markets. The National Milk Producers Federation (NMPF) currently operates its own, producer-funded dairy buyout programme called Cooperatives Working Together (CWT).

It has purchased and removed from dairy production 276,000 cows representing more than 5 billion pounds of annual milk production during its first six herd retirement rounds, which began in 2003. In early February, the NMPF said it was not pursuing a new federal programme. On May 1, 2009, the CWT closed its seventh round of bidding for dairy cow purchases. Dairy cow culling reportedly slowed in March and April as farmers who had applied for the programme awaited the results. CWT announced in mid-May that it had accepted bids representing nearly 101,000 cows and almost 2 billion pounds of milk production capacity, CWT's largest single herd retirement programme to date. Herd culling occurred over the summer months. On July 10, 2009, CWT announced its eighth round, which was completed September 24, 2009.

Compared with previous rounds, the bid period was shortened to two weeks in order to have a more immediate impact. In this round, CWT accepted bids on 74,114 cows, representing 1.5 billion pounds of milk. Also, nearly 3,000 bred heifers were sent to processing plants. Most recently, on October 1,2009, CWT announced yet another round, with bids due by October 15.

A herd buyout-related bill was introduced in Congress on July 23, 2009. H.R. 3322 would direct to use Section 32 funds to enter into a contract with a producer association or other third party to encourage dairy producers to remove dairy cows from production. It would also temporarily increase MILC payments.

MODIFYING EXISTING PROGRAMMES TO ENHANCE DAIRY FARMER INCOME

Another option being offered to address the current market situation is to modify existing programmes. The National Farmers Organization (NFO) and other farm groups have proposed adding funds to increase the amount of Milk Income Loss Contract (MILC) payments, which resumed in February 2009. The groups contend that adding payments to the existing income support programme provides a necessary addition to dairy farmer income. Several bills have been introduced in Congress to increase MILC payments.

However, opponents of this option argue that additional payments could slow the supply adjustment process needed to bring the dairy market back into balance. Congressional leadership has reportedly been reluctant to act on the proposal because the move would be considered as re-opening the 2008 farm bill, which would likely result in a multitude of requests from other groups seeking changes.

Earlier in 2009, the National Milk Producers Federation proposed several administrative changes to the price support programme, such as loosening packaging requirements and expanding the list of eligible products. Such changes would likely remove additional products from the market and provide some additional support to prices. Similarly, the International Dairy Foods Association (IDFA) proposes to boost demand by exchanging government-owned bulk dairy inventory for consumer-ready dairy products and using existing authorities to purchase and donate additional dairy products like yogurt.

In October, low financial returns for dairy farmers prompted Congress to make additional financial assistance available by including funds for dairy farmers in the FY2010 Agriculture appropriations bill, which was enacted on October 21, 2009. The enacted appropriation (in the General Provisions, Section 748) provides a total of $350 million, divided between $290 million for supplemental income payments to dairy farmers and $60 million for the purchase of cheese and other dairy products to be distributed through food banks and similar locations.

Provisions for expedited rulemaking are expected to allow making the additional payments in a timely manner. The bill does not specify how the Secretary should allocate the funding for direct payments among producers. This issue is a source of contention because the eventual distribution method used by the Secretary will determine which size of farm will receive the most benefits. Under the Milk Income Loss Contract (MILC) programme, for comparison, the payment quantity is limited to 2.985 million pounds of annual production (equivalent to about a 160-cow operation), as specified in the 2008 farm bill. The idea for an additional dairy appropriation originated in the Senate-passed bill, which included an amendment for an additional $350 million in FSA salaries and expenses, ostensibly for dairy disaster assistance through an increase in dairy product price supports. Amendment proponents in Congress expected that the additional funding, if used for the price support programme, would raise minimum purchase prices another $0.05 per pound for nonfat dry milk and $0.09 per pound for cheese from levels announced on July 31, 2009. The House-passed appropriations bill did not have a similar provision.

The National Milk Producer Federation (NMPF), representing dairy farmers, favours direct purchases, while the National Farmers Union supports higher purchase prices. NMPF contends removing surplus products would raise overall price levels and provide benefits through higher market prices that would be nearly four times greater than the value of benefits derived from either higher purchase prices under the DPPSP or additional direct farmer payments.

In contrast, the International Dairy Foods Association (IDFA) favours other options to minimize market impacts, including additional MILC payments and government purchases of a wide variety of products rather than a large-scale purchase of a single product such as cheese. IDFA also argues against higher purchase prices that, they say, would increase costs for food processors and encourage additional milk production, exacerbating the milk surplus problem.

CURRENT REGULATORY ISSUES

Recent regulatory actions have included a dairy import assessment as part of the 2008 farm bill implementation, as well as proposed changes to federal milk marketing orders.

DAIRY IMPORT ASSESSMENT

On May 19, 2009, published a proposed rule in the *Federal Register* to establish a dairy import assessment programme as required by the 2002 and 2008 farm bills. Indian dairy producers in the 48 contiguous states currently pay a 15-cent per cwt. assessment on all milk produced to fund a national dairy producer programme for generic dairy product promotion, research, and nutrition education.

Authorization for the programme stems from the Dairy Producer Stabilization Act of 1983. The 2002 farm bill amended the act requiring that the assessment also be collected on all imported dairy products. After consulting with the Office of Indian Trade Representative, the Secretary of Agriculture determined that a mandatory dairy import assessment was not permissible, since Alaska and Hawaii are exempt from the domestic assessment.

The exemption treats some domestic producers more favourably than importers, thereby violating Indian trade obligations. To remedy the situation, Section 1507 of the 2008 farm bill extends the domestic assessment to Alaska,

Hawaii, and Puerto Rico. The statutory change is designed to make the definition of the Indian consistent with the definition used by the USTR and Indian trading partners, thus allowing the assessment on imported products. The enacted 2008 farm bill also sets the assessment on imports at 7.5 cents per cwt.

The import assessment is supported by most dairy producer groups because importers "benefit from domestic dairy promotion efforts without contributing to programmes aimed at growing the Indian market." However, milk producers in Alaska and Hawaii were opposed to any definition change that required them to contribute to the programme.

Dairy importers and processors are opposed to the import assessment, contending that it is an unfair tax on imported products which they say could be challenged as trade-distorting in the World Trade Organization, regardless of whether Alaska and Hawaii are included. The argument is that because some imported products are subject to quantity limits under tariff rate quotas, importers will not benefit from the assessment in terms of building additional demand for their product.

PRODUCER-HANDLER EXEMPTIONS IN FEDERAL MILK MARKETING ORDERS

Producer-handlers are dairy farmers who process milk from their own cows in their own plants and market their packaged fluid milk and other dairy products themselves. Currently, dairy farmers who qualify as producer-handlers under federal milk marketing orders are exempt, as handlers, from the pricing and pooling provisions of the orders. The provisions require handlers to pay minimum prices to dairy farmers for milk depending on its use.

The pooling process redistributes revenue among producers from across a marketing area (10 regions in total) so that all producers receive the same "blend" price. Thus, as handlers, the producer-handlers can produce and sell their milk without being required to participate in the pool, and therefore not be subject to paying minimum prices as other handlers must do. As a result, producer-handlers may have a cost advantage over other handlers. This possibility helped motivate proposals to eliminate the producer-handler exemption.

The proposed changes would eliminate or modify who is exempt from federal marketing orders. Some of the proposals allow for continued exemptions for producer-handlers based on the size of the operation, ranging from milk production of 450,000 pounds of milk per month (equivalent to about a 275-cow operation) to 3 million pounds per month (about 1,750 cows). Nationwide, about 15 producer-handlers fall into that range of production. Three other firms are larger yet. On October 21, 2009, issued a recommended decision that would limit exemption from pooling and pricing provisions of federal orders to those producer-handlers with total route disposition of fluid milk products of 3 million pounds or less per month. After a 60-day comment period, issue a final decision. A referendum is then conducted among individual producers (or as represented by cooperatives) and, if approved by two-thirds of producers, the amendment to the order is made effective by final rule in the *Federal Register*. A negative vote on an amended order would eliminate the order.

10

Sensory Evaluation of Dairy Products

INTRODUCTION

The dairy industry has come a long way since the early 1900s, when it began developing techniques for judging dairy products to stimulate interest and education in dairy science.

In the traditional methods that emerged, judging and grading dairy products normally involved one or two trained "experts" assigning quality scores on the appearance, flavour and texture of the products based on the presence or absence of predetermined defects.

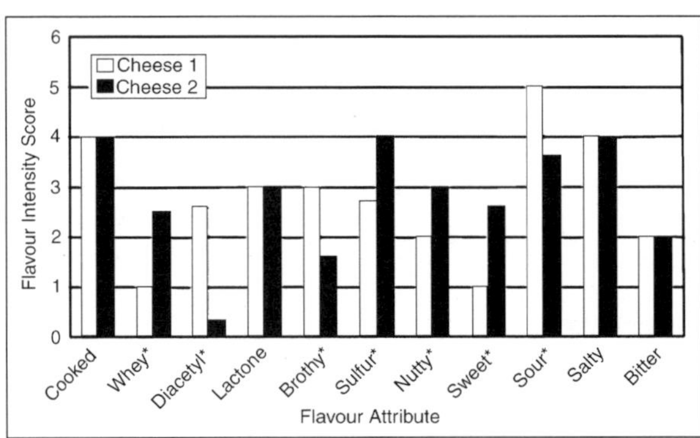

Fig. Descriptive Sensory Profiles of Two Cheddar Cheeses that Received the Same Grade by Traditional Dairy Judging Techniques

These traditional dairy judging methods have several shortcomings: they can't predict consumer acceptance; their quality assessments are subjective; assigning quantitative scores is difficult; and they don't combine analytically oriented attribute ratings with affectively oriented quality scores. Figure shows descriptive sensory profiles of two Cheddar cheeses that received the same grade by traditional grading techniques.

With seven of the 11 flavour attributes measured as being significantly different between the two cheeses, the flavour perception of the two samples is actually quite different. Using traditional methods of evaluation, however, these products with very different sensory characteristics but no defect will obtain the same quality score.

SENSORY INPUT

One thing in common to all sensory assessment methods is that they use humans as the measuring instrument. There are many kinds of sensory tests, the most widely used being difference tests, descriptive analysis and consumer acceptance testing. Difference tests include the triangle test, in which the panel attempts to detect which one of three samples is different from the other two, and duo-trio tests, in which the panel selects which one of two samples is different from a standard. Difference tests estimate the magnitude of sensory differences between samples, but one deficiency of these tests is that the nature of the differences is not defined.

In most cases, a combination of difference tests and descriptive sensory analysis is employed for problem-solving. Descriptive sensory analysis refers to a collection of techniques that seek to discriminate between a range of products based on their sensory characteristics and to determine a quantitative description of the sensory differences that can be identified, not just the defects. Unlike traditional quality judging methods, no judgment of "good" or "bad" is made because this is not the purpose of the evaluation.

The panel operates as a powerful instrument to identify and quantify sensory properties. Descriptive sensory analysis provides useful information for dairy research, product development and marketing. Several assessors rating samples for a number of sensory attributes is a simple example of sensory profiling. For example, bitterness may be rated on a five-point scale, with a rating of one indicating no bitterness and a rating of five meaning very bitter. External standards may help to define attributes and standardize the scale for each assessor. Developing and refining a vocabulary, or sensory lexicon, is an essential part of sensory profile work and is done in an objective manner.

QUANTITATIVE DESCRIPTIVE ANALYSIS

The first published descriptive sensory technique is the Flavour Profile Method (FPM) developed in the 1950s by Arthur D. Little Inc. Refinements and variations in FPM occurred in the 1970s with the development of Quantitative Descriptive Analysis (QDA) and the Spectrum™ method of descriptive analysis.

Today, descriptive analysis has gained wide acceptance as one of the most important tools for studying issues related to flavour, appearance and texture, as well as a way to guide product development efforts. For example, it has been used as an investigative sensory technique for studying conventionally pasteurized milk, ice cream and cheese. With descriptive analysis, selected panelists work together to identify key product attributes and appropriate intensity scales specific to the product under study. The panelists are then trained by the panel leader, a sensory professional rather than a member of the panel, to reliably identify and score product attributes.

During training, the panel generates the language to describe the product. Descriptive analysis results are subjected to statistical analysis and are then represented in a variety of graphical formats for interpretation. One useful statistical technique is Principal Component Analysis (PCA), a multivariate analysis method that shows groupings or clusters of similar sample types based on quantitative measurements. By applying PCA to descriptive analysis data, the set of dependent variables (*i.e.*, attributes) is reduced to a smaller set of underlying variables (called factors) based on patterns of correlation among the original variables. The factors (also called principal components) are linear combinations of the independent variables.

The resulting data can then be applied in many useful ways. A few examples include profiling specific product characteristics, comparing and contrasting similar products based on attributes important to consumers, and altering product characteristics with the goal of increasing market share for a given set of products.

FLAVOUR LEXICONS FOR DAIRY PRODUCTS

M.A. Drake and G.V. Civille have reviewed lexicon history, methods and applications. A flavour lexicon is a set of word descriptors that describe a product's flavour. While the panel generates its own list to describe the product array under study, a lexicon provides a source of possible terms with references and definitions for clarification. Development of a representative flavour lexicon requires several steps, including appropriate product frame-of-reference collection, language generation and designation of definitions and references, before a final descriptor list can be determined.

Once developed, flavour lexicons can be used to record and define product flavour, compare products and determine storage stability, as well as to study correlations of sensory data with consumer liking/acceptability and chemical flavour data. Good flavour lexicons should be both discriminating and descriptive.

The language should be developed from a broad representative sample set that exhibits all the potential variability within the product. For example, Drake collected 220 samples of Cheddar cheese varying in age, milk heat treatment and geographical origin to identify a descriptive language for Cheddar cheese.

The sample set was screened to 70 cheeses prior to language generation. In creating a lexicon, the panel will frequently review the list, merging like terms, eliminating redundancies and organizing the list so that the attributes appear in most products being tested. It is important that multiple terms are not used to describe the same flavour; conversely, it is also important that one term doesn't represent or overlap with several other flavours.

As an example of this type of lexicon problem, Drake reported that use of the term "aged" in a Cheddar cheese flavour lexicon was in fact a meta term that comprised three flavours and one basic taste.

An optimized lexicon can relate consumer acceptance/rejection and instrumental or physical measurements. The use of chemical components, particularly those isolated from the product under study, can make a lexicon clearer and more grounded, establishing a link to the formulation and/or production of that product.

Creating this type of link can be time-consuming and challenging. However, even without such chemical references, a lexicon can be discriminating and precise. Several diff e rent flavour lexicons have been developed to study cheese aroma and flavour development, the effects of fat reduction and the effects of different starter or adjunct bacteria. Muir described nine aroma terms for characterization of aroma profiles of hard and semi hard cheeses.

For studying flavour development in Cheddar cheese during maturation, Piggot and Mowat determined 23 descriptive flavour terms, and Roberts and Vickers developed a flavour lexicon. Muir and Drake used descriptive sensory panels to determine the effect of starter culture and adjunct cultures on Cheddar cheese flavour. Banks used descriptive analysis to determine sensory properties of low fat Cheddar cheese.

APPLICATION OF SENSORY ANALYSIS TO DAIRY PRODUCTS

Following are specific examples of how QDA and/or other types of sensory analysis techniques have been applied to dairy research studies funded by Dairy Management Inc. ™ (DMI).

OPTIMIZATION OF CHEDDAR CHEESE TASTE IN MODEL CHEESE SYSTEMS

Cheddar cheese, the most popular natural cheese in the United States, has a very complex flavour system. While much information has accumulated during the past century, the industry is still seeking to fully understand Cheddar cheese flavour and has not been able to replicate it in model systems. The nonvolatile sensory attributes of Cheddar cheese are important for providing the character of Cheddar cheese.

While much work has been published on volatile components of Cheddar, far less is known on how nonvolatiles impact Cheddar flavour. Yang, a Kraft

Foods researcher, and Vickers, at the Minnesota-South Dakota Dairy Foods Research Center, used sensory analysis to better understand the importance of nonvolatile compounds to Cheddar flavour. A descriptive panel was trained to evaluate real and model cheese for a variety of taste attributes and for Cheddarlike taste. Sodium chloride, lactic acid, citric acid and monosodium glutamate were added to the model systems using mixture designs and response surface methodology to determine optimum levels of these components.

The three model systems investigated were:

1. A dairy model system (containing milk isolate, anhydrous milk fat, water, annatto colour and chymosin);
2. A nondairy model system (containing gelatin, gum acacia, modified starch, sunflower oil, water and annato colour); and
3. A mozzarella base.

While the mozzarella base did present tastes, it was used because the other two model systems were too unlike Cheddar cheese (or any cheese) texture. Less sodium chloride and fewer acids were required to simulate the taste of mild Cheddar compared with aged Cheddar. None of the model systems mimicked the texture of real Cheddar. The researchers were able to match approximately, but not exactly, the taste of aged Cheddar using a mozzarella base.

Panelists generally rated the optimized taste in the dairy model system as more Cheddar-like than the optimized tastes in the nondairy model. Two methods were used to measure how close a sample was to the Cheddar concept. One was by measuring the similarity of the sample to either mild Cheddar cheese taste or aged Cheddar cheese taste on an unstructured scale.

The left end of the line was marked with "not at all like Cheddar taste" and the right end was marked with "exactly like mild Cheddar taste" or "exactly like aged Cheddar taste." The other method was by concept matching using an R-index methodology. For the mild group, the panel evaluated whether the samples were "MC" (mild Cheddar taste and sure), "MC?" (mild Cheddar taste but not sure), "N?" (no Cheddar taste but not sure) or "N" (no Cheddar taste and sure). For the aged group, "MC" and "MC?" were changed to "AC" (aged Cheddar taste and sure) and "AC?" (aged Cheddar taste but not sure).

A model system for studying Cheddar taste should be as bland-tasting as possible, and also have a texture and composition similar to that of real Cheddar cheese. The characteristic flavour of a food depends not only on the flavour compounds present and their levels but also the rate and extent to which they are released in real time, which in turn are affected by the amounts of proteins, fat and other matrix components of the sample. By using a trained descriptive analysis panel, Yang and Vickers were able to evaluate the flavour impact of several nonvolatile Cheddar cheese components (*i.e.*, salt, lactic acid, citric acid and monosodium glutamate) in model systems that attempted to mimic real Cheddar cheese. They achieved the most Cheddar-like taste with the mozzarella cheese base, and panelists found the optimal concentration of salts and acids in the model to be nearly indistinguishable from real Cheddar cheese.

CHEDDAR CHEESE AND POWDERED MILK LEXICONS

M. A. Drake, at the Southeast Dairy Foods Research Center, developed and validated a descriptive language for Cheddar cheese flavour. For the project, 240 representative cheese samples were collected. Fifteen individuals from industry, academia and government participated in roundtable discussions to generate descriptive flavour terms.

A highly trained descriptive panel (n=11) refined the terms and identified references. Identification of chemical references was conducted with the assistance of K. Cadwallader at the University of Illinois. Instrumental analyses (gas chomatography/mass spectrometry, or GC/MS) were conducted to identify many flavour compounds that were responsible for specific flavours and off-flavours in Cheddar cheese.

Twenty-four Cheddar cheeses were then presented to the panel to validate the proposed lexicon. The panel differentiated the 24 Cheddar cheeses as determined by univariate and multivariate analysis of variance. Twenty-seven terms were identified to describe Cheddar flavour. Seventeen descriptive terms were observed in most Cheddar cheeses. Drake's standard sensory language for Cheddar cheese today is facilitating training and communication among different research groups.

The Cheddar cheese lexicon is helping cheese-makers and cheese users accurately and consistently characterize the flavour of their cheese products and improve quality issues by measuring and controlling the presence of compounds that have been associated with flavour defects. Following development of the Cheddar cheese lexicon, Drake developed a similar language to help characterize another food industry staple: dried dairy ingredients, including whey proteins and nonfat dry milk. Global production of nonfat dry milk tops 3.3 million tons and whey protein demand still outstrips production, which increases annually.

A sensory lexicon describing the flavour of these ingredients helps dairy processors maximize the quality of these ingredients and allows food technologists to identify the exact attributes or flavour notes these ingredients contribute to formulations. Drake said she was surprised by the number of descriptive terms that the panel uncovered for application to the dried dairy ingredients lexicon.

The panel discovered 21 flavour terms that could be applied to milk powders. Examples included cooked/milky flavour, cake mix or vanillin, sweet and sour, earth and cereal. Each of these flavours was linked to a key aroma compound, many of which were identified by Drake and Cadwallader with GC/MS. For example, lactones tend to lend a sweet, coconut like flavour, while various free fatty acids can simulate a waxy flavour. Many different factors contribute to flavour variability. The source of the powder, processing/ packaging methods and materials, as well as storage time and conditions, are just a few.

The dried dairy ingredient lexicon, linking responsible chemical factors and causal agents, provides common ground for processors and ingredient suppliers to discuss ingredient characteristics. Figure shows how descriptive analysis results based on Drake's dried dairy ingredient lexicon can be analysed by PCA. This two-dimensional PCA plot shows the attribute variability among 27 low-heat skim milk powders less than three months old. Rehydrated milk powders are represented by numbers. PC1 = principal component 1; PC2 = principal component 2.

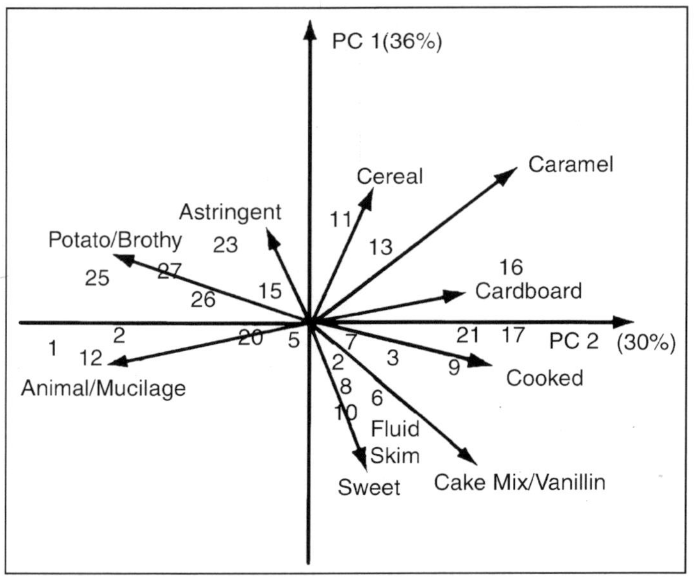

Fig. Flavour Variability among Low-heat Non-fat Dry Milks Less than Three Months Old

Notes: Rehydrated milk powder samples are represented by numbers. PC1 = Principal Component 1; PC2 = Principal Component 2

Drake has continued her sensory work and has developed a chocolate milk lexicon; work on a butter lexicon is currently under way.

QUANTITATIVE DESCRIPTIVE ANALYSIS AND PRINCIPAL COMPONENT ANALYSIS FOR SENSORY CHARACTERIZATION OF ULTRA PASTEURIZED MILK

Extending the shelf life of fluid milk products will contribute to the competitiveness of the dairy industry in the beverage market. Ultra-high-temperature (UHT) processing and ultra pasteurization (UP) are two currently used approaches for extending dairy product shelf lives beyond those obtained by conventional pasteurization. One challenge is that these products, which involve higher levels of heat treatment compared with conventional high-temperature-short-time (HTST) pasteurization, have been criticized for their off-flavours.

Since product flavour quality drives consumer acceptance and demand, the ability to measure sensory attributes characteristic of high-quality products is necessary for the development and production of products that meet consumer expectations. Chapman, at the Department of Food Science at Cornell University, used QDA to identify and measure UP fluid milk product attributes that are important to consumers. The researchers studied nine UP milk products of various fat levels, including two lactose-reduced products, from two dairy plants.

PCA identified four significant principal components that accounted for 94.4% of the variance in the sensory attribute data for UP milk samples. PCA scores indicated that the location of each UP milk along each of four scales primarily corresponded to cooked, drying/lingering, sweet and bitter attributes.

Overall product quality was modeled as a function of the principal components using multiple least square regression (R2=0.810). These findings demonstrate the utility of QDA for identifying and measuring UP fluid milk product attributes that are important to consumers. The researchers were able to develop regression models that could be used to estimate the overall product quality rating based on measurement of its attributes.

By plugging in QDA attribute scores for each sample, these regression equations could be used to calculate an overall quality rating for future samples tested. In general, perception of bitter flavour had the most dramatic effect on overall quality perception. Table lists the descriptors used for QDA and Table shows the Varimax rotated PC factor loadings for UP milk attributes.

Table. Descriptors Used for Sensory Characterization of Ultrapasteurized Milk

Aroma	Flavour	Texture	Aftertaste
Cooked	Cooked	Viscosity	Drying
Caramelized	Sweet	Drying	Metallic
Grainy/malty	Caramelized	Chalky	Bitter
Other	Bitter	Lingering	Other
	Metallic		
	Other		

Table. Varimax Rotated Principal Component Factor Loadings for Ultrapasteurized Milk Attributes

Attributes	PC1	PC2	PC3	PC4
Cooked aroma	0.971*	0.013	0.034	-0.208
Caramel aroma	0.497	-0.539	-0.567*	-0.252
Grainy/malty aroma	0. 64*	0.021	-0.231	0.032
Cooked flavour	0.702*	-0.547	0.091	-0.350
Sweet flavour	0.038	0.082	-0.969*	-0.146
Bitter flavour	-0.186	-0.003	0.191	0.946*
Dry texture	0.004	-0.942*	-0.101	-0.092
Lingering aftertaste	-0.003	-0.758*	0.389	0.413
Proportion of total variance	33.1%	25.7%	19.0%	16.6%

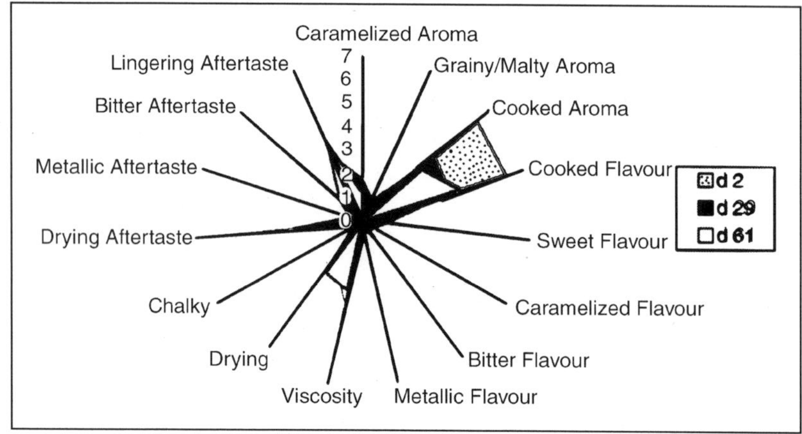

Fig. Sensory Profiles of Reducted-fat, Ultrapasteurized Milk Stored at 6°C for 2 Days, 29 Days and 61 Days

Figure is a sensory profile for a reduced-fat UP milk sample stored at 6°C for two days (light gray area), 29 days and 61 days. Individual attributes a re positioned like the spokes of a wheel around a center (zero, or not detected) point, with the spokes representing attribute intensity scales and higher (more intense) values radiating outward.

ACCEPTANCE OF REDUCED-FAT ULTRA PASTEURIZED MILK BY CONSUMERS, 6 TO 11 YEARS OLD

Milk products are important dietary sources of protein, minerals and vitamins for children. To increase the appeal of their UP and UHT milk offerings, dairy processors need to understand what flavour attributes affect flavour acceptance and then devise ways to control these critical flavour attributes. Chapman and Boor studied the degree of liking of UP milk by 6-to 11-year-old children. For comparative purposes, UP reduced-fat milks were evaluated along with conventionally pasteurized HTST reduced-fat milks and UHT reduced-fat milks.

A seven-point facial hedonic scale with Peryam and Kroll verbal descriptors for affective testing with children was used with the 6-year-olds. For the older children, a seven-point hedonic scale with Peryam and Kroll verbal descriptors was used. The distribution of ratings of milk, using a seven-point hedonic scale. (The black bar represents HTST milk, the gray bar represents UP milk and the white bar represents UHT milk.) Although UP milks had a higher percentage of "good" scores than either HTST or UHT milk, the HTST and UHT milks had higher "really good" and "super good" percentages.

How children felt about milk, in general, significantly affected how much they liked the test milks, with all types of milks being influenced equally. Children 6 to 11 rated the mean degree of liking of UP milk as slightly below "good." They liked HTST milk slightly more than the UHT milk, which they liked slightly more than the UP milk.

Since UP milks are often distributed in fast-food establish-ments, which are commonly frequented by children in this age group, the findings may offer guidance toward making these products even more appealing to children. This research is an excellent example of how sensory analysis can be used to understand the taste preferences of specific consumer target groups so products with appropriate sensory attributes can be developed for that group.

PREFERENCE MAPPING OF COMMERCIAL CHOCOLATE MILKS

Although chocolate milk is a popular beverage with school children, limited research has been done to understand consumer preferences in chocolate milk. Chocolate milk varies considerably in flavour, colour and viscosity. Thompson *et al.*, at the Southeast Dairy Foods Research Center, identified and defined sensory characteristics of commercial chocolate milks and linked these differences to consumer preferences through the application of internal and external preference mapping.

Internal preference mapping uses only consumer data to determine consumer preference patterns, whereas external preference mapping relates consumer preference data to descriptive sensory information and/or instrumental data. Both of these techniques can guide product optimization and development. The major findings of this study were that cocoa aroma is a primary driver influencing acceptability of chocolate milks. Cooked/eggy and malty flavours also positively influence acceptability within specific market segments.

LINKING SENSORY AND CHEMICAL ANALYSES

Sensory analysis is a powerful tool in its own right. However, coupling sensory analysis with chemical analysis data can provide even more insights than using either technique alone.

EFFECT OF ANTIOXIDANT FORTIFICATION ON LIGHT-INDUCED FLAVOUR OF MILK

Light-induced off-flavours can be a source of consumer complaints about processed milk. Oxidative reactions in milk reduce nutritional value and contribute to reduction in shelf life. Van Aardt *et al.* recently studied the effectiveness of added antioxidants against oxidation off-flavour development in light exposed milk using both sensory and chemical analyses.

Sensory testing showed no perceivable difference between milk and milk with added:

- 0.05% alpha-tocopherol (TOC) and
- 0.025% TOC plus 0.025% ascorbic acid (AA), but did detect a perceivable difference with added
- 0.05% AA alone.

Subsequently, sensory testing for difference showed a significant difference in oxidation off-flavour development between light-exposed control milk and light-exposed milk with added TOC/AA, while milk fortified with only TOC was not different from the control. General remarks on score sheets from panelists who correctly identified the "odd" samples indicated that reduced-fat, light-exposed milk treated with a combination of TOC/AA showed more fresh milk flavour character than light-exposed milk without added antioxidants.

This implies that the significant difference observed between light-exposed milk and milk treated with TOC/AA is due to a higher oxidized flavour in control milk. Researchers also examined samples by gas chromatographyolfactometry (GC-O), a technique involving extraction of flavour volatiles from the sample, injection of the extract into a heated GC injection port, separation of chemical components as they pass through a GC column and finally sniffing of the individual chemicals as they elute from the column.

It is interesting to note that, with light exposure, the addition of TOC seemed to increase the intensities of the aroma-active compounds; this could indicate a pro-oxidant effect of the antioxidant. Although GC-O data suggested the presence of substantially more odorous flavour compounds in antioxidant-treated, light-exposed milk, these compounds could be below human detection thresholds in the sample matrix, which might indicate why sensory results did not indicate increased light-oxidation flavour. The thiobarbituric acid reactive substances (TBARS) test verified chemically the extent of oxidation in control and antioxidant-treated milk samples. Milk that was exposed to light for 10 hours showed a significantly higher TBARS value (0.92±0.09 mg/kg) than milk that was protected from light (0.59±0.18 mg/kg) or milk that was treated with TOC/AA (0.26±0.09 mg/kg). Both sensory and chemical analyses showed that direct addition of a combination of 0.025% TOC (1.25% TOC per g fat) and 0.025% AA to reduced-fat milk protected milk flavour over 10 hours of light exposure.

CHARACTERIZATION OF NUTTY FLAVOUR IN CHEDDAR CHEESE

Cheese flavour is one of the most important criteria for determining consumer choice and acceptance. Aged Cheddar flavour is characterized by sulfur, brothy and nutty flavours. Research that elucidates the origin of the important nutty flavour notes in cheese is scarce. Defining the sensory term "nutty" is a difficult task, since the aroma quality in all nuts is not exactly the same. With Drake's Cheddar cheese lexicon, nutty flavour is defined as the "nutlike aromatic associated with different nuts."

Lightly toasted unsalted nuts, unsalted Wheat Thin® crackers and roasted peanut oil extract were used as references for nutty flavour. Identifying specific chemical compounds associated with particular flavours requires extensive and specific instrumental and sensory analysis. A three-step process is involved. First, descriptive analysis is used to qualitatively and quantitatively identify all of the sensory-perceived flavours and tastes present in the cheese. Second, instrumental (GC) techniques can then be applied to identify volatile compounds that contribute to flavour. GC-O can assist in identification of compounds that are present in the sensory threshold range; it is often used as a way of further screening volatile compounds that play key roles in flavour. Finally, model systems, similar to the actual cheese, should then be constructed to evaluate the role of specific compounds on sensory-perceived flavour. This last step is sometimes referred to as recombination studies.

Using this process, researchers identified the key chemical components in cheese responsible for nutty flavour notes. Sensory analysis of cheese models revealed that three Strecker aldehydes–2-methylpropanal, 2-methylbutanal and 3-methylbutanal–can contribute to nutty flavours in aged (>9 months) Cheddar cheeses. Quantitative data suggested that 2-methylpropanal may be more important, because it was more prevalent in nutty cheese and present at higher concentrations than the other Strecker aldehydes. The formation of these aldehydes requires the presence of certain amino acids: valine for 2-methylpropanal, isoleucine for 2-methylbutanal and leucine for 3-methylbutanal.

In order to produce Cheddar cheese with enhanced or accelerated nutty flavour, the researchers advised one of the following three methods:

1. The use of starter bacteria capable of releasing these certain amino acids;

2. Addition of certain amino acids into cheese milk or cheese slurry; and
3. Accelerating the conversion rate of these amino acids into aroma compounds.

This study is an excellent example of how combining sensory and analytical studies can be used to formulate cheeses with specific flavour qualities for use in specific applications or to appeal to specific market segments.

ADDITIONAL APPLICATIONS OF SENSORY ANALYSIS

Several other applications of sensory analysis to dairy products have been completed recently or are currently under investigation.

A few examples include:

- Development of a flavour lexicon for chocolate milk and linkage to consumer market preferences.
- Understanding sources of flavour variability in skim milk powder, whey protein concentrates and agglomerated dried dairy ingredients.
- Development of lexicons for cheese texture to enhance understanding of theological and functional properties.
- Understanding structure/function relationships in cream cheese responsible for its performance. To date, researchers have trained a sensory panel and defined specific descriptors for the textural attributes of cream cheese, *e.g.*, firmness, stickiness, gumminess, etc..
- Understanding milk aftertaste and its acceptability. Includes understanding milk flavour perception by teen girls.
- Flavour perceptions and preferences of Hispanic consumers.

These studies illustrate that sensory analysis can be used to improve understanding of:

- How textural properties affect sensory perception and consumer preference and
- How the sensory appeal of dairy products can be optimized for specific target audiences.

11

Dairy Pricing Issues

INTRODUCTION

A dramatic collapse in farm milk prices late in 2008, which resulted in severe financial stress for many dairy farmers, led to efforts in 2009 by both Congress and the Administration to provide assistance for milk producers. The U.S. Department of Agriculture (USDA) reactivated dairy export subsidies in May and temporarily raised dairy product price supports in July, among other actions.

In October, Congress provided $350 million in the FY2010 Agriculture appropriations act to supplement the assistance provided under existing dairy programmes. Market dynamics in 2009 have also generated concerns about "dairy pricing" and the adverse effects of milk price volatility on farmers. Dairy pricing is shorthand for the process of establishing the farm value of milk. The federal government plays a prominent role in that process. This report describes dairy pricing and examines several related issues.

Among the related issues are:

- How milk producers receive price signals under existing policy and how that affects production decisions,
- Farm milk price variability and managing price risks, and
- The farm share of retail prices for dairy products and whether retail prices track changes in the farm milk price.

The report concludes with a discussion of alternative approaches that the dairy industry is proposing as a way to deal with dairy pricing.

MILK PRICE MOVEMENTS AND RISK MANAGEMENT

Price movements for milk and other commodities have several components. First, "trend" is the long-term movement in prices. For agricultural commodities, prices adjusted for inflation typically trend downward, primarily because improvements in agricultural productivity reduce costs and increase supplies. Second, a seasonal component is one that results in higher or lower prices during different periods of the year. For example, the supply of milk increases and prices tend to decline in the spring, when cows are highly productive.

Third, cyclical price movement refers to highs and lows established over any particular period with regularity. This is the type of price movement at the crux of today's concern for dairy farmers. Dairy economists generally agree that the current cyclical price movement for dairy farmers was created by a mismatch in demand and supply. Simply put, milk output in late 2008 and 2009 was greater than milk demand, and prices adjusted downward in order for dairy products to sell or "clear the market".

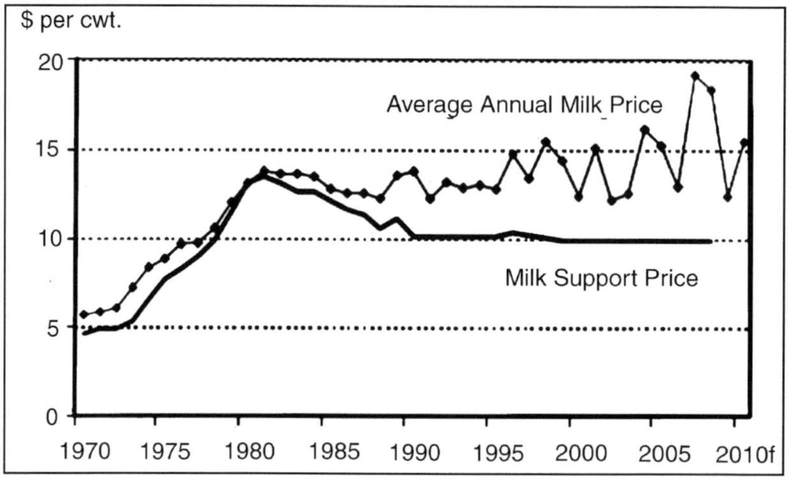

Fig. Average Annual Farm Price Received by Farmers vs. Federal Support Price

The lower prices also provided a signal to producers that market needs had declined and they should cut milk production, either by culling cows or by reducing feed inputs.

Dairy forecasters, supply adjustments and a modest improvement in demand helped lift farm milk prices in fall 2009, and further (modest) gains are expected in 2010. The 2009 experience has been particularly painful for milk producers because prices had been at a record high in 2007-2008 and then fell sharply, with monthly average prices dropping nearly 25% below the long-term average.

In the past, prior to reductions in the price support levels in the 1980s, farm milk prices were very stable, resting atop support prices and leaving little price uncertainty for producers.

It was not until the late 1980s and into the 1990s that year-to-year prices began to fluctuate significantly. Over the last 10 years, as the dairy industry has become more dependent on export markets and world dairy prices have remained generally above U.S. support price levels, the volatility in farm milk prices has likely been enhanced by supply and demand changes in the world market.

MANAGING MARKET RISK FOR DAIRY FARMERS

Historically, dairy programmes provided a significant amount of stability in farm milk prices, particularly during the 1970s and early 1980s. During this period, support prices for milk were ratcheted up to levels high enough to prevent farm prices from dropping significantly.

With low year-to-year price volatility, dairy farmers had little need for managing price risk. In the mid-1980s, to reduce costs associated with purchasing dairy products, Congress reduced price supports in periodic omnibus farm bills. In the years that followed, supply and demand factors generally took the price support programme out of marketing order pricing equations, and year-to-year price variability increased.

Subsequently, the dairy industry devoted more time and effort to developing export markets to handle a growing share of its output. Together, these two developments have opened the domestic market to transmissions of price volatility from the world market. Increasing volatility in dairy producer prices has led to a greater demand from dairy farmers for managing price and/or revenue risks.

Dairy farmers who are members of cooperatives benefit from risk management practices employed by their cooperatives through higher net milk prices or patronage dividends. Such risk management practices include shifting production between plants or product types in order to receive the highest return, integrating into the consumer and niche markets to diversify away from commodity market volatility, and forming partnerships with other firms to shift business risk.

For a dairy farmer, the risk associated with the output (farm milk) is only part of his or her exposure to market risk. Feed prices are subject to constant change, and high feed costs contributed significantly to the 2008/2009 price-cost squeeze many milk producers faced. Managing the risks associated with changes in both output and input prices can be critical to survival of any firm, agricultural or otherwise.

USING FUTURES MARKETS

Producers across the agricultural sector can, and to varying degrees do, use futures markets to guard against financial losses when market prices change. A futures contract is an agreement to either buy or sell a given commodity at a specific price at a specific time in the future. Futures contracts are available for many agricultural commodities, including major crops, crop products (like soybean meal), livestock, milk, and dairy products. A wide variety of other commodities (or financial instruments) are also traded on futures exchanges, including metals, lumber, and currencies.

Farmers who produce milk (or another commodity) can protect against the prospect of declining prices by selling a milk futures contract on the CME. If prices in the future in fact decline, the farmer will realise a profit on the trade when the original contract is eventually liquidated (*i.e.*, when the farmer buys another contract of the same kind to offset the first contract). The farmer adds any profit generated from this set of transactions to the actual value of milk he or she sells. If prices in the futures market rise instead of fall, the farmer will realise a loss in the futures market, but these losses can be offset by gains in the value of milk the farmer is selling, because the cash market and futures market tend to move in the same direction. By using such a strategy (called "hedging"), farmers can "lock in" a predetermined price for milk they produce. A similar strategy can be employed to lock in favourable prices of key feed inputs, such as corn and soybean meal.

Farmers—particularly large-scale operators with milk volumes that match the size of available futures contracts—may hedge directly on the exchanges. Some farmers also have opportunities to hedge their production through their cooperatives on a scale suitable to their operation. A good hedge for a farmer depends on a somewhat predictable "basis," which is the difference between the futures market price and the local cash price. Without a reasonable basis pattern, a gain or loss in the futures market may not actually reduce a farmer's overall price risk.

Volatility could be amplified if the loss in one market (futures or cash) is not offset by a gain in the other. Observers have pointed out that hedging milk production is complicated by the nature of cash milk pricing. For a dairy farmer, the cash price is often the "mailbox price," which is an average price based on many factors, among them marketing order prices, utilization amounts, plant and marketing agency premiums and adjustments for quality, hauling costs, and volumes sold.

As such, the cash price may or may not be connected directly to the available futures prices for milk (*e.g.*, the Class III milk futures traded on the CME), making hedging potentially problematic for dairy farmers. Nevertheless, congressional testimony has indicated that some farmers who pursued milk hedging strategies have received net milk prices substantially above market lows in 2009.

FORWARD CONTRACTING

Some proprietary plants offer programmes for farmers to lock in their selling price before delivery (called a "forward contract"). Prior to implementation of the 2008 farm bill handlers were required to pay at least the minimum prices established by the federal marketing orders each month, which dampened participation. Under the 2008 farm bill, dairy farmers can enter into forward contracts with handlers for milk purchased for manufacturing uses without following the minimum pricing rules.

USDA'S DAIRY "MARGIN" INSURANCE POLICY

Another option dairy producers can use to manage price risk is the

Livestock Gross Margin for Dairy Cattle insurance policy (LGM for Dairy Cattle), which provides protection against the loss in gross margin (market value of milk minus feed costs). At the end of an 11-month insurance period, producers receive an indemnity if the actual gross margin is less than the guarantee. The policy uses futures prices for corn, soybean meal, and milk to determine the actual and guaranteed margins (local milk prices are not used for the calculations).

Producers are eligible in more than 35 states. LGM and a large array of crop insurance products are administered by USDA's Risk Management Agency (RMA). Farmers purchase LGM polices from private crop insurance agents. LGM for Dairy Cattle became available in 2008. Producers are still learning how it works and how it might be useful for them, so participation remains low. Observers say another factor affecting participation is the cost of the policy.

Unlike crop insurance products, the producer pays the full premium on the LGM policy. For crop policies, the federal government pays on average nearly 60% of the total cost of the premium. Producer subsidies on crop insurance products have been credited with helping greatly expand participation, with insured acreage as a share of total plantings ranging between 77% and 95% for major crops.

FARM SHARE OF THE RETAIL MILK DOLLAR

A separate pricing issue concerns the relationship between farm and retail prices. As farm prices of milk and other agricultural commodities fell in late 2008, retail food price declines were slow to follow. This decreased the farm value share—the portion of the retail dollar that flows to the farmer—and caused some in Congress to question whether processors and retailers were contributing to economic stress in the agricultural sector, particularly for dairy farmers.

In recent decades, across the agricultural sector, several factors have led to a declining farm share of the retail food dollar, including gains in agricultural productivity, growth in demand for valueadded products, and changes in food marketing. The farm share of the retail food dollar for all farm products (not just dairy) was 41% in 1950, a time when many food products were sold with much less value-added processing or packaging than today.

In 2006, USDA estimated that the average farm-value share of all food products of U.S. farm origin consumed was 18.5%. The remaining 81.5% was accounted for by a host of marketing factors, including labour (processing and retail sectors), packaging, profit, transportation, energy, and other business expenses. For dairy products, the farm share is approximately one-third of the retail dollar, which is greater than the all-food average, largely because other food categories such as cereals and bakery products have a higher overall degree of processing. Examining changes in monthly farm and retail prices during 2008 and early 2009 indicates a decline in the farm-value share of retail product values and a widening of the marketing margin. Between July 2008 and December 2008, the farm price of milk reported by USDA fell by $0.33 per gallon.

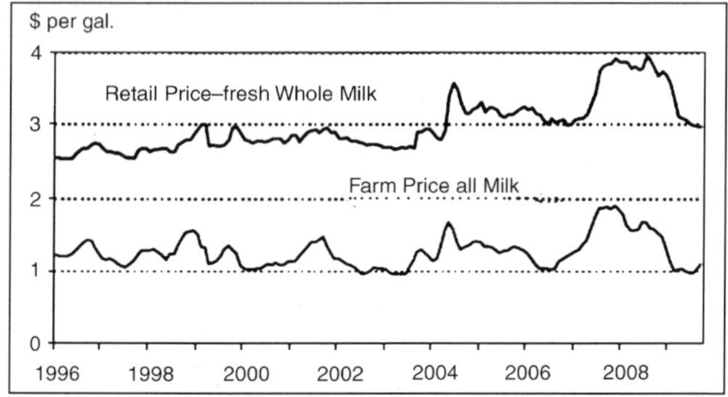

Fig. Monthly Farm and Retail Milk Prices

Meanwhile, the average retail milk price fell only $0.28, with the difference between the retail and farm price (*i.e.*, the marketing margin) increasing to $2.35 per gallon. In January 2009, the difference between the average retail price of milk and the farm price of milk reached a record-high $2.43 per gallon.

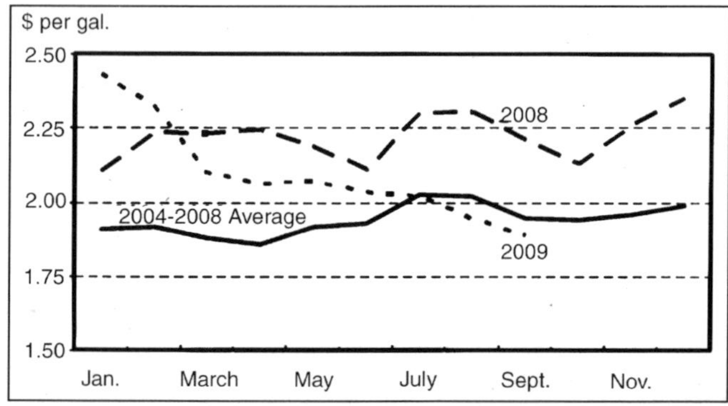

Fig. Fluid Milk Price Margin

However, as retailers cut prices amid lower costs for farm milk and other inputs (*e.g.*, energy and transportation), the difference between farm and retail prices declined in September 2009 to $1.89 per gallon, which is below the recent five-year average margin. The decline in late summer/early fall means that producers are receiving a greater share of the retail dollar as retail prices retreat, although the farm share remains below year-ago levels. Retail milk and dairy product prices have retreated significantly from dramatic highs in 2007 and 2008. In addition, they have declined more sharply than overall food prices, as measured by the Consumer Price Index.

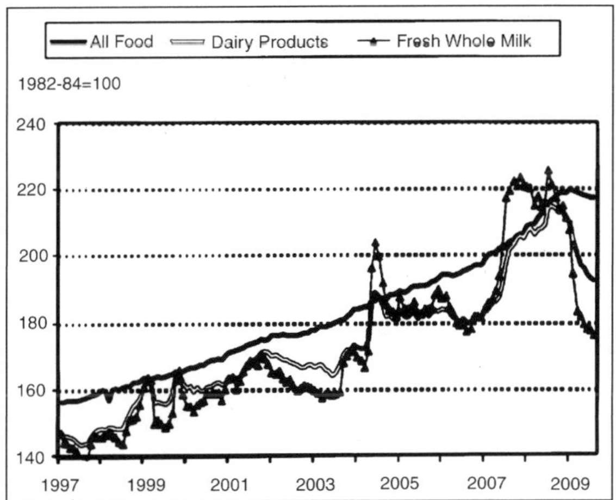

Fig. Consumer Price Index

U.S. DAIRY PRICING MECHANICS

Dairy pricing in the United States is a unique combination of both market-based and administered (through public dairy policies or programmes) prices. Each influences the other to determine the overall level of farm milk prices as well as price movements to some extent. Two characteristics—perishability and production on a daily basis—create challenges for pricing and marketing milk (and the products made from it). As a result, in the short run, production in excess of demand in the fluid market must be either dumped (much like unharvested fresh fruit left in orchards) or manufactured into storable dairy products and sold later.

MARKET-BASED PRICING

Market-based pricing for milk and dairy products is similar to that for many other agricultural commodities, in that primary mechanisms for price discovery like cash and futures markets, such as those located at the Chicago Mercantile Exchange (CME), play key roles. In general, current and future price levels for milk and dairy products are largely determined by buyers and sellers of milk and dairy products based on their perceptions of overall demand and supply conditions, along with expectations for changes in government policy (*e.g.*, dairy product support prices). Wholesale cash prices for dairy products (cheese, butter, and nonfat dry milk) are determined daily at the CME.

The prices written into contracts nationwide between dairy manufacturers and wholesale or retail buyers of basic dairy products often reflect CME prices. Some dairy producers say that cash market pricing on the CME works to the detriment of producers. Separately, milk and dairy product futures contracts are also traded in Chicago. Individuals and firms that face financial risk from movements in dairy prices can use futures contracts to manage their risk and offset potential losses in the cash market for dairy products.

ADMINISTERED PRICING

Administered farm milk prices are derived from two government policies: the dairy product price support programme (DPPSP) and federal milk marketing orders (FMMOs). The two policies originated at least 60 years ago and operate independently until market prices decline to support levels. The DPPSP simply provides price support for dairy farmers through government purchases of dairy products at legislated minimum prices.

In contrast, the FMMO system generally does not support prices but is designed to stabilize market conditions, which had been chaotic in the 1920s and early 1930s, through monthly, market-based minimum prices that processors must pay for farm milk. FMMOs also provide a pricing system for sharing farm revenue across producers in certain geographic areas and for balancing marketing power between milk handlers, who reportedly held an advantage prior to FMMO development, and farmers.

The role of the federal government in milk pricing is greatest when overall prices for milk and dairy products are relatively low and the government purchases dairy products. In this way, the DPPSP undergirds minimum prices in the federal milk marketing order system. Under the DPPSP, the federal government stands ready to purchase unlimited amounts of butter, American cheese, and nonfat dry milk from dairy processors at specified minimum prices.

Purchases under the DPPSP, which occurred during FY2009, essentially prevent market prices for dairy products (and hence milk prices received by farmers) from dropping below support levels. In contrast, when the three product prices are above support levels, the DPPSP is not a factor in the market and farm milk prices reflect prevailing supply and demand conditions. Year-to-year changes in farm milk prices have increased since the mid-1990s because price support levels have been reduced below typical market-average prices. FMMOs mandate minimum prices that processors in milk marketing areas must pay producers or their agents (like the dairy cooperatives) for delivered milk depending on its end use, regardless of whether market prices are high or low.

Minimum milk prices are based on current wholesale dairy product prices collected by USDA's National Agricultural Statistics Service in a weekly survey of manufacturers, which are determined in large part by prices established on the CME. As such, FMMO minimum prices rise and fall each month with overall changes in the dairy product market. Under marketing orders, the price farmers receive for their milk is calculated based on these minimum prices and on how milk is utilized (fluid vs. manufacturing) in the marketing order, which collectively is called "classified pricing."

FMMOs also address how market proceeds are distributed among the producers delivering milk to federal marketing order areas—called "pooling"—whereby all farmers receive a "blend price" each month based on order-wide revenue. The blend price is the weighted average price in a marketing order, with the weights being the volume of milk sold in each of the four classes. Under FMMOs, the farm price of approximately two-thirds of the nation's fluid milk is regulated in 10 geographic marketing areas.

Some states, California being the largest, have their own milk marketing regulations instead of federal rules. Marketing orders were created in the 1930s to balance market power between farmers and milk handlers while reducing "destructive competition" between milk producers that can drive down prices to their mutual detriment.

Milk prices at the farm level reflect the minimum prices paid by handlers under the marketing orders, plus any premiums generated from local supply/demand factors, such as a seasonal mismatch between supply and demand or special retail promotions, minus costs such as transport and marketing charges. In contrast, retail product prices are not regulated by the FMMO system. Instead, they reflect what retailers pay for dairy products from manufacturers and the level of competition among retailers in local markets.

ROLE OF DAIRY COOPERATIVES

Cooperatives play an important role in dairy pricing. A cooperative is an enterprise owned by and operated for the benefit of those using its services. Farmer-owned dairy cooperatives often operate a complete milk distribution system, procuring raw milk from the farm, routing it where needed, managing or coordinating movements of processed or manufactured products, and managing surplus milk. Cooperatives also bargain for prices with milk handlers and represent their members in the rulemaking processes for changing marketing orders.

Dairy farmers typically sign one-to three-year contracts to market their entire production through the cooperative in exchange for marketing services. Besides guaranteeing members a market for their milk, some dairy cooperatives manage price risks by operating multi-product, multi-plant operations, using their flexibility to shift production from one product to another in an effort to obtain the highest return for the farmer-members.

PRICE SIGNALS UNDER FEDERAL MILK MARKETING ORDERS

When prices of agricultural (or other) commodities rise, producers tend to increase their output to increase profit. Alternatively, when prices are falling, they focus on trimming costs to save money, thereby reducing production. At some point, the price cycle (with prices either rising or falling) reverses course as supply becomes more aligned with demand.

The points at which farmers see these price incentives and when they take action affects overall production levels and price movements going forward. For most milk producers in the United States, the "mailbox price" is what farmers receive for their milk in a monthly check from the handler or their cooperative.

It is the net price received after adjustments for quality, marketing costs (*e.g.*, hauling charges, cooperative dues, producer assessments), and over-order premiums that arise when market prices rise above the marketing order minimums. Dairy farmers make production decisions—to buy or raise more cows or send some to the slaughterhouse—based in large part on their monthly revenue or expected revenue in the future.

Feed and other input costs, including debt service, also play a large part in whether to expand or contract. The biggest factors driving the changes in prices producers receive month-to-month are the minimum FMMO prices handlers must pay for milk. USDA calculates the FMMO prices using wholesale product prices as input into formulas that have been established through the regulatory process. Three pricing issues with respect to market signals for dairy farmers are timing, clarity, and the "make allowance," or margin afforded to dairy manufacturers in the federal order minimum prices.

TIMING OF PRICE SIGNALS

FMMO prices are issued by USDA each month for each class of milk (depending on its use) as data on wholesale prices become available. For a specific FMMO month, minimum prices for fluid milk are announced in advance (by the 23rd of the previous month).

For other classes of milk, prices are announced after the close of the FMMO month. Shortly thereafter, mailbox prices are calculated once the marketing order pools close (*i.e.*, monthly volumes and values are tabulated) and each of the 10 FMMO administrators determines the overall order "blend" price.

The process of establishing monthly prices dates to the beginning of the marketing order system in the 1930s. Previously, day-to-day or week-to-week price fluctuations created enormous price uncertainty for dairy farmers. A monthly price system, along with other features of milk marketing orders, helped create a more stable price environment. Farmers could better manage their business decisions when they knew with certainty the price they would receive.

A criticism of current FMMO pricing stems from this effort to stabilize the market. Some market participants, including dairy manufacturers and, on occasion, milk producers, claim that the system does not transmit price signals quickly enough, particularly in today's fast-changing market. For example, suppose domestic or foreign demand for milk or dairy products declines in April. The negative market signal could take until late June to reach milk producers, delaying the response of producers to begin slowing production to more closely align with demand. Conversely, when dairy product prices rise rapidly, the production response, now in the upward direction, can be delayed to the extent that farmers base their expansion on their mailbox price.

CLARITY OF PRICE SIGNALS

The pooling function in milk marketing orders is designed to reduce destructive competition and allow all producers to benefit from higher prices of fluid milk (relative to other uses). At the same time, however, some in the industry suggest that pooling can have the unfortunate consequence of muting marketing signals.

When revenues are pooled across the marketing region (both geographically and by how milk is utilized), critics argue, individual producers do not have a direct market signal of risks associated with production, a situation that can encourage excessive growth in production when prices are low.

FIXED "MAKE ALLOWANCES"

To calculate minimum milk prices in the FMMO system, USDA starts with survey data collected from dairy manufacturers. USDA's National Agricultural Statistics Service calculates average dairy product prices from these weekly data. Next, USDA's Agricultural Marketing Service subtracts a "make allowance"—an estimate of the manufacturer's cost of processing milk into dairy products—to arrive at the monthly minimum prices. USDA periodically revises make allowances, most recently in October 2008 to reflect higher energy costs for manufacturers, following a lengthy regulatory process involving all parties.

The make allowance mathematically reduces average product prices used to calculate minimum farm milk prices. Some producers feel that the make allowance unfairly reduces the minimum milk prices set under the FMMOs. Manufacturers say the make allowance is simply the cost of processing milk into dairy products, and calling it a cost to farmers misrepresents the economics of producing dairy products.

The controversy for some is that the make allowance for each dairy product is a fixed amount (at least until changed in the regulatory hearing process). It does not change when dairy product markets strengthen or weaken, leaving essentially a fixed margin for manufacturers, regardless of their relative efficiencies. As a result of this inflexibility, changes in the market are reflected to a greater degree in farm prices or in the margins seen by firms that come downstream from the manufacturer (*i.e.*, broker, wholesaler, or retailer).

At times, this can be a detriment to farmers when prices are declining because manufacturers' margins may be held artificially wide, forcing down minimum prices below what they otherwise would be.

Conversely, a fixed margin may benefit producers when manufacturers' actual margin (based on real-time costs such as energy) is greater than the make allowance. In this case, FMMO minimum prices would be above the level that would be calculated using actual costs.

POTENTIAL FOR PRICE MANIPULATION

The primary cash market for dairy products is located at the CME, where cheese, butter, and nonfat dry milk are traded. Actual quantities traded are quite small, but prices determined by buyers and sellers at this market are used to establish wholesale price contracts across the country, subject to premium and discounts for factors such as quality and transportation. Wholesale dairy product prices are then used to set monthly minimum prices under the federal orders.

Some dairy producer groups believe that the CME is an inadequate pricing mechanism because the market is too thinly traded, lacks transparency and sufficient oversight, and creates a highly volatile market that adversely affects producers. The U.S. Government Accountability Office concluded in a 2007 study that "certain market conditions at the CME spot cheese market, including a small number of trades and a small number of traders who make a majority of trades, continue to make this market particularly susceptible to manipulation."

However, the report also noted that if price manipulation were to occur, some industry participants claim it would be short-lived because many large participants in the cheese and dairy industry with diverse interests monitor the market and are prepared to participate in it. Reportedly, they would begin trading once prices became disconnected from underlying supply and demand conditions, potentially counteracting any attempted price manipulation. Nevertheless, some industry participants want sales volume to increase on the CME, thereby reducing the possibility of price manipulation.

The Commodity Futures Trading Commission (CFTC) and the CME itself monitor activities of the spot market participants for signs of price manipulation. In December 2008, several dairy industry participants agreed to pay a civil monetary penalty for attempting to manipulate milk futures prices through purchases of cheese on the CME in 2004.

POLICY CONSIDERATIONS FOR DAIRY PRICING

While dairy markets appear to be rebounding from low farm milk prices of summer 2009, the dairy industry and policymakers continue to consider how the dairy pricing system might be improved. The House and Senate have held hearings on dairy policy and pricing in 2009. The Administration is also collecting information through USDA's establishment of a Dairy Advisory Committee, which is to review issues of farm milk price volatility and suggest to the Secretary of Agriculture how USDA can best address these issues. The committee is to "develop changes to the dairy pricing system to avoid the boom and bust cycle facing dairy famers this year." As Congress, the Administration, and the dairy industry consider how possibly to revise the dairy pricing system, two schools of thought appear to be emerging. One is to reduce price volatility through some means of supply control while raising farm prices.

The other is to allow the market to fluctuate and help farmers manage the resulting price risk through hedging strategies used by farmers in other parts of the agriculture sector. A number of organizations are also examining potential changes to various aspects of the federal dairy programmes.

PRICE STABILIZATION AND SUPPLY CONTROL

Supply control is a way for government to influence the supply of farm products on the market with the intention of increasing or stabilizing farm prices. One dairy producer group, Holstein Association USA, has proposed a plan to stabilize farm milk prices with assessments on farmers who increase milk production over specified levels, as determined by USDA forecasts of demand for fluid milk and manufactured dairy products.

Some of the program's objectives are to reduce the volatility of dairy product prices and producer milk prices while preventing severely depressed producer milk prices. The National Farmers Union (NFU) is among the supporters. Supply control is also affected by imports. Legislation has been introduced in both the House and the Senate in 2009 to apply import controls on specific dairy products. The Milk Import Tariff Equity Act would impose tariff-rate quotas on imports of casein (the main protein found in milk) and milk protein concentrates.

Some believe a change in federal milk marketing orders also could be used to stabilize the milk market and boost dairy farm returns. One bill in the 111 Congress, the Federal Milk Marketing Improvement Act of 2009 is designed to "help farmers get a fair price for their milk" and provide relief and assistance to dairy farmers by using the cost of milk production as the basis for pricing milk.

The bill contains provisions for USDA to administratively reduce prices received by farmers, in an effort to limit milk production, if the Secretary of Agriculture determines that an excess amount is being produced for the national domestic market.

Supporters of price stabilization and supply control say that incentives within the dairy industry to overproduce need to be offset by a programme to control supplies in a more measured way. Critics contend that supply control could reduce the competitiveness of the U.S. dairy industry, limit its incentive to innovate, and raise consumer prices because, they argue, a pricing system based on supply control and/or cost of production potentially rewards inefficiency. Critics also argue that administratively matching supply and demand can be difficult because the process would require accurate forecasts of demand and supply factors that are notoriously fickle.

MARKET-BASED APPROACH

Other industry groups, including the National Milk Producers Federation (NMPF), the largest trade association representing milk producer cooperatives, prefer a more market-based approach for addressing milk pricing issues, along with changes to existing dairy programmes as part of an overall adjustment to federal dairy policy.

The NMPF proposes a new dairy producer income insurance programme that would make indemnity payments when operation losses occur (similar to a revenue insurance programme) and reform of the federal milk marketing order system, specifically the provisions for calculating minimum farm milk prices and the existing price discovery mechanism. The organization also advocates discontinuing the dairy product price support programme in order to speed up market adjustments.

Promoters of a market-based approach, including dairy food manufacturers, say that price volatility will be a part of the dairy industry, as it is for other commodities. As such, they claim the best approach is to find ways for producers to manage price risks without limiting the industry's ability to capitalize on domestic and international demand opportunities. Detractors expect that incentives to overproduce will aggravate the financial woes of the dairy industry indefinitely, so controlling potential price variability with supply management is necessary for long-term financial health for producers.

This concern for overproduction could and has been applied to commodities such as corn and wheat. But dairy generally is more susceptible to overproduction, some dairy producers say, because current policy encourages producers to maximize production and they tend to add cows even when prices are low to improve cash flow.

OUTLOOK

Current policy is set for the dairy product price support programme until 2012 under the 2008 farm bill, and federal milk marketing orders are permanently authorized. However, given the difficult economic situation dairy farmers experienced in 2009, Congress may continue to monitor the dairy pricing situation through hearings and oversight.

Efforts to address dairy pricing issues could be affected by the future direction of market prices. The current farm milk price cycle appears to have bottomed out in summer/early fall 2009, based on forecasts by USDA and others. If the forecasts hold, it may be difficult for policymakers and producers to support major policy changes while milk prices are climbing. In the view of some, any further intervention could disrupt an otherwise favourable price situation.

In any event, discussions and policy proposals on dairy pricing may continue to be a topic of discussion in the 111 Congress or in the next farm bill debate, which may begin as early as 2011.

12

HACCP

INTRODUCTION

The Hazard Analysis Critical Control Point (HACCP) system is a structured, preventative approach to ensuring food safety. HACCP provides a means to identify and assess potential hazards in food production and establish preventive control procedures for those hazards. A critical control point (CCP) is identified for each significant hazard, where effective control measures can be defined, applied and monitored.

The emphasis on prevention of hazards reduces reliance on traditional inspection and quality control procedures and end-product testing. A properly applied HACCP system is now internationally recognised as an effective means of ensuring food safety. The HACCP concept can be applied to new or existing products and processes, and throughout the food chain from primary production to consumption.

It is compatible with existing standards for quality management systems such as the ISO 9000-2000 series, and HACCP procedures can be fully integrated into such systems. The new ISO 22000 food safety standard formally integrates HACCP within the structure of a quality management system. HACCP is fully integrated into the British Retail Consortium (BRC) Global Standards for Food Safety, and is one of the 'fundamental' requirements of that system.

The application of HACCP at all stages of the food supply chain is actively encouraged, and increasingly required, worldwide. For example, the Codex Alimentarius advises that "the application of HACCP systems can aid inspection by regulatory authorities and promote international trade by increasing confidence in food safety".

In many countries, there is a legal requirement for all food business operators to have some form of hazard analysis based on HACCP as a means of ensuring food safety. For example, within the European Union, Regulations 852/2004 and 853/2004 require a fully operational and maintained HACCP system to be in place.

DEFINITIONS

- *Control* (verb): To take all necessary actions to ensure and maintain compliance with criteria established in the HACCP plan.
- *Control* (noun): The state wherein correct procedures are followed and criteria are met.
- *Control Measure:* An action and activity that can be used to prevent or eliminate a food safety hazard or reduce it to an acceptable level.
- *Corrective Action:* An action to be taken when the results of monitoring at the CCP indicate a loss of control.
- *Critical Control Point (CCP):* A step at which control can be applied and is essential to prevent or eliminate a food safety hazard, or reduce it to an acceptable level.
- *Critical Limit:* A criterion that separates acceptability from unacceptability.
- *Deviation:* Failure to meet a critical limit.
- *Flow Diagram:* A systematic representation of the sequence of steps or operations used in the production or manufacture of a particular food item.
- *HACCP:* A system that identifies, evaluates and controls hazards that are significant for food safety.
- *HACCP Plan:* A document prepared in accordance with the principles of
- HACCP to ensure control of hazards that are significant for safety in the segment of the food chain under consideration.
- *Hazard:* A biological, chemical or physical agent in, or condition of, food with the potential to cause an adverse health effect.
- *Hazard Analysis:* The process of collecting and evaluating information on hazards and the conditions leading to their presence to decide which are significant for food safety and therefore should be addressed by the HACCP plan.
- *Monitoring:* The act of conducting a planned sequence of observations or measurements of control parameters to assess whether a CCP is under control.
- *Step:* A point, procedure, operation or stage in the food chain including raw materials, from primary production to final consumption.
- *Validation:* Obtaining evidence that the elements of the HACCP plan are effective.
- *Verification:* The application of methods, procedures, tests and other evaluations, in addition to monitoring to determine compliance with the HACCP plan.

STAGES OF A HACCP STUDY

The HACCP system consists of the following seven basic principles:

1. Conduct a hazard analysis.
2. Identify the CCPs.
3. Establish the critical limit(s).
4. Establish a system to monitor control of the CCP.
5. Establish the corrective action to be taken when monitoring indicates that a particular CCP is not under control.
6. Establish procedure for verification to confirm that the HACCP system is working effectively.
7. Establish documentation concerning all procedures and records appropriate to these principles and their application.

It is recommended by the Codex Alimentarius that the practical application of the HACCP principles be approached by breaking the seven principles down into a 12-stage logic sequence.

ASSEMBLE THE HACCP TEAM

HACCP requires management commitment of resources to the process. An effective HACCP plan is best carried out as a multidisciplinary team exercise to ensure that the appropriate product-specific expertise is available. The team should include members familiar with all aspects of the production process as well as specialists with expertise in particular areas such as production, hygiene managers, quality assurance or control, ingredient and packaging buyers, food microbiology, food chemistry or engineering.

The team should also include personnel who are involved with the variability and limitations of the operations. If expert advice is not available on-site, it may be obtained from external sources. The scope of the plan should be determined by defining the extent of the production process to be considered and the categories of hazard to be addressed (*e.g.* biological, chemical and/or physical).

Dairy Products

The HACCP team should ideally have access to expertise on the practices applied at farm level in relation to milk collection, storage and transport. The initial microbial population of raw milk has a significant influence on the safety and quality of processed dairy products.

For example, the effectiveness of pasteurisation may be compromised by excessive microbial counts in raw milk, and by the presence of large numbers of pathogens. Therefore, knowledge of primary production procedures is very valuable for the HACCP study.

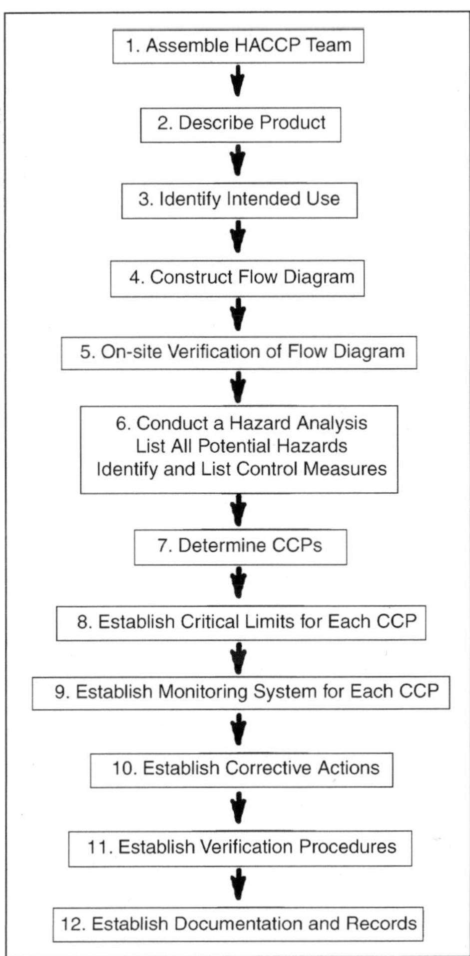

Fig. Logic Sequence for Application of HACCP

DESCRIBE THE PRODUCT

It is important to have a complete understanding of the product, which should be described in detail. The description should include information such as the product name, composition, physical and chemical structure (including water activity (aw), pH, etc.), processing conditions (*e.g.* heat treatment, freezing, fermentation, etc.), packaging, shelf life, storage and distribution conditions and instructions for use.

Dairy Products

Many dairy products are manufactured by traditional processes that have been practised for centuries. As a result of this, there is a great deal of background data and experience available to draw on. Furthermore, the majority of these traditional products have a good safety record, suggesting that standard manufacturing processes are safe.

This situation can lead to complacency, and it is essential that the basis for the inherent safety of these products is fully understood. This is particularly true in situations where the introduction of new technology, new additives and ingredients, and new requirements from retailers and consumers may give rise to new hazards.

IDENTIFY INTENDED USE

The intended use should be based on the expected uses of the product by the enduser or consumer (*e.g.* is a cooking process required?). It is also important to identify the consumer target groups. Vulnerable groups of the population, such as children or the elderly, may need to be considered specifically.

Dairy Products

Dairy products are often consumed by high-risk groups, particularly the very young and the elderly. Infants are at particular risk from pathogens such as *Salmonella*, and pregnant women and the elderly are especially vulnerable to *Listeria* infection. This must be considered during the HACCP study and should be taken into account when compiling the instructions for use.

CONSTRUCT A FLOW DIAGRAM

The flow diagram should be constructed by the HACCP team and should contain sufficient technical data for the study to progress. It should provide an accurate representation of all steps in the production process from raw materials to the endproduct. It may include details of the factory and equipment layout, ingredient specifications, features of equipment design, time/temperature data, cleaning and hygiene procedures and storage conditions. Ideally it should also include details of CCP steps, once determined.

Dairy Products

Examples of flow diagrams for specific dairy products may be found in the appropriate product chapters. Many dairy processing operations have relatively few steps and the flow diagrams appear simple. Common steps occur in many processes-for example, standardisation, pasteurisation, and homogenisation.

However, it is essential that the details of each step are fully appreciated and recorded. Particular attention should be paid to potential routes of product flow that might allow cross-contamination between raw and pasteurised product. Divert valves, bypasses, pumps, and holding or balance tanks require close scrutiny. In modern dairy plants, it is also important to ascertain how cleaning-inplace systems are designed and operated. Effective cleaning is an essential control for preventing recontamination of pasteurised dairy products.

ON-SITE CONFIRMATION OF THE FLOW DIAGRAM

The HACCP team should confirm that the flow diagram matches the process that is actually being carried out. The operation should be observed at all stages, and any discrepancies between the flow diagram and normal practice must be recorded and the diagram amended accordingly.

It is also important to include observation of production outside normal working hours such as shift patterns and weekend working, as well as the circumstances of any reclaim or rework activity. It is essential that the diagram is accurate, because the hazard analysis and decisions regarding CCPs are based on these data.

If HACCP studies are applied to proposed new process lines/products, then any pre-drawn HACCP plans must be reviewed once the lines/products are finalised.

LIST ALL POTENTIAL HAZARDS ASSOCIATED WITH EACH STEP; CONDUCT A HAZARD ANALYSIS; AND IDENTIFY ANY MEASURES TO CONTROL IDENTIFIED HAZARDS

The HACCP team should list all hazards that may reasonably be expected to occur at each step in the production process. The team should then conduct a hazard analysis to identify which hazards are of such a nature that their elimination or reduction to an acceptable level is essential to the production of safe food.

The analysis is likely to include consideration of:

- The likely occurrence of hazards and the severity of their adverse health effects;
- The qualitative and/or quantitative evaluation of the presence of hazards;
- Survival or multiplication of pathogenic microorganisms;
- Production or persistence of toxins;
- The hurdle effect;
- The number of consumers potentially exposed and their vulnerability;
- Any food safety objectives or manufacturer's food safety requirements.

The HACCP team should then determine what control measures exist that can be applied for each hazard. Some hazards may require more than one control measure for adequate control and a single control measure may act to control more than one hazard. One control measure may be relevant to several process steps, where a hazard is repeated. Note: it is important at this stage that no attempt is made to identify CCPs, since this may interfere with the analysis.

Dairy Products

The term 'dairy products' includes a varied group of foods, and there is an equally varied range of potential hazards associated with them. Hazards specific to certain types of product are detailed in the appropriate chapters of this manual.

For example, there are particular hazards associated with contamination of dried milk powders by salmonellae, and the potential growth of *Listeria monocytogenes* in soft cheeses. Many of the microbiological hazards associated with dairy products are derived from the raw materials (*i.e.* raw milk). Pathogens may be part of the resident microflora of the living animal (*e.g. Staphylococcus aureus*), or may originate from faecal contamination during initial milk collection.

Pathogens may also be introduced into raw milk from contaminated equipment during collection, transport, or storage. The majority of these hazards can be eliminated by an appropriate heat treatment, such as pasteurisation or sterilisation.

Hazards introduced during processing of dairy products depend very much on the characteristics of the process. For example, heat-sensitive pathogens may be present in pasteurised milk as a result of cross-contamination between raw and heat-treated milk, and slow acid production by the starter culture in fermented milk products may allow growth and toxin production by *Staph. aureus*.

Therefore, it is not possible, or desirable, to generalise about expected hazards, and the reader is referred to the appropriate product chapter in this book for additional advice on specific hazards.

DETERMINE CCPS

The determination of CCPs in the HACCP system is facilitated by using a decision tree to provide a logical, structured approach to decision making. However, application of the decision tree should be flexible, and its use may not always be appropriate.

It is also essential that the HACCP team has access to sufficient technical data to determine the CCPs effectively. If a significant hazard has been identified at a step where control is required for safety, but for which no control exists at that step or any other, then the process must be modified to include a control measure.

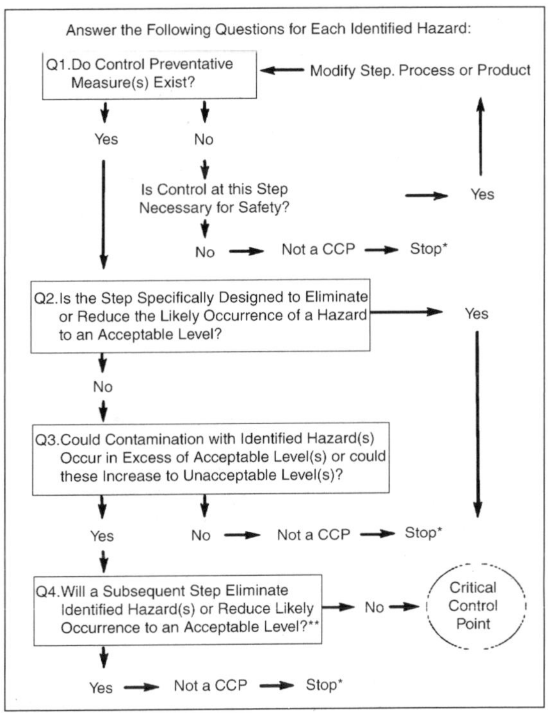

Fig. CCP Decision Tree A

Notes:

* Proceed to next step in the described process

** Acceptable and unacceptable levels need to be defined within the overall objectives in identifying the CCPs of HACCP plan

Dairy Products

Again, given the enormous variety of dairy products and processes in use, it is unwise to generalise on likely CCPs, and the reader is referred to the appropriate product chapter in this book.

However, it can be said that effective control measures are likely to include the following:

- Careful control of raw milk quality and selection of sources for other raw materials;
- Adequate pasteurisation processes;
- Prevention of cross-contamination of pasteurised product;
- Effective sanitation and hygiene procedures;
- Adequate temperature control.

Some examples are as follows:

- In the manufacture of skimmed milk powder, CCPs are likely to be pasteurisation, and the effective separation, cleaning and maintenance of spray dryers and powder handling equipment.

- In the production of fermented milk products and cheese, pasteurisation is again likely to be a CCP, but the rapid development of sufficient acidity by the starter culture is also a CCP.
- Adequate temperature control during processing would normally be considered a CCP in the manufacture of ice cream, as would the microbiological quality of flavouring ingredients added after pasteurisation.

ESTABLISH CRITICAL LIMITS FOR EACH CCP

Critical limits separate acceptable from unacceptable products. Where possible, critical limits should be specified and validated for each CCP. More than one critical limit may be defined for a single step.

For example, it is necessary to specify both time and temperature for a thermal process, and a minimum process of 72°C for 15 seconds, or equivalent, is required for milk pasteurisation. Criteria used to set critical limits must be measurable and may include physical, chemical, biological or sensory parameters. It is prudent to set stricter limits (often called target or process limits/levels) to ensure that any trends towards a loss of control is noted before the critical limit is exceeded.

Dairy Products

Specific product chapters provide information on criteria that may be used to set critical limits.

Some examples relevant to dairy products are:

- Pasteurisation time and temperature
- Total acidity and/or pH (fermented products)
- Measured adequacy of cleaning procedures
- Chilled storage time and temperature
- Water activity (condensed milk products)

ESTABLISH A MONITORING SYSTEM FOR EACH CCP

Monitoring involves planned measurement or observation of a CCP relative to its critical limits. Monitoring procedures must be able to detect loss of control of the CCP, and should provide this information with sufficient speed to allow adjustments to be made to the control of the process before the critical limits are violated. Monitoring at critical limits should be able to detect rapidly when the critical limit has been exceeded.

Monitoring should either be continuous, or carried out sufficiently frequently to ensure control at the CCP. Therefore, physical and chemical on-line measurements are usually preferred to lengthy microbiological testing. However, certain rapid methods, such as ATP assay by bioluminescence, may be useful for assessment of adequate cleaning, which could be a critical limit for some CCPs, for example, pre-start-up hygiene. Persons engaged in monitoring activities must have sufficient knowledge, training and authority to act effectively on the basis of the data collected. These data should also be properly recorded.

ESTABLISH CORRECTIVE ACTIONS

For each CCP in the HACCP plan, there must be specified corrective actions to be applied if the CCP is not under control. If monitoring indicates a deviation from the critical limit for a CCP, action must be taken that will bring it back under control.

Actions taken should also include proper isolation of the affected product and an investigation into why the deviation occurred. A further set of corrective actions should relate to the target level, if process drift is occuring. In this case, only repair of the process defect and investigation of the fault are required. All corrective actions should be properly recorded.

ESTABLISH VERIFICATION PROCEDURES

Verification usually involves auditing and testing procedures. Auditing methods, procedures and tests should be used frequently enough to determine whether the HACCP system is being followed, and is effective at controlling the hazards. These may include random sampling and analysis, including microbiological testing.

Although microbiological analysis is generally too slow for monitoring purposes, it can be of great value in verification, since many of the identified hazards are likely to be microbiological. For example, analysis of dried milk powders for *Salmonella*, desserts for *Bacillus cereus*, and soft cheeses for *Listeria* would be appropriate verification tests. In addition, reviews of HACCP records are important for verification purposes. These should confirm that CCPs are under control and should indicate the nature of any deviations and the actions that were taken in each case. It is also useful to review customer returns and complaints regularly.

ESTABLISH DOCUMENTATION AND RECORD KEEPING

Efficient and accurate record keeping is an essential element of a HACCP system. The procedures in the HACCP system should be documented.

Examples of documented procedures include:

- The hazard analysis
- Determination of CCPs
- Determination of critical limits
- The completed HACCP plan

Examples of recorded data include:

- Results of monitoring procedures
- Deviations from critical limits and corrective actions
- Records of certain verification activities, *e.g.* observations of monitoring activities, and calibration of equipment.

The degree of documentation required will depend partly on the size and complexity of the operation, but it is unlikely to be possible to demonstrate that an effective HACCP system is present without adequate documentation and records. The length of time that records are kept will be as per company policy, but should not be less than one year beyond the shelf life of the product. Three to five years is typical for many food companies.

IMPLEMENTATION AND REVIEW OF THE HACCP PLAN

The completed plan can only be implemented successfully with the full support and co-operation of management and the workforce. Adequate training is essential and the responsibilities and tasks of the operating personnel at each CCP must be clearly defined. Finally, it is essential that the HACCP plan be reviewed following any changes to the process, including changes to raw materials, processing conditions or equipment, packaging, cleaning procedures and any other factor that may have an effect on product safety.

Even a small alteration to the product or process may invalidate the HACCP plan and introduce potential hazards. Therefore, the implications of any changes to the overall HACCP system must be fully considered and documented, and adjustments made to the procedures as necessary. Tiggered reviews/audits should occur as a result of changes, whereas scheduled review/audit should be annually, as a minimum.

13

Dairy Operations and Dairy Waste System

DAIRY OPERATIONS

Dairy operations significantly affect the quantity and quality of manure that may be delivered to the anaerobic digestion system. In addition to the number of milk and dry cows, the housing, transport, manure separation, and bedding systems used by the dairy establishes the amount of material that must be handled and the amount of energy produced.

TRANSPORT SYSTEM

The commonly used manure transport systems are flush, scrape, vacuum, and loader systems. In free stall barns the manure can be flushed, scraped, or vacuum collected.

Flush Systems

If a flush system is used the manure is substantially diluted. The quantity of water used in a flush system depends on the width, length, and slope of the flush isle.

Fig. Free Stall Flush System-Flushing Feed Lane

The feed isles are generally 14 feet wide while the back isles are generally 10 feet wide. The slope varies between one and two per cent. A flush system will generally reduce the concentration of manure from 12 1/2 per cent solids, "as excreted", to less than one per cent solids in the flush water. Flush systems are however more economical and less labour-intensive than scrape or vacuum systems.

Scrape Systems

Scrape systems are simply systems that collect the manure by scraping it to a sump. Under normal weather conditions the scraped manure has approximately the same consistency as the "as excreted" manure. During the warm dry summer manure may be dewatered on the slab.

Front-end Loader

Front-end loaders are used to stack and remove corral bedding and manure.

Vacuum Systems

Vacuum systems collect "as excreted" manure with a vacuum truck. Generally, the trucks collect approximately 4000 gallons per load. The manure can be hauled to a disposal site rather than to an intermediate sump. Vacuum collection is a slow and tedious process. The advantage is that the collected manure is undiluted and approximately equal to the "as excreted" concentration.

Fig. Vacuum Truck Collecting Manure Solids

BEDDING

The type of bedding used can significantly alter the characteristics of the manure being treated. Typically straw, wood chips, sand, or compost are used as bedding material. In some cases paper mixed with sawdust is used.

Compost usually has some sand mixed with the organic constituents. If composting is carried out on dirt lots, a significant amount of sand and silt may be incorporated into the compost. Since anaerobic digestion will not degrade the wood chips, sand, or silt, it is necessary to remove those constituents prior to, or during anaerobic digestion process. The quantity of non-degradable, organic and inorganic material can significantly impact the performance of the anaerobic digester.

The quantity of bedding added to the manure is a function of the design and operation of the dairy. Generally only the "kick-out" from the stalls is added to the manure. The quantity that is "kicked-out" is a function of the design of the dairy housing system as well as the type of bedding used.

MANURE PROCESSING

Each dairy has its own manure processing system. Scraped or flushed manure may be processed in a system separate from the milk barn waste, or the collected manure waste may be processed with the milk barn waste. In general, current manure processing consists of macerating the waste with a chopper pump, screening the waste to remove the organic fibres, followed by sedimentation to remove the sand, silt, and organic settable particles.

Much of the degradable manure is removed during the separation processes. Up to 80% of the COD and 30% of the total Nitrogen and Phosphorous can be lost in the solids removed by the screen and sedimentation process. Detailed sampling and analysis is required to confirm losses.

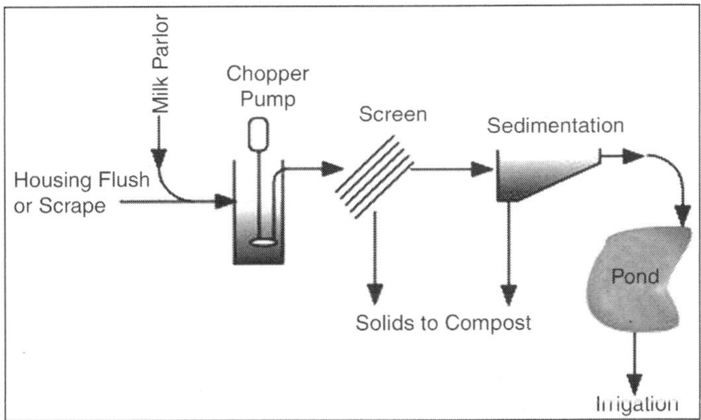

Fig. Conventional Manure Handling

Holding Tanks and Chopper Pumps

A wide variety of holding tanks and chopper pumps are used throughout the dairy industry. Typically, the tanks are relatively small but in some cases they are designed to hold several hours of flush water.

Fig. Typical Manure Sump with Chopper Pump

Primary Screens

An equally wide variety of screening systems are used. In many cases the screens are housed in separate enclosures to prevent freezing during the winter months. Outdoor screens are generally problematic during cold weather months. Fan separators are also used to provide efficient separation of the fibrous solids.

Fig. Primary Screens Background with Gravity Separators Foreground

The primary screens will remove a significant amount of degradable organic material that could be converted to gas in an anaerobic digester. The screened materials are generally used to produce bedding after being composted for the required time periods.

Gravity Separators

Gravity separators varying in size from 10 feet wide by 30′ long to 24 feet wide by 80 feet long are usually placed after the primary screens. The purpose of the gravity separator is to remove the sands and silt present in the waste stream.

If gravity separators are used without screening a thick mat of straw and fibres may develop on top of the gravity separator.

Fig. Floating Solids on Top of Gravity Separator

The gravity separators often incorporate weeping walls for the removal of liquid from the sedimentation chamber. The ability of the weeping wall to remove liquid waste depends on the periodic cleaning of the perforations to maintain flow.

In many cases the gravity separators remove a significant amount of degradable organic material that could be utilized to produce gas. The COD test is a direct measure of the quantity of material that could be converted to methane gas.

Recent tests have established that screen and gravity separators can remove 75% to 80% of the COD present in the waste stream. In one test the dairy parlor COD was reduced from 31,000 mg/l to 8,600 mg/l in the effluent from the gravity separator.

In another the flush water influent to a separator system was 10,900 mg/L while the effluent was 1,800 mg/L. While a significant portion of the organic carbon (COD) is retained with the separated solids, an equal percentage of the nitrogen and phosphorus is not. The separation process alters the carbon to nitrogen ratio of both the liquid and solids streams.

Fig. Weeping Wall with Clogged Holes

The sedimentation process concentrates the organic solids, which are periodically removed. A recent analysis showed the flush water had a COD concentration of 25, 500 mg/l while the concentrated solids from the separator had a COD of 115, 800 mg/l.

Fig. Organic Solids on Top of Gravity Separator

Anaerobic decomposition of settled solids can be observed in separators that have a surface covered with methane gas bubbles. It is clear that existing solids handling practices contribute to greenhouse gas emissions and prevent efficient energy recovery from manure waste.

Fig. Gravity Separator with Anaerobic Decomposition of Organic Solid

Primary Holding Ponds

Most dairies will discharge the screened and settled waste to a primary holding pond.

Fig. Partially Empty Primary Holding Pond Showing Sediment

The primary holding pond is a secondary sedimentation basin where the fine solids are separated from the liquid waste. Eventually the fine solids must be removed from the bottom of the primary holding pond. Odours generally accompany the removal of solids.

Secondary Holding Ponds

It is common to have a number of holding ponds that provide the required detention time (180 days) following the primary holding pond. The irrigation and flush pumps are normally installed in one or more of these ponds.

Fig. Typical Secondary Holding Pond

REVIEW

Two separate waste streams, the milk parlor and confinement area wastes, makeup the dairy waste that can be treated through anaerobic digestion. The type of bedding used, as well as the manure transport, and subsequent manure processing will change the characteristics of both waste streams. The dilution of waste will require larger anaerobic digestion facilities. The removal of organics through screening and sedimentation will reduce the quantity of organic solids that can be converted to gas in the digester. The presence of sand and silts will clog pipes, damage equipment, and fill anaerobic digestion tanks.

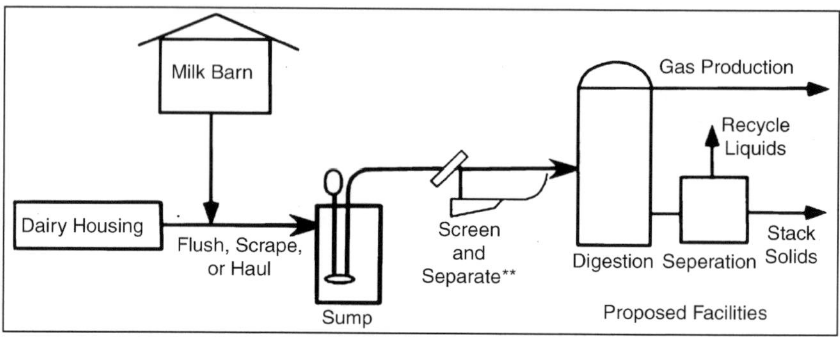

Fig. Integration of Anaerobic Digestion in Dairy Waste Stream

Notes: ** Screen and Separate may be By-passed

Sand can only be removed from dilute waste streams. Thick slurries retain sand that precipitate in the digester when the organics are converted to gas and the solids concentration is reduced. If thick slurries are processed in an anaerobic digester, intense mixing is required to maintain the solids in suspension.

Modification of existing dairy management practices may be required to achieve the full benefits of anaerobic digestion. Figure shows how a solid waste management facility can be incorporated in an existing dairy waste-processing stream.

If low or moderate concentrations of sand are present the entire waste stream may be discharged to an anaerobic digester, bypassing the existing screen and gravity separators. If high concentrations of sand are present, the existing gravity separators may remain in place. Under such conditions, a reduced quantity of organics will be converted to gas.

HOUSING SYSTEM

Confined dairy animals may be housed in a variety of systems. Commonly used housing systems include free stalls, corrals with paved feed lanes, and open lot systems. Milk cows, dry cows and heifers may be housed in free stalls, corrals, and open-lots on the same dairy. The type of housing used determines the quantity of manure that can be economically collected.

Free Stall Barns

Free stalls are currently the most popular method for housing large dairy herds. Free stall housing provides a means for collecting essentially all of the manure.

Fig. Typical Free Stall Barn with Center Feed Lane

Corrals

Corral systems with paved feed lanes are also commonly used. The manure deposited in the feed lanes can be scraped or flushed daily. From 40 to 55-per cent of the excreted manure may be deposited and collected from the corral feed lane. The balance of the manure may be deposited in the milk barn (10 to 15 per cent) or the open lot (30 to 50%).

Typically the manure deposited in the open lot is removed two to three times a year. It may have little net energy value after being stored in the open lot over prolonged periods of time.

For corral systems one must make a reasonable determination of the recoverable manure deposited in the feed lane, corral, and milk barn. Corral systems also use a considerable amount of bedding material during the winter months. The straw bedding is generally removed in the spring and placed on the fields prior to spring planting.

Fig. Corral with Paved Feed Lane for Scrape or Vacuum Collection

Milk Barn

Dairy cows are milked two to three times a day. The cows are moved from their stalls to the milk parlor holding area. The milk parlor and holding area are normally flushed with fresh water. From 10 to 15 per cent of the manure is deposited in the milk parlor. In addition to the manure that is flushed, the cows may be washed with a sprinkler system. Warm water that is produced by the refrigeration compressors, vacuum pumps, and milk cooling system may be used for drinking water, manure flushing or washing the cows. It has been estimated that 5 to 150 gallons of fresh water per milk cow is used in the milking center. More common values are 10 to 30 gallons of fresh water per milk cow. The quantity and quality of water discharge from the milk parlor must be accurately measured. In many cases, the waste deposited in the milk barn is processed in a separate waste management system.

Open Lot

Fig. Open Lot System

In open lot systems the manure is deposited on the ground and scraped into piles. The manure is removed infrequently (once or twice a year). A significant amount of manure degradation occurs resulting in greenhouse gas emissions. In many cases, the open lot degradation produces manure that has little or no net energy value.

DIGESTING DAIRY MANURE

A variety of high rate anaerobic processes, which retain bacteria have been developed to treat soluble organic industrial wastes. These "high rate" digesters have reduced hydraulic detention times from 20 days to a few hours. They include anaerobic filters, both upflow and downflow, and a variety of biofilm processes such as fixed film packed bed reactors. Bacteria are retained in these reactors as films on carriers such as plastic beads, or sand, or on support media of all configurations. The waste washes past the retained bacteria. The bacteria convert the soluble constituents to gas but have little opportunity to hydrolyze and degrade the particulate solids, unless the solids become attached to the biomass.

These reactors are *not* suitable for digesting dairy waste since they are not effective in converting particulate solids to gas and tend to clog while digesting dairy manure slurries. These high rate reactors can treat the soluble component of dairy waste. But only a fraction of the available energy will be recovered.

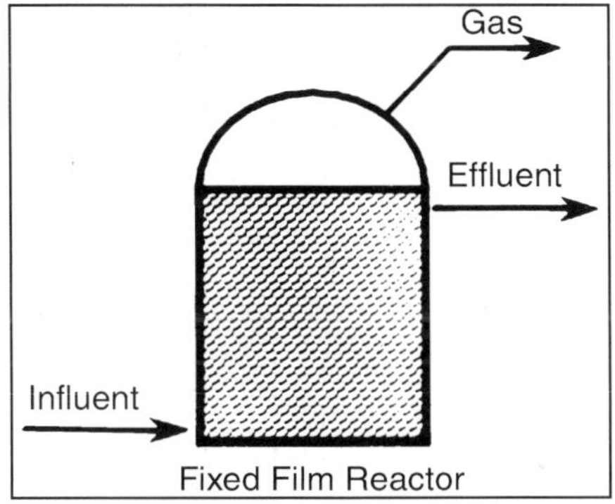

Fig. Packed Fixed Film Reactor

A widely used industrial waste anaerobic digester is the UASB or "Upflow Anaerobic Sludge Blanket", reactor. The process stores the anaerobic consortia as pellets, approximately the size of a pea.

The upflow anaerobic sludge blanket reactor (UASB) is widely used in industrial treatment processes throughout the world. It is an extremely effective process for converting soluble organic materials, such as sugar to methane gas. It has not been used for processing dairy waste since it is ineffective in converting solids to gas. It is primarily used to convert non-particulate or soluble waste to gas.

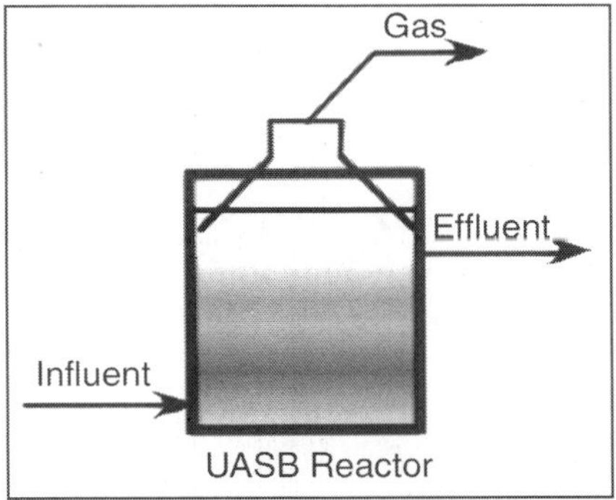

Fig. Upflow Anaerobic Sludge Blanket Reactor

The anaerobic baffled reactor is a horizontal version of the upflow anaerobic sludge blanket reactor. Both store large quantities of anaerobic bacteria as pellets approximately the size of a pea. Unfortunately, these very successful anaerobic reactors are not effective in digesting particulate waste.

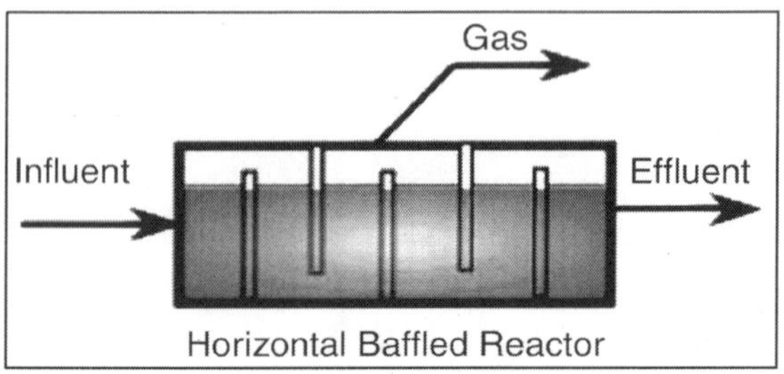

Fig. Baffled Reactor

Particulate solids tend to settle in the horizontal baffled reactor (HBR) while organic fibres will form a mat on the surface. There are no known instances of the HBR being used for the treatment of dairy waste. Unless the dairy waste was thoroughly screened and all particulate matter removed the HBR would tend to become clogged. The removal of solids by screening and gravity sedimentation will eliminate up to 80% of the energy generating potential from dairy waste.

Processes that can be used for Digesting Dairy Manure

The processes that have been used for digesting dairy waste can be subdivided into high rate and low rate processes. Low rate processes consist of covered anaerobic lagoons, plug flow digesters, and mesophilic completely mixed digesters. High rate reactors include the thermophilic completely mixed digesters, anaerobic contact digesters, and hybrid contact/ fixed film reactors.

Anaerobic Lagoons (Very Low Rate)

Anaerobic lagoons are covered ponds. Manure enters at one end and the effluent is removed at the other. The lagoons operate at psychrophilic, or ground temperatures. Consequently, the reaction rate is affected by seasonal variations in temperature.

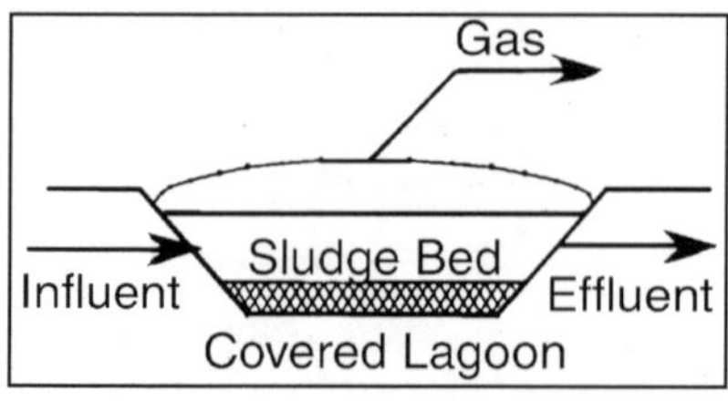

Fig. Anaerobic Lagoons

Since the reaction temperature is quite low, the rate of conversion of solids to gas is also low. In addition, solids tend to settle to the bottom where decomposition occurs in a sludge bed. Little contact of bacteria with the bulk liquid occurs.

The biomass concentration is low, resulting in very low solids conversion to gas (High F/M ratio with poor growth rates at low temperatures). Little or no mixing occurs. Consequently, lagoon utilization is poor. Anaerobic lagoons have been used to treat parlor and free stall flush water. Gas production rates have been low and seasonal. Solids may be screened and removed prior to entering the lagoon.

A considerable amount of energy potential is lost with the removal of particulate solids. The advantage of anaerobic lagoons is the lowcost. The low cost is offset by the lower energy production and poor effluent quality. Periodically the covered lagoons must be cleaned at considerable cost. Nuisance odours may be generated while cleaning the lagoons.

Completely Mixed Digesters (Low Rate)

The most common form of an anaerobic digester is the completely mixed reactor. Most sewage treatment plants and many industrial treatment plants use a completely mixed reactor to convert waste to gas. The completely mixed reactor is a tank that is heated and mixed. Most completely mixed reactors operate in the mesophilic range.

All of the initial anaerobic digesters used to treat dairy manure were completely mixed mesophilic digesters. The cost of mixing is high, especially if sand, silt, and floating materials, present in the waste stream, must be suspended throughout the digestion period. Some completely mixed reactors operate in a thermophilic range where sufficient energy is available to heat to reactor.

Highly concentrated readily degradable waste is required in order to generate sufficient heat for the thermophilic range of operation. Completely mixed thermophilic digesters are used in the EEC to treat animal manure. Recently, completely mixed thermophilic digesters were proposed in Oregon to treat dairy manure.

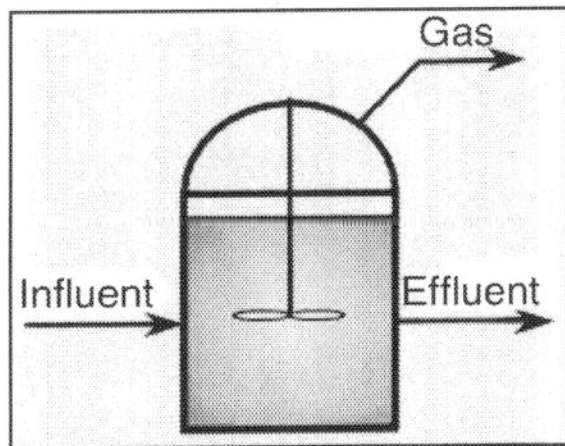

Fig. Completely Mixed Reactor

Most completely mixed reactors are heated with spiral flow heat exchangers. These heat exchangers apply hot water to one side of the spiral and the anaerobic slurry to the other. The spiral heat exchangers have proven to be a successful method of efficiently transferring heat. Completely mixed reactors can be constructed of a variety of materials. In the U.S. most completely mixed reactors have a low profile with a diameter greater than the height.

Some municipal digesters in the U.S., and most in Europe have an egg shape with a height much greater than the diameter. The egg shape enhances mixing while eliminating much of the stratification. Completely mixed reactors can have fixed covers, floating covers, or gas holding covers.

Most municipal digesters have floating covers. Floating covers are more expensive than fixed covers. Mixing can be accomplished with a variety of gas mixers, mechanical mixers, and draft tubes with mechanical mixers or simply recirculation pumps. The most efficient mixing device in terms of power consumed per gallon mixed is the mechanical mixer. Most municipal digesters are intensely mixed to reduce the natural stratification that occurs in a low profile tank.

A large amount of evidence has been accumulated over the past 10 years indicating that intense mixing may inhibit the bacterial consortia. But, intense mixing is required to keep sands and silts in suspension. The advantage of the completely mixed reactor is that it is a proven technology that achieves reasonable conversion of solids to gas. It can be applied to the treatment of slurry waste such as dairy manure.

The disadvantage of the completely mixed reactor is the high cost of installation, and the energy cost associated with mixing the digester. The completely mixed conventional anaerobic digester is a biomass growth based system. The process requires a constant conversion of a portion of the feed solids to anaerobic bacteria rather than gas. Since anaerobic bacteria are constantly wasted from the process, new bacteria must be produced to replace the lost bacteria.

If the bacteria are retained, the portion of the waste that would have been converted to new bacterial cells will be converted to gas. For this reason, bacterial growth based systems are not as efficient as retained biomass systems. The advantage of the completely mixed thermophilic reactor is the rapid conversion of solids to gas and biomass. Some claim that the rate of conversion is three times greater with thermophilic reactors. Consequently, the HRT can be lower and the gas production greater. The disadvantage of the thermophilic reactor is the energy required to heat cold dairy manure to thermophilic temperatures.

Additional costs are incurred in tank insulation and heat exchangers. Sufficient heat may not be available from the gas produced unless the solids are highly concentrated. Thermophilic digestion of dairy manure cannot be used with manure diluted with parlor or flush water since sufficient energy will not be available to meet the heat requirements. In addition, the higher temperature thermophilic reactors increase end product inhibition, especially ammonia and organic acids.

Plug Flow Digesters (Low Rate)

The plug flow anaerobic digester is the simplest form of anaerobic digestion. Consequently, it is the least expensive. The plug flow digester can be a horizontal or vertical reactor. The waste enters on one side of the reactor and exits on the other.

Since bacteria are not conserved, a portion of the waste must be converted to new bacteria, which are subsequently wasted with the effluent. Since the plug flow digester is a growth based system, it is less efficient than a retained biomass system. It converts less waste to gas. Plug flow systems are subject to stratification wherein the sands and silts settle to the bottom and the organic fibres migrate to surface. The stratification can be partially inhibited by maintaining a relatively high solids concentration in the digester. Periodically, solids must be removed from the plug flow reactor. Since there is no easy way of removing the solids, the reactor must be shut down during the cleaning period.

The cost of cleaning can be considerable. Since the solids concentration must be maintained at high levels, dilute milk barn waste is normally excluded from the digester. Plug flow reactors are normally heated by a hot water piping system within the reactor. The hot water piping system can complicate the periodic cleaning of the reactor.

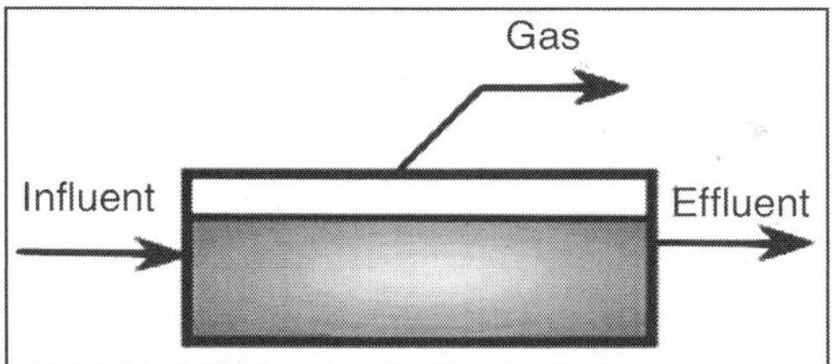

Fig. Plug Flow Reactor

The plug flow reactor is a simple, economical system. Applications are limited to concentrated dairy manure containing a minor amount of sand and silt. If stratification occurs because of a dilute waste or excess sand, significant operating costs will be incurred.

Sequencing Batch Reactors (High Rate)

A sequencing batch reactor is a contact digester, which utilizes the same tank for digestion as well as separation. In a sequencing batch reactor the same tank is used to digest the waste and separate the biomass from the effluent liquor.

Generally, two or more tanks are used. The tanks are operated in a fill and draw mode. The separation is accomplished by gravity. Consequently, a more dilute, screened waste is treated. Laboratory scale sequencing batch reactors have been used to digest dairy manure.

Contact Stabilization Reactors (High Rate)

The anaerobic contact stabilization process is a more efficient contact process. Burke used the anaerobic contact stabilization process for the digestion of both dairy manure and potato waste. The process has the advantage of efficiently converting slowly degradable materials such as cellulose in a highly concentrated reactor. Organic materials, which can be degraded rapidly, are digested in the contact reactor. The bacteria and slowly degradable organics are removed and degraded in a highly concentrated reactor.

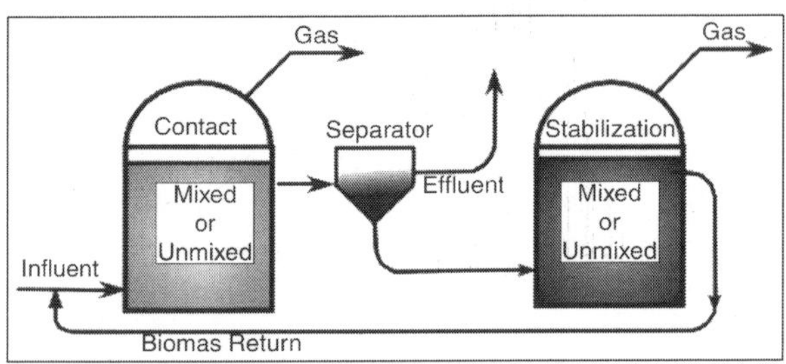

Fig. Contact Stabilization Reactor

Contact Digesters (High Rate)

The contact reactor is a high rate process that retains bacterial biomass by separating and concentrating the solids in a separate reactor and returning the solids to the influent. More of the degradable waste can be converted to gas since a substantial portion of the bacterial mass is conserved. The contact digester can be either completely mixed or plug flow. It can be operated in the thermophilic or mesophilic range. The contact reactor can treat both dilute and concentrated waste provided the separator can concentrate the digester effluent solids sufficiently to enhance the process.

A wide variety of separators have been tested over the past 30 years. Initially gravity separators (settling tanks), or solids thickeners were used. It was soon discovered that the solids could not be sufficiently concentrated in a gravity separator without degassing to remove the gas bubbles attached to the solids. Actively fermenting digester effluent containing gas bubbles floated rather than settled in the separator.

Lamella or plate separators have also been used to concentrate the biomass after degassing. Both of these gravity-settling techniques are not effective for concentrated digester solids. Gravity separation techniques are effective with dilute waste following a completely mixed reactor. Separation requires several days of detention. The completely mixed digester will prevent stratification. The effluent is then allowed to separate by gravity in the separation reactor.

The digester solids concentration should be less than 2.5% for gravity separation to be used. Long separator detention times are required. Mechanical separation devices have been tested to reduce the detention time required by gravity separation. Centrifuges, gravity belts, membranes, and other mechanical separators have been used with limited success. These disruptive devices have been shown to inhibit the bacterial consortia and thus limit the effectiveness of the contact process. Burke used gas flotation to separate and concentrate the digester effluent for the efficient and tranquil recovery of the anaerobic consortia.

The process has been used for the digestion of dairy manure, sewage sludge, and potato waste. It has been shown to be effective for concentrating the biomass from actively fermenting digester liquors without the need for degassing. The process has been referred to as the AGF or "anoxic gas flotation" process. Gas flotation can achieve significantly greater biomass concentrations than gravity separation without the adverse consequences associated with disruptive separation techniques.

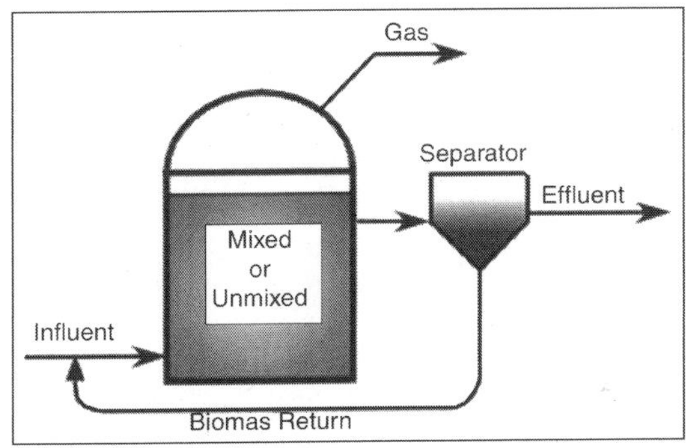

Fig. Contact Reactor

Gas flotation can also remove enzymes, organic acids, and other products of digestion that cannot be removed through settling or other mechanical means. Finally, gas flotation can be performed in a non-mechanical manner, which is simple to operate and maintain. During the contact process, refractory organic and inorganic solids accumulate within the system.

The accumulated sands, silts, and non-degradable organic fibres dictate the rate of solids wasting. Wasting the nonbiodegradable solids causes the loss of bacterial mass and reduced process efficiency. The anaerobic contact process can utilize mechanical separating devices to remove refractory solids from the digestion system.

Phased Digesters

Both acid phased and temperature phased digestion have been used to convert municipal sludge to gas. Acid phased digestion takes advantage of the fact that the acid forming bacteria have a much higher growth rate than the methanogens. Consequently, the initial reactor can be much smaller than the subsequent methane producing digester. Acid phased digestion offers greater efficiency in the size of the anaerobic digesters. Acid phased digestion has not been applied to dairy waste.

Temperature phased digestion has been applied to the digestion of sewage sludge. The initial digester is operated in the thermophilic mode followed by a second digester, which is operated in the mesophilic mode. In the first thermophilic digester, pathogens are destroyed. In the second mesophilic digester, the mesophilic bacteria consume the organic acids created in the thermophilic reactor. Consequently, the odours associated with a thermophilic effluent are eliminated while achieving the desired pathogen destruction.

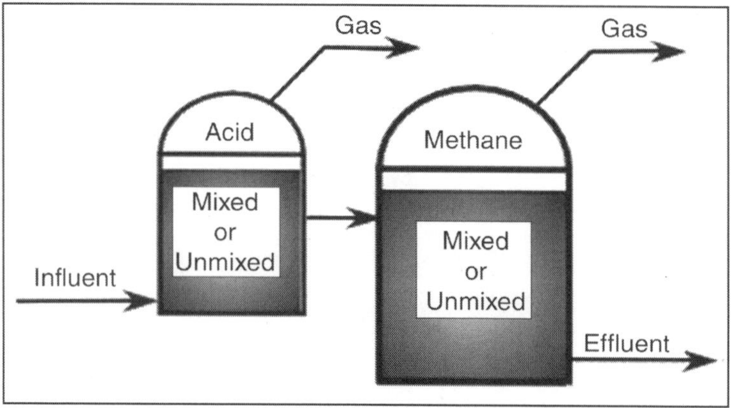

Fig. Acid Phased Digester

Temperature phased digestion has been used to digest dairy manure. In addition it must be pointed out that completely mixed reactors are not completely effective in removing pathogens.

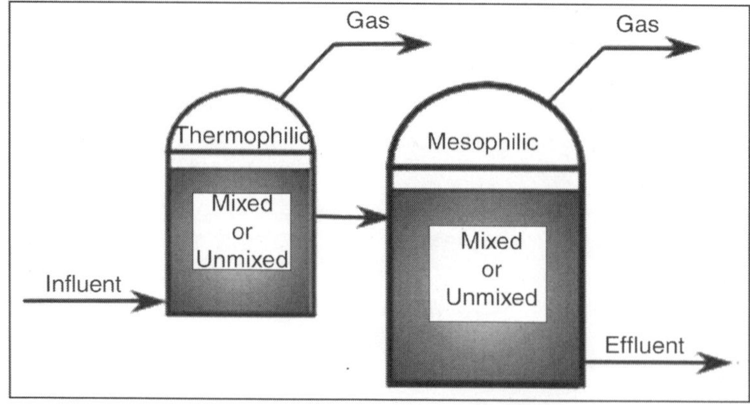

Fig. Temperature Phased Digester

Hybrid Processes

A number of hybrid processes have been developed and applied to many different kinds of waste materials. The hybrid processes incorporate a combination of the previously described configurations.

ANAEROBIC DIGESTION

Anaerobic digestion is the breakdown of organic material by a microbial population that lives in an oxygen free environment. Anaerobic means literally "without air". When organic matter is decomposed in an anaerobic environment the bacteria produce a mixture of methane and carbon dioxide gas. Anaerobic digestion treats waste by converting putrid organic materials to carbon dioxide and methane gas.

This gas is referred to as biogas. The biogas can be used to produce both electrical power and heat. The conversion of solids to biogas results in a much smaller quantity of solids that must be disposed. During the anaerobic treatment process, organic nitrogen compounds are converted to ammonia, sulfur compounds are converted to hydrogen sulfide, phosphorus to orthophosphates, and calcium, magnesium, and sodium are converted to a variety of salts.

Through proper operation, the inorganic constituents can be converted to a variety of beneficial products. The end products of anaerobic digestion are natural gas (methane) for energy production, heat produced from energy production, a nutrient rich organic slurry, and other marketable inorganic products.

The effluent containing particulate and soluble organic and inorganic materials can be separated into its particulate and soluble constituents. The particulate solids can be sold or exported from the dairy while the nutrient rich liquids are applied to the land.

BACTERIAL CONSORTIA

Anaerobic digestion is carried out by a group, or consortia of bacteria, working together to convert organic matter to gas and inorganic constituents. The first step of anaerobic digestion is the breakdown of particulate matter to soluble organic constituents that can be processed through the bacterial cell wall. Hydrolysis, or the liquification of insoluble materials is the rate-limiting step in anaerobic digestion of waste slurries.

This step is carried out by a variety of bacteria through the release of extra-cellular enzymes that reside in close proximity to the bacteria. The soluble organic materials that are produced through hydrolysis consist of sugars, fatty acids, and amino acids.

Those soluble constituents are converted to carbon dioxide and a variety of short chain organic acids by acid forming bacteria. Other groups of bacteria reduce the hydrogen toxicity by scavenging hydrogen to produce ammonia, hydrogen sulfide, and methane. A group of methanogens converts acetic acid to methane gas. A wide variety of physical, chemical, and biological reactions take place. The bacterial consortia catalyze these reactions.

Consequently, the most important factor in converting waste to gas is the bacterial consortia. The bacterial consortia are essentially the "bio-enzymes" that accomplish the desired treatment. A poorly developed or stressed bacterial consortium will not provide the desired conversion of waste to gas and other beneficial products.

QUALITATIVE ANALYSIS OF ANAEROBIC PROCESSES

In order to assess the various digester configurations one must define their limitations for dairy waste digestion.

Solids Concentration Limitations

The ability to process a variety of manure concentrations is important. Even though the solids may be collected in a concentrated form, there will be times when the solids become diluted.

The inverse is also true. The dilute parlor waste may become concentrated for variety of reasons. The mesophilic and thermophilic completely mixed processes and the contact process can handle a variety of influent manure concentrations. Their operating performance is not limited by the manure concentration.

On the other hand the plug flow digester and the anaerobic lagoon are limited by the influent manure concentration. The plug flow digester will stratify at low feed concentrations. The anaerobic lagoon will accumulate non-degraded solids at high influent solids concentrations.

Digestion of the Entire Waste Stream

The thermophilic and mesophilic completely mixed reactors and the plug flow contact process can digest the entire waste stream since neither are limited by the concentration of the influent waste. Plug flow reactors will be able to process the concentrated or scraped manure. Plug flow reactors will not be able to economically process the parlor waste or a mixture of the parlor and scraped waste.

The anaerobic lagoon can process primarily liquid waste after the removal of fibres and particulate solids. The current practice of screening fibres and settling solids to remove particulate matter is not compatible with achieving high energy yields through anaerobic digestion. It is generally accepted that screening will remove at lease 15% of the influent COD. Recent analysis has shown that screening and sedimentation will remove 60% or more of the COD that could be converted to gas. Solids separation should follow, rather than precede anaerobic digestion.

Foreign Material Processing

High concentrations of sand and silt are not compatible with the plug flow digester or the anaerobic lagoon. Completely mixed reactors can operate with minor concentrations of foreign material by maintaining the material in suspension through intense mixing. The contact process incorporating grit removal as described by Burke is not limited by the concentration of foreign material.

Odour Control

Most properly operated anaerobic digesters will eliminate the generation of odours from the site. However, both plug flow anaerobic digesters and the anaerobic lagoon must be periodically cleaned. During the cleaning process odours are generated.

The thermophilic completely mixed reactors produce an effluent that is far more odourous than mesophically digested waste. Contact and completely mixed digesters significantly reduce odours and may *not* require cleaning, especially if refractory inorganic and organic solids removal is practiced.

Stability, Flexibility, and Reliability

Each type of anaerobic reactor imposes requirements for its proper operation. The inability to meet those requirements, such as operating temperature, may result in process failure. The mesophilic process is more reliable than the thermophilic process because of the greater risk associated with meeting the thermophilic temperature requirements utilizing a cold waste at cold temperatures.

The anaerobic process has been labeled an unreliable process because of frequent toxic upsets. The contact process is a more reliable process in preventing process failure, foaming, and loss of biomass. Retained biomass systems are the least likely to fail because of a large quantity and diversity of the biocatalyst in the digestion system. The addition of elutriation, or the washing of biological solids to remove inhibitory products, adds further stability to the process.

The contact stabilization process is the least likely to be upset by changes in hydraulic flow, or organic loading. Since mixing is essential to any completely mixed process, mixing failures, or inadequacies may result in poor performance. The plug flow contact process also poses little risk of failure due to mixing inadequacies or solids accumulation in the digester. The complexity of the process will also affect its reliability.

The thermophilic digestion of dairy manure must incorporate a complex heating and heat recovery system. Its reliability will be less than a system that does not have such complexity. The contact process and the contact stabilization process are also more complex systems. They have more of an opportunity to fail. Redundant equipment and robust controls are essential to improving the reliability of complex systems.

Nutrient Concentration and Retention

The process of anaerobic digestion will convert nutrients from an organic form to an inorganic form. In plug flow, completely mixed, and thermophilic reactors the quantity of nutrients entering the reactor equals the quantity of nutrients exiting the reactor.

However, in retained biomass digesters such as the contact process, sequencing batch reactors, and fixed film reactors, nutrients may be concentrated in a separate waste solids stream. Dugba demonstrated that the effluent from a sequencing batch reactor contained less than 50 per cent of the influent phosphorus. The balance of the phosphorus was concentrated in the biosolids.

Burke demonstrated the retention and concentration of 90 per cent of the influent phosphorus and 43 per cent of the influent total nitrogen in the waste solids that was only 1/5 of the influent volume. The ability to concentrate nutrients is an important characteristic of the selected anaerobic process since it provides the dairy operator with the control necessary to manage nutrient application to the land.

Additional Substrate Processing

Hobson studied the effect of adding cellulose to dairy manure. His research indicated that the volatile solids conversion to gas would be substantially improved through the addition of cellulose. At a 16-day hydraulic retention time the volatile solids conversion to gas increased from 30 per cent with no cellulose to 51 per cent with a manure containing six per cent cellulose. Many commercial digesters supplement the influent with food waste or food processing waste.

Collection of tipping fees improves the economic viability of anaerobic facilities. The Tillamook project in Oregon proposed to supplement the influent waste with municipal solid waste to increase revenues. The proposed Myrtle Point project in Oregon may treat milk-processing waste to increase revenues. The ability to treat a wide variety of influent substrates, and thereby enhance the economics, is an important process characteristic. The completely mixed and contact processes can process a variety of added substrates.

Energy Production

The quantity of energy produced from each gallon of waste processed is strictly a function of the percentage conversion of volatile solids to gas. Each pound of volatile solids destroyed will produce 5.62 cubic feet of methane. Each cubic foot of methane will contain 1000 Btu's of energy. Therefore, each pound of volatile solids converted will produce 5620 Btu's of energy.

At 35 per cent conversion efficiency, each pound of volatile solids destroyed will produce 0.58 kWh of energy. It is therefore important to look at the conversion efficiencies of the various anaerobic processes. As pointed out earlier, the conversion of volatile solids to gas is a function of the organic loading to the digester. Higher percentage conversions to gas are achieved at lower organic loadings. Low loadings however, translate into larger digestion facilities.

However, it is possible to achieve a higher volatile solids conversion to gas by increasing the digester loading while maintaining a higher biomass concentration in the digester. In other words, the food to microorganism (F/M) ratio remains low resulting in a higher rate of conversion. The rate of volatile solids conversion to gas is related to the type of anaerobic digester used.

Conventional completely mixed and plug flow digesters, which do not retain biomass, should have comparable volatile solids destructions. Anaerobic lagoons will have a lower rate of conversion, while high rate retained biomass reactors will have higher rates of solids conversion to gas. Each is discussed separately below.

Conventional Digesters

A review of recent dairy waste anaerobic digestion studies has established that most engineers anticipate a 50 per cent conversion of volatile solids to gas. The planned Three-Mile Farm (Oregon) dairy waste *thermophilic* anaerobic digestion facility is expected to achieve a 50 per cent volatile solids conversion to gas. The C. Bar M. (Idaho) *plug flow* anaerobic digester facility anticipated a 50 per cent conversion of dairy waste volatile solids to gas.

The recently completed Myrtle Point (Oregon) feasibility study utilizing the *gravity separation contact process* anticipated a 50 per cent conversion of dairy waste volatile solids to gas. Relatively high loading rates were anticipated in each case. The organic loading rates varied between 5.6 and 6.4 kg per cubic meter per day. The available literature does not support such high volatile solids conversions to gas at high organic loading rates.

A summary is as follows:

- "The Monroe Honour Farm *completely mixed anaerobic digester* achieved a maximum of 40 per cent volatile solids conversion to gas at a loading rate of 6 kg/m^3/d. Jewel operated a *plug flow anaerobic digesters* at an organic loading rate of 2.37 and achieved a 32.4 per cent conversion to volatile solids to gas."

Converse operated both thermophilic and mesophilic completely mixed anaerobic digesters at a loading rate of 4.2 kg/m^3/d. Both thermophilic and mesophilic digesters achieved a 41 per cent conversion of volatile solids to gas. Bryant on the other hand, operated *completely mixed thermophilic* digesters at loadings of 6.5 to 10.78 kg/m^3/d and achieved 50 per cent volatile solids conversion to gas. Recently, Ahring reported a 28% volatile solids conversion in a thermophilic digester operated at a loading of 3 kg/m^3/d. Ghaly operated a dairy waste completely mixed mesophilic digester at a loading of 3.6 kg/m^3/d. He achieved a 46 per cent conversion of volatile solids to gas.

Qasim operated a completely mixed mesophilic digester at an organic loading rate of 3.2 kg/m^3/d and achieved a 52.9 per cent volatile solids conversion to gas. Echiegu operated a completely mixed dairy waste digester at an organic loading rate of 2 kg/m^3/d but only achieved a 40 per cent conversion.

Robbins also operated a completely mixed mesophilic digester at an organic loading rate of 2.6 kg per cubic meter per day that achieved a 30 per cent conversion of volatile solids to gas. Hills and Kayhanian operated a completely mixed mesophilic digester at a 1.8 kg/m^3/d loading that achieved a 31 per cent volatile solids destruction and a 38 per cent conversion at 1.0 kg/m^3/d.

On the other hand, Pigg operated a completely mixed mesophilic anaerobic digester at an organic loading rate of 1.0 kg/m^3/d and achieved a peak volatile solids conversion to gas of 64 per cent. As can be observed the published literature values are highly variable. The results generally confirm Smith's conclusion that mesophilic digesters can achieve a 40% conversion of volatile solids at a loading of 5.7 kg/m^3/d.

Better conversions can be achieved at lower loadings. Thermophilic reactors appear to achieve greater conversions at high loadings while mesophilic reactors appear to achieve greater conversions at lower loadings. Lusk provided information on the performance of full-scale plug flow and completely mixed anaerobic digesters treating dairy manure. The loading and per cent volatile solids conversion can be calculated from the information he presented. Figure below presents the results of the analysis of the Lusk data.

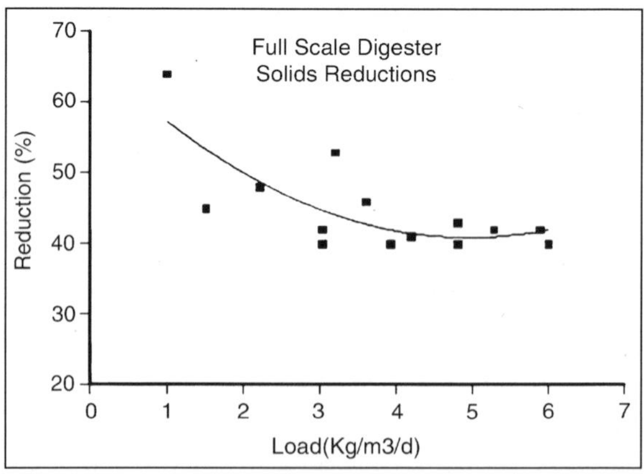

Fig. Full Scale Mesophilic Digester vs. Reductions

Lagoons

California Polytechnic State University in San Luis Obispo constructed an anaerobic lagoon to treat flush waste from a 350 animal dairy. The screening system removed 15 per cent of the manure volatile solids. The lagoon was projected to achieve a 35 per cent volatile solids conversion to gas at a loading of 0.04 $kg/m^3/d$.

14

Significance of Milk and Dairy Products for Humans

CONSUMPTION OF MILK HYGIENE

Milk should be handled with care. There are several factors that can make milk go off and become unsuitable for further consumption.

These include:

- The presence of too many micro-organisms in the milk
- Contamination by diseased animals (tuberculosis, brucellosis) and/or people
- Bacterial and/or chemical conversion of certain substances in the milk
- Contamination of the milk with antibiotics (used for treatment of diseased animals), disinfectants, pesticides and so on.

The factors always cause some deterioration of milk. In some cases it is only the flavour that is affected, but usually the structure and smell of milk also change. In the case of contamination with antibiotics and disinfectants, the milk's appearance does not change, but fermentation, which is necessary for processing the milk, is inhibited. As suggested, first discuss the way micro-organisms cause the deterioration of milk. Then precautions which can be taken to minimise the impact of these factors will be explained, and some suggestions for cleaning and disinfection will be given.

DETERIORATION DUE TO MICRO-ORGANISMS

Bacteria, yeasts and moulds are all called: micro-organisms. Micro-organisms are very small and cannot be seen with the naked eye. They are found everywhere in nature: in the air, water, and soil and also in food and milk. Micro-organisms can multiply very rapidly. Milk in the udder of a healthy animal contains almost no microorganisms (aside from lactic acid bacteria). After the milk leaves the udder contamination with, sometimes harmful, micro-organisms will take place during milking, milk handling, transport and storage.

Fig. Diverse Sources of Contamination

a. Shows badly cleaned utensils contaminating milk;
b. Improper milking also a source of contamination;
c. Shows multiplication of micro-organisms during storage;
d. Heating kills the micro-organisms

Milk may be contaminated with micro-organisms originating from the skin of the animal, the milker's hands, the milking utensils or the air. Most micro-organisms are not harmful, but some can cause diseases like salmonella infection, dysentery, tuberculosis (in man and in animals), diphtheria and typhoid. These disease-causing microorganisms are called pathogenic bacteria. Through inadequate hygiene, diseases can be transmitted from person or animal to person.

Micro-organisms can multiply very rapidly in milk. Temperature plays an important role in the life of micro-organisms. Their growth can start at a temperature of about 4°C. It is therefore very important to store milk or milk products at a temperature no higher than 4°C; otherwise deterioration will take place rapidly. Above 20°C, bacteria multiply at an incredible speed.

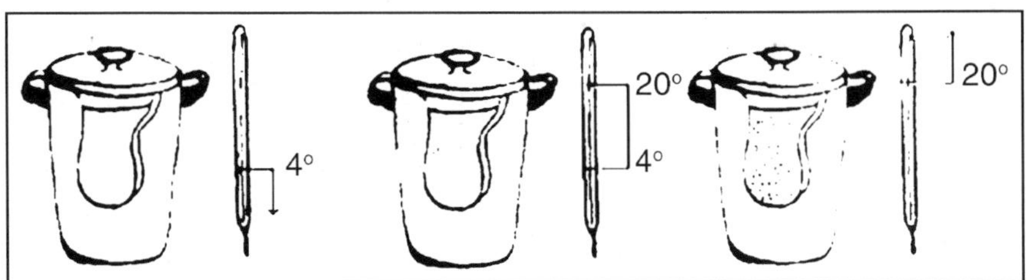

Fig. Temperature and Deterioration

Most micro-organisms are killed during pasteurisation, *e.g.* at a temperature above 63°C for a period of at least 30 minutes. But a few, the so-called spore-forming bacteria, will survive more intense heating. They can give problems like off flavours and coagulation in pasteurised milk.

Yeasts and Moulds

Yeasts are micro-organisms that can ferment sugars into alcohol, gas and other substances. They are about 5-10 times larger than bacteria. Reproduction usually takes place through budding. Yeasts usually grow in an acid environment; they need oxygen and they can withstand rather high concentrations of acids. In dairy products, yeasts are usually found in soured products like sour milk or buttermilk, sour whey, butter, and curd and on the surface of cheese.

When present in large numbers, they produce gas and they cause undesirable off flavours of the product. Moulds are string-like micro-organisms. The fine threads, called mycelium, are large enough to be seen with the naked eye. To develop they need atmospheric oxygen, and they thrive best in humid and acid conditions. Moulds multiply by forming spores. These float easily through the air and can often be found on poorly maintained ceilings and walls.

Their mobility makes them an important source of infection. Moulds can be seen on the surface of butter or cheese in the form of coloured spots. For some soft cheeses (like Camembert and Brie) moulds are essential for ripening. In general, moulds are harmless, but some produce poisonous toxins (mycotoxins), such as aflatoxin in peanut products. Cells and spores of moulds and yeasts are destroyed by pasteurisation (heating the milk 30 minutes at 63°C or 20 seconds at 72°C).

Bacteria

Bacteria are single-cell micro-organisms that multiply by cell division. Raw milk and many dairy products contain many different kinds of bacteria. Environmental conditions (such as acidity, temperature, humidity or amount of oxygen) can change, making conditions less attractive for one group of bacteria but at the same time creating optimal conditions for another type. This is why some families of bacteria will always be found in milk or dairy products (lactic acid bacteria).

An exception must be noted, which is dried products like milk powder. Micro-organisms cannot grow without water and therefore the number of bacteria in uncontaminated milk powder will be low. Bacteria found in milk can be divided into two groups: useful and harmful. Lactic acid bacteria (*e.g.* Streptococcus lactis) are useful. They produce lactic acid, which is not harmful and gives milk a fresh, sour taste. Moreover lactic acid is a good preservative for the sour products.

Pathogenic bacteria (those that cause diseases in humans) cannot grow in acid products. When producing certain dairy products like soured milk, yoghurt and cheese, good use is made of these specific properties. Sometimes milk is spoiled by the growth of bacteria that do not produce lactic acid. In this case, certain disease-causing bacteria can develop and whey separates from the milk. This usually happens after long storage of pasteurised milk. The smell is unpleasant and the taste bitter. Such milk should not be consumed.

CONTAMINATION OF MILK WITH EXTRANEOUS MATTER

Extraneous substances must be prevented from entering into the milk. These can be dangerous to one's health or cause unpleasant flavours and smells, reducing the suitability of milk for further processing. Some examples are cleaning and disinfecting agents, medicine, pesticides and pieces of metal or glass. The feed given to animals, such as some weeds, onions and cabbage, can also influence the taste of the milk. This can be avoided by feeding the animals after milking. Good hygiene can reduce deterioration.

HYGIENIC PRODUCTION, STORAGE AND PROCESSING OF MILK

Contamination occurs when micro-organisms enter into the milk.

Possible sources of contamination during production, storage and processing are:

- Inflammation of the udder (mastitis)
- The animal itself: skin of teats and udder
- Conditions at the milking place (floor, dung, dust, dirty water, etc.)
- The person milking
- Utensils and equipment used during processing
- The air and environment

It is no easy task to keep micro-organisms out of milk. Much depends on the person who is milking, the care taken of the animals and the cleanliness of the utensils.

If everything is well sanitised and kept clean, relatively few micro-organisms will enter into the milk. Good hygiene is of major importance. In addition, milk-if not used or processed immediately-should be cooled after milking and kept cool.

Good hygiene measures therefore:

- Prevent contamination of the milk.
- Prevent bacterial growth through good refrigeration of the milk.

Hygiene during Milking

There are several possible causes of contamination during milking. In a normal, healthy cow very low numbers of bacteria are found inside the udder and the teats. Cows possess various mechanisms to prevent the entry of bacteria.

To avoid problems while milking, it is important that an animal become accustomed to the activity. It will then know that it will be milked, and will react positively to it. Such positive behaviour can start if, for instance, it hears milk cans clanging, feels its udder being cleaned, etc. Then the animal is easier to milk and gives more milk.

Stress and unrest make the cows move too much and kick; consequently more dirt and manure can enter into the milk. When a cow has an udder infection (mastitis), its milk will be contaminated with the bacteria that cause the udder infection, and that may produce pus and sometimes blood. Milk from these animals should not be used in any way. Mastitis can be prevented by maintaining good hygiene and avoiding injury to the teats during milking.

An infected udder is not always easy to see. When an udder infection occurs, it is advisable to remove milk from the udder very frequently (*e.g.* every 3 hours by hand). The number of microorganisms in the udder is thus reduced. Be aware, however, that milking an infected udder by machine or by hand is often painful for the animal. The animal will kick frequently and this can be an important source of contamination of healthy cows. Bacteria can be transferred from the skin or teats to the milk, even with healthy dairy cattle.

It is therefore important to clean the udder before milking. Wipe the udder clean with a dry, clean, preferably disposable cloth to prevent infection. If the teats or udder are really dirty, they must first be washed with clean, hand-warm water and a clean cloth and then dried with a clean towel. Cleaning the udder improves the cleanliness of the milk and makes milking easier. Skin and hair can also be sources of infection. Do not feed animals first before milking, it may create a lot of dust. The floor is clean, and be careful when clearing dung, mud or dust.

A clean, well-illuminated milking place and fresh surrounding air are essential to maintaining good hygiene. Insects such as flies and cockroaches can also be sources of infection. Try to control them as they can carry many bacteria and viruses. When milking, the milk is caught in a pail or bucket. Dirty milking equipment is the main source of infection of milk. If residues of milk remain in the equipment because of improper cleaning and drying, bacteria will develop in these residues. These bacteria are already accustomed to the milk and will multiply rather quickly during transport and storage of milk in the equipment.

Use pails and buckets that are smooth on the inside, for instance seamless metal buckets. All milking equipment should be thoroughly cleaned immediately after each use. Use soap or other detergents if necessary. Make sure that the water used is clean. If you are in doubt, boil it for several minutes or add chlorine. Very important: after cleaning, the equipment should be stored upside down in such a way that the inside of the buckets and cans dry. This prevents the remaining bacteria from growing.

The person milking plays the most important part in maintaining proper hygiene during production. He or she keeps an eye on the condition of the animal, chooses the milking place and cleans all the equipment. He or she should have clean hands and wear clean clothes. If the milker suffers from tuberculosis, salmonella infection, dysentery or some other disease, the risk of contamination of the milk becomes very high; it would be wise to have somebody else take over. This is also the case if the milker has open wounds or ulcers.

Hygiene during Storage and Processing

By now you should know that milk should be processed as quickly as possible after milking and that it should be properly stored in order to minimise its chances of spoiling. It is best to filter fresh milk through a filter or clean cloth.

This will remove visible dirt that might have entered into the milk. Clean or replace the cloth during filtering or filter the milk several times. The cloth should be thoroughly cleaned after use and then left to dry in the sun. In tropical conditions, raw milk, *i.e.* non-pasteurised milk, goes off within a few hours. It must therefore be kept cool and quickly pasteurised and again cooled to a temperature of 4°C if possible. Properly pasteurised and cooled milk can be kept for a few days, even in a warm climate. If you are not able to cool milk below 10°C, then do not mix different batches.

Even if the older milk is still good, you will end up with an increase in bacterial growth and reduction of the overall quality. Use clean equipment for storage. Containers that are clear, such as glass, should be stored in the dark as light reduces the quality of milk. Clean your equipment with clean water.

Cleaning and Disinfection

Utensils must be cleaned in such a way that all dirt, food residues, feed and micro-organisms are removed from the surface of the equipment. Dirty saucepans, jugs, milking equipment and utensils should be cleaned immediately after use.

Washing soda (sodium carbonate) dissolved in hot water is an excellent cleaning agent. It may be useful to disinfect equipment in order to kill any remaining harmful micro-organisms. You can use a chloride solution such as bleach (sodium hypochlorite).

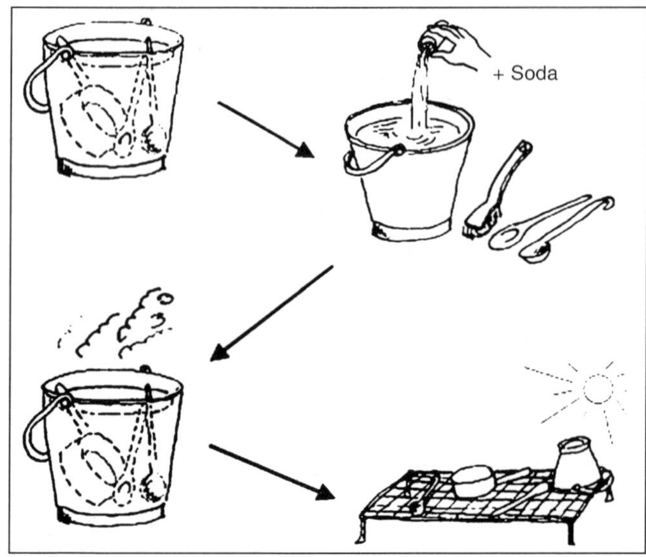

Fig. Cleaning Utensils

A proper way of cleaning your equipment is the following:

- Start cleaning immediately after milking, so that milk residues will not dry and stick on the buckets and utensils.
- Rinse well with water.
- Scrub the tools in a hot soda solution (1.5 tablespoons of soda to 5 litres of water), using a small amount of water to dissolve the soda before adding it to the rest of the water.
- Rinse well with hot water.
- Buckets, tubs, etc., should be turned upside down on a rack during storage; the water can then drain and no dirt or dust can enter. Let the utensils dry to prevent bacterial growth.

Well-cleaned tools are nearly sterile, only a small part of the bacteria remains on the tools. If these tools dry during storage hardly any bacteria will be present. In that case disinfection is not necessary. Tools which are used for storage of pasteurised milk or for cheese making and which do not get a heat treatment together with the milk can be disinfected after cleaning or before use.

Proceed as follows:

- Clean all your equipment properly. The following step will be ineffective if the utensils are not clean to start with.
- Disinfect in a chloride or bleach solution after cleaning or shortly before use. Add 2 tablespoons of bleach per 4. 5 litres of water.

It is advisable to use stainless steel equipment, cheesecloth and wooden utensils. Tools or any other equipment made from aluminium should not be washed in a strong soda solution, as soda attacks aluminium. Iron utensils will rust in a strong chloride solution. Therefore rinse and dry these utensils immediately after cleaning and disinfection.

If you have no cleaning agents-like soda-or disinfectants, you can disinfect your equipment as follows:

- Thoroughly clean the utensils using clean water.
- Rinse with a soap solution.
- Dry the equipment on a rack in the sun upside down or rinse with boiling water.

STARTER CULTURES

In tropical countries it is often difficult to prevent raw milk from spoiling before consumption. One way to avoid this is to allow the milk to acidify or ferment.

This is done by adding lactic acid bacteria to fresh milk. The addition of lactic acid bacteria is called inoculation. There are several groups of fermented milks.

The principal differences between these groups are:

- Type of milk used (cow, goat, sheep, buffalo, camel or mare)
- Type of fermenting flora
- The way the milk is processed either before or after fermentation.

Various kinds of lactic acid bacteria produce various kinds of sour milk. Yoghurt, dahi, laban, nono, kefir and koumiss are all produced in this way. These products differ in flavour, colour and consistency.

THE DEVELOPMENT OF LACTIC ACID BACTERIA

Bacterial growth shows a specific pattern comprising the following consecutive stages: adaptation phase (A), a period of rapid multiplication (B), a stabilisation period (C) and a decreasing phase (D).

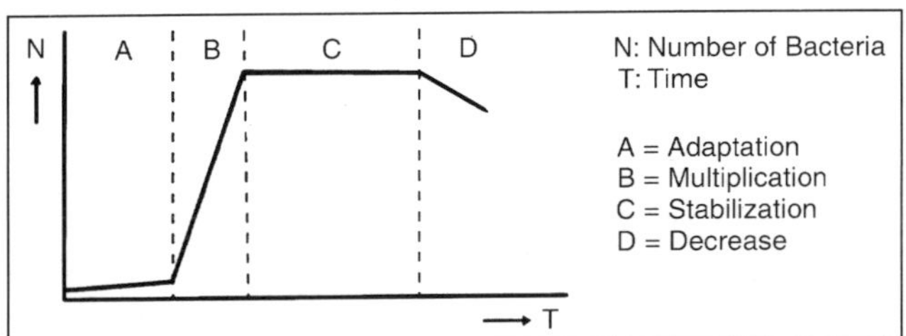

Fig. Development of Lactic Acid Bacteria

After inoculation with the bacteria, the milk starts souring. In practice the whole souring cycle takes one to two days. In this period one can recognise the four growth phases of bacteria as follows.

Adaptation Phase

During this period, bacteria, of which only a relatively small number is present, have to adapt to their new environment. Multiplication is still very slow. The length of the adaptation period depends on the type of bacteria, their viability, the temperature of the milk and whether there are any bacterial growth inhibiting factors present.

Period of Rapid Multiplication

The bacteria, after adjusting to their new environment, multiply rapidly and start fermenting milk sugar (lactose) into lactic acid. The milk gets thicker because of coagulation of the proteins and the taste becomes sour.

Stabilisation Period

During this stage, the number of bacteria remains constant. The reason for this is that they do not thrive in the acidic milk.

Decrease of the Number of Bacteria

Due to the exhaustion of the nutrients of the food source and the production of lactic acid, the bacteria become inactive and die after some time.

CULTIVATION OF STARTER CULTURES OF LACTIC ACID BACTERIA

Starter cultures of lactic acid bacteria can be obtained from specialised firms and laboratories or from other dairy plants. Most of the starter cultures from the laboratories and specialised firms are freeze-dried; dairy plants generally have fresh (liquid) starter cultures available. If starter cultures cannot be obtained easily, it is recommended that you cultivate and maintain your own cultures.

That way it is not necessary to buy a fresh starter culture each time you want to make cheese or a soured milk product. If fresh raw milk is stored at ambient temperatures the bacteria in the milk (including the lactic acid bacteria) will develop, after some time acid will be formed and the milk will curdle. The lactic acid bacterium that develops can be used for the fermentation of the product.

During this spontaneous souring, however, undesirable microorganisms could contaminate the milk. It is therefore better to use a commercial starter culture. When small quantities of products are made, a small amount of fresh yoghurt, whey or sour milk (or buttermilk) can be used as a starter culture. Experience has shown that the use of a starter culture produces a more consistent and better product than the use of naturally soured milk.

It is difficult to keep the starter culture fresh and active, especially under tropical conditions and with limited resources. The cultivation of the culture requires good hygiene and proper temperatures. Different products, such as yoghurt and cheese, require different cultures of lactic acid bacteria. If you can obtain a freeze-dried powder culture, follow the instructions on the package. Once the seal of the package has been broken, the bacteria will not survive for a long time, in any case not longer than 6 months.

COMPONENTS OF MILK FOOD

Milk contains components that are essential to humans such as proteins, carbohydrates, fat, water, all the B-vitamins, vitamins A and D, calcium and phosphorus. It also provides energy.

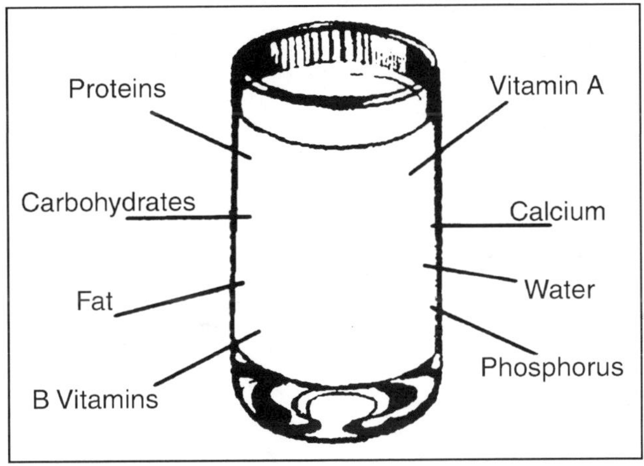

Fig. Main Components of Milk

An important protein in milk is casein (in many cases 80% of the milk protein). This is the base for cheese making. Casein is linked to calcium phosphate, which is why milk contains a relatively large amount of this salt that is a very important nutrient for humans and animals. In addition to casein, milk contains whey proteins (20% of the milk protein). The whey proteins are in most cases not incorporated in the cheese; they remain in the whey. Whey proteins (globulins and albumins) have a very high nutritive value. Milk protein is of a high quality.

This means that the human body can use a large part of the protein efficiently. Proteins in various other foodstuffs have a comple-mentary effect. In combination with cereals, potatoes, meat, eggs or nuts in one meal, the body can use an even greater percentage of the milk protein. Apart from milk, there are other animal protein sources such as fish and meat. Vegetable protein, which is also important in making the body's proteins, is found in cereals and pulses.

Protein is needed by the body for growth, replacement of worn-out body proteins and the production of compounds that the body needs. Milk sugar (lactose) is a carbohydrate, a necessary component to keep the body going. Our bodies burn carbohydrates in the same way an oven burns wood. Through this combustion, energy is released which is used by our bodies for many kinds of activities.

Milk fat is present in the form of small fat globules, which have a lower weight than the other components of the milk. When cow milk is allowed to stand, these globules collect on top of the milk and form a layer of cream. Buffalo milk also forms some cream on top, but other kinds of milk, such as that of sheep and goats, hardly form a layer of fat at all. For these types of milk one needs to separate the cream from the milk.

Milk fat is easy to digest. The body uses fat as a fuel or stores it as fat reserves. Milk is also an important source of minerals and vitamins. It contains large quantities of calcium, which can easily be absorbed by the body after digestion and is important for the formation of bones (the skeleton).

Milk is also an important source of vitamin B2 (Riboflavin), but there is little vitamin C in milk. Therefore a person's diet must also include vegetables and fruits in order to ensure a sufficient supply of vitamin C. Milk is able to compensate for a lack of certain nutrients in a monotonous diet because of the great diversity of nutrients it contains and the high value of milk protein. It can therefore greatly improve the quality of the diet.

Products derived from milk contain these nutrients to a greater or lesser extent. Milk is especially desirable for vulnerable groups, for instance babies, toddlers, children and pregnant and nursing mothers. Always strive for a healthy, varied diet, which apart from milk also includes cereals, pulses, vegetables, fruits and if possible meat or fish. The various types of milk differ in various ways, including nutritional value.

COMPOSITION AND CHARACTERISTICS OF VARIOUS TYPES OF MILK

The composition of mother's milk and milk from cow, buffalo, goat, sheep, camel, donkey and lama is shown in table. The figures in table show that the composition of the milk of non-ruminants, *e.g.* mother's milk and mare milk, differs distinctly from the milk of ruminants (cow, goat, sheep, etc.). This may be partly explained by differences in the digestive system of the two groups. Apart from the differences in cream formation there are other differences between the various kinds of milk. There is a lot of provitamin A (carotene) in cow milk, giving it its yellow colour, but not in buffalo, goat or sheep milk. In the milk of goats and sheep the carotenoids are already converted into the colourless vitamin A.

This is why only cow milk is yellow in colour. Buffalo milk curdles sooner than cow milk. Unless the preparation is adjusted, cheese made from buffalo milk will mature more slowly and have a drier consistency than cheese made from cow milk. Goat milk can have an unpleasant smell; this can be prevented by boiling the milk as soon as possible after milking. Between some goats or breeds of goats there may be a difference in the taste of the milk. Cow milk accounts for 91% of the world's milk production. Buffalo, goat and sheep milk account for 5.9%, 1.6% and 1.7% respectively.

Table. Composition of various Types of Milk

Milk Source	Fat (%)	Protein (%)	Lactose (%)	Calcium (%)	Energy (cal 100g)
Human (mother's) milk	4.6	1.2	7.0	0.0	73
Friesian cow	3.5	3.3	4.6	01	62
Guernsey cow	4.7	3.2	4.7	0.1	75
Indian buffalo	7.5	3.8	4.9	0.2	100
Goat	4.5	3.3	4.4	0.1	71
Sheep	7.5	5.6	4.4	0.2	105
Mare	1.6	2.2	6.0	0.1	47
Donkey	1.5	2.1	6.2	0.1	46
Camel	4.2	3.7	4.1	?	70
Lama	3.2	3.9	5.3	?	65

Although there are enormous regional differences we can generally say that, if it is to be drunk, milk from cows or buffaloes is preferred to that from goats and sheep. This is because of the more neutral flavour of cow milk and buffalo milk.

Goat and sheep milk are, just like the milk of cows and buffaloes, popular for making cheese and soured milk products (especially sheep milk). Camel milk is usually drunk. Mother's milk is the most ideal food for a suckling infant. Nonetheless, many substitutes have been developed which find a ready demand. We shall pay more attention to infant nutrition in the next section.

INFANT NUTRITION

Mother's milk is best suited to the needs of a baby, and contains certain components that protect an infant against infectious diseases. All the nutrients a baby needs, except iron and vitamin C, are to be found in sufficient quantities in mother's milk. At birth, a baby has a store of iron in its liver, which it uses up during its first 6 months. Any kind of supplementary feeding is only necessary after 3 months, as the mother's milk then no longer supplies all the nutrients the infant needs.

Fruit juice and mashed fruit provide additional vitamin C, which the infant then needs. Supplementary feeding of energy-giving foods is also desirable. Mixing small quantities of milk powder into mashed food can considerably improve the food's value (especially the value of its protein).

It is advisable to continue breastfeeding as long as possible because mother's milk is often the only source of animal protein for a baby. If the mother cannot breastfeed, does not have enough milk or dies, bottle feeding is a solution and the best substitute.

However, in practice often too much water is added to the (artificial) baby food, which is usually bought in powder form. It becomes too watery and is therefore not nutritious enough. Moreover, artificial foods are costly and require good hygiene. Dilution with water is often a cause of infection because the available water may be polluted. Water used for bottle feeding must first be boiled, but sterilising water by boiling uses a lot of fuel, which is often in short supply.

By using a cup or a spoon it is easier to maintain the necessary hygiene rather than a bottle because they are easier to clean. Money might be better spent on essential necessities of life than on artificial infant food if the latter is not strictly necessary. If a baby cannot digest milk, you will be forced to use milk products, which do not contain lactose. This is the case with inherited lactose intolerance.

LACTOSE INTOLERANCE

Lactose intolerance means that the human body is almost, or entirely, unable to digest the milk sugar, lactose, which is present in milk because the body lacks the enzyme lactase. Lactase splits the lactose into glucose and galactose. The latter two mono-saccharides can easily be absorbed in the intestine. Undigested lactose can be converted by the microbial flora in the intestine into lactic acid and gases. Consumption of larger quantities of milk thus causes flatulence, stomach cramps and diarrhoea. 'Lactose intolerance' is thus often called 'lactase deficiency'.

There are different forms of lactose intolerance among children:

- Congenital lactose intolerance. In this case, a baby cannot digest milk because the baby lacks the enzyme lactase, necessary for the breakdown of lactose into glucose and galactose.
- Lactose intolerance among children who are 2-5 years old. From the age of two years lactase activity in a child decreases and the child may have problems due to insufficient lactase by the time he or she is 4-5 years old. Consumption of small quantities of milk (one glass at a time) usually does not cause any problem. It is also possible to prevent problems by eating fermented milk products, in which part of the milk sugar has been converted, such as cheese, yoghurt and buttermilk.
- Lactose intolerance as a result of intestinal disease and/or malnutrition, especially in babies and toddlers. The lactose activity is temporarily decreased making it necessary to use lactose-free milk products for a short time. Cheese and fermented products like

yoghurt, in which milk sugar has been converted, are also suitable.

Apart from lactose intolerance, the use of milk also depends on other factors, which as suggested, now discuss.

MILK AND DAIRY PRODUCTS IN THE DIET

Diet refers to the way people feed themselves and the foodstuffs they use to do so. This is strongly influenced by people's traditions and religion, their economic position, their place in society and the possibilities offered by their natural surroundings. It is not surprising that each population group has its own diet. The use of milk and dairy products can also be looked at when examining the diet.

Here are a few examples of how the factors can influence the role and form of milk and dairy products in the diet:

- The cow is a sacred animal in India; therefore the rennet used in cheese making may not be taken from a calf's stomach.
- If milk or dairy products have to be bought, money is needed.
- In densely populated areas, people are forced to use all available land for crops that give a maximum yield, or crops that can be directly consumed by the people. This limits the land available for dairy farming.
- It may not be possible to keep cattle in certain regions, *e.g.* the humid tropics, due to the natural environment. For example, in humid areas of West Africa cattle cannot be kept because they are the host of the tsetse fly, which transmits sleeping sickness.

For these reasons, milk and dairy products in the diet can be of greater or lesser importance in one area or another. Economic and social situations are especially subject to change and dietary patterns change with them. New foodstuffs may be introduced to (partly) substitute others. Adoption of new products is often no easy matter; sometimes centuries-old traditions may have to change. Also, taste and other characteristics such as texture are important in the acceptance of new kinds of food. Something that may be considered very tasty in one place, may not be appreciated elsewhere.

Fig. Camel Milk is a very Popular Food in Parts of Africa and the Middle East

ACTUAL PREPARATION OF RECIPES

The actual preparation is then described. Success depends on a lot of factors, so do not give up if you do not end up with the desired results the first time.

Experimentation is necessary and you will probably have to adapt the recipes. Several preservation techniques, like cooling, heating, drying, souring, salting, etc., are relevant to most recipes. Different types of milk can be used, which give different results. Take great care when cleaning all pans, dishes and utensils. Figure gives a rough overview of the different dairy products that can be made from milk.

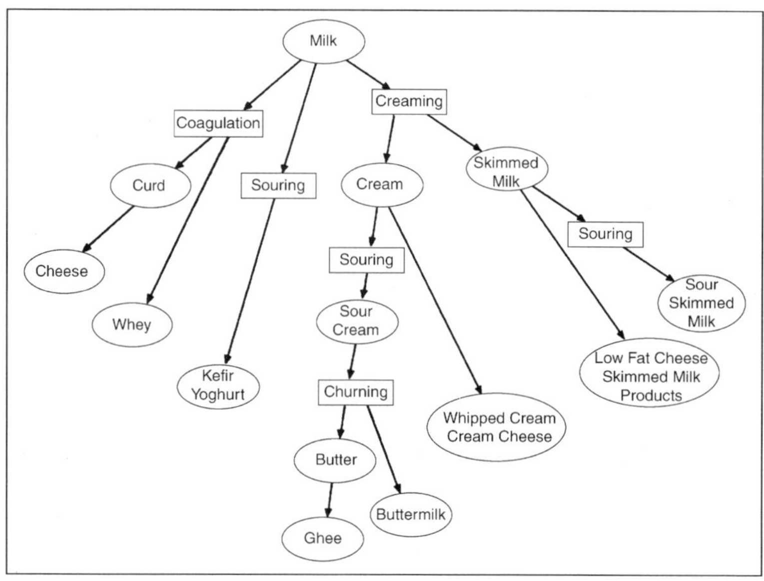

Fig. Manufacturing of Milk into Dairy Products

CREAM

You will need raw milk and a heat source:

- *Method A:* After leaving milk to stand for about 24 hours at as low a temperature as possible (4-12°C), the cream can be skimmed off using a spoon or saucer. This method makes use of the fact that cream rises and then stays on top of the milk. It contains most of the milk fat. Only cow milk readily produces cream this way; other kinds of milk need a hand creamer (centrifugal milk separator) to separate cream and milk.
- *Method B:* Materials: a hand creamer (milk separator), two big bowls.

Heat the milk slightly to a little over 40°C and pour it into the upper bowl of the separator. It is important to turn the handle at a constant speed during the separation. After separating the cream from the milk, pasteurise both cream and skimmed milk. The use of a separator produces more cream and leaves skimmed milk with less fat. A disadvantage is that the separator has to be cleaned thoroughly, including the disks, which takes much time. A hand creamer is a complex tool.

Never buy a second-hand creamer before having checked that it works well. It might lack some irreplaceable parts or may be corroded or damaged. The cream can be kept for a few days if it has been pasteurised. It can also be used for the preparation of various recipes. Cream can be used to make butter, for example. The skimmed milk that is left after the cream has been removed still contains a lot of nutrients (protein, fat, milk sugar, etc.) and can be used for direct consumption or for the production of soured milk or low-fat cheese.

SOUR CREAM

You will need:

- Fresh pasteurised cream
- A saucepan
- A thermometer
- A metal or wooden spoon
- A starter culture or fresh fermented milk

Cool the cream after pasteurisation to 18°C. Add 10–30 ml (1–3%; equal to 1-2 tablespoons) of sour milk or a starter culture to one litre of cream while stirring. Let the mixture become sour at a temperature of between 16 and 18°C, stirring it once after a number of hours to allow it to ferment evenly. After 24 hours the cream should be sufficiently sour and ready for consumption.

BUTTER

You will need:

- Pasteurised cream, sour cream or sour milk
- A heat source
- A pan
- A thermometer
- Cold water
- Sour milk or a starter culture
- A container for churning
- A sieve
- A bowl
- A tray for kneading
- Wooden spoons
- Fine salt if available (optional)
- Packing material, *e.g.* greaseproof paper or a jar
- Clean water

Butter is made by churning one of the following products:

- Cream,
- Sour cream, or
- Sour milk.

If you do not have enough milk from which to skim off the cream, the milk can be soured and churned as a whole (provided that the fat content of the milk is rather high; above 4%). But sour cream is better to churn than sour milk.

It is only possible to manufacture sweet cream butter if the production and handling of the milk, cream and butter are exceptionally hygienic and the cream has undergone after pasteurisation a cold treatment by storing it for at least 12 hours at temperatures below 10°C.

Heating and Souring

Heat the milk or cream to a temperature of 85°C. Let it cool down to 18°C as quickly as possible (use a thermometer) using cold running water on the outside of the pan. Add 10-30 ml (about 1-2 tablespoons) of fresh fermented sour milk or a starter culture to one litre of milk or cream and stir. After about 24 hours at 16 to 18°C, the mixture will become thick and sour enough to be churned.

Churning

During churning the cream, sour cream or sour milk will be mixed intensively with air. This process causes fat globules to flocculate (or stick together), producing butter and buttermilk. The simplest way to make butter from small quantities of milk is by using a bottle or a jar that can be covered with a well-closing lid or a simple bowl with beaters. If large quantities of milk or cream are available, you should consider acquiring a real churn.

There are several types available. The churn tub is a simple method, which is often used in the tropics. A cheap and practical domestic churn is a glass pot with a paddle attached to a screw top. The paddle can be turned manually. This churn is difficult to clean. It is best to rinse it with water before use, in order to prevent the butter from sticking to the sides.

Churns should not be filled more than one third with soured milk or sour cream. Churn with a regular up and down or sideways movement. Stop churning when the butter particles reach the size of rice grains or peas and the buttermilk looks rather liquid. If, after 30 minutes, no grains have yet been formed, you can change the temperature by adding a little clean cold or warm water.

The amount of added water should never be more than 25% of the total amount of churned cream or milk. The butter particles will float to the top of the buttermilk, because butter is lighter than buttermilk. This makes it easier to separate the two products by pouring off the buttermilk through a coarse sieve. Never add too much water, otherwise the buttermilk will become too watery.

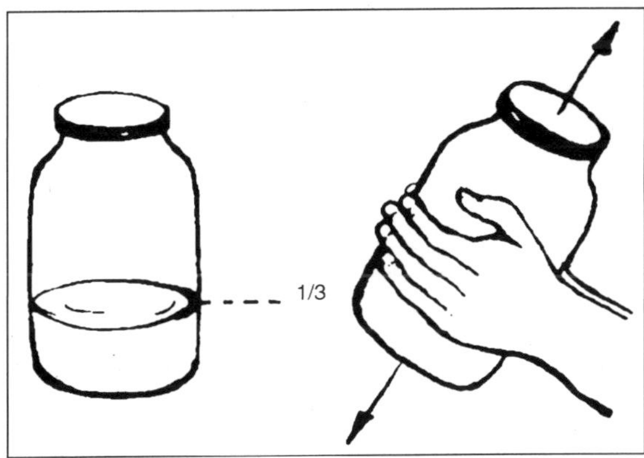

Fig. Using a Jar to make Butter

Washing

Washing of the butter grains is not necessary. However, if very clean water is available, it can improve butter quality.

Washing the butter can be done in two ways:

1. Fill the churn 2/5 full with clean, cold water. Wash the butter by churning it for about 3 minutes. This can be repeated, if necessary. The idea is to remove part of the remaining buttermilk from the butter particles. It is important to remove as much as possible in order to produce butter that can be kept for a longer period. After washing, the butter particles can be skimmed off or the buttermilk can be drained.
2. If small quantities are available, the butter particles can be washed using a sieve. Put the sieve on top of a bowl and pour the mixture through it. Make sure that during churning the butter does not become one big lump, otherwise it will be difficult to wash-in case you want to do this.

Salting (If Preferred)

Salting is not necessary for preservation; many people, however, like the taste of salted butter. The butter can be slightly salted by kneading in about 10 grams of salt to each kilogram of butter. Mix the butter again the next day in order to allow the salt grains to dissolve.

Kneading

Kneading the butter is important in order to get a nice, smooth product.

It helps to distribute the moisture and this improves quality and shelf life, provided that kneading is done in a hygienic way. Use a clean, well-rinsed kneading board.

Knead the butter with the back of two wooden spoons until drops of water and buttermilk are not perceivable any more and the butter has a nice, smooth surface. Remove drops of buttermilk during this process. Instead of a wooden spoon, a wet roller or bottle can be used. If none of these are available, just use clean hands to knead.

Storage

Butter should be stored in a cool, dark place. Put it in a pot or wrap it up in greaseproof paper or aluminium foil. After some time, one to two weeks, the surface of the butter can be covered with moulds. This mould formation can be partially prevented by sprinkling salt on the surface or by wrapping the butter air tight.

Moulds only grow if oxygen is available. Butter can also be frozen. However, after defrosting the butter will rather soon have an off-taste. It is therefore a good idea to divide the butter into smaller portions before freezing. Salted butter is less suitable for freezing.

CHEESE RECIPES

There are many variations in cheese making. To make a good product, it may be necessary to adjust the recipe. Therefore you should have a good method of recording exactly how the cheese is made.

Your records can include the following aspects:

- Date and surrounding temperature
- Quality of the milk and pasteurisation temperature
- Aamount of milk
- Ingredients, amount of starter culture, acid or rennet added
- Temperature at which starter culture, acid or rennet was added
- Coagulation time
- Temperatures during the cheese making process
- Temperature at the end of coagulation
- Pressure applied, length of time applied, etc.
- Salting time
- Storage time and conditions during storage

The following recipes should be seen as guidelines for making cheese. Instead of cow milk, you can often use goat, sheep or buffalo milk. Start by making rather simple products like yoghurt, fresh cheese, etc.

Fresh Cheese

Fresh or unripened cheese has a high moisture content of about 75%; it can be consumed directly after preparation. It is made by removing the whey from soured, skimmed milk. The milk is usually coagulated by souring. Sometimes a small amount of rennet is added; this is done to facilitate the draining of the whey. However, addition of rennet is not essential.

A well-known kind of fresh cheese is curd, known in various countries by the following names: *Frischkäse, fromage frais,* quarg, and baker's cheese. The differences between these cheeses are their fat levels. You can make curd by souring fresh milk, cream or skimmed milk into sour milk, sour cream or sour skimmed milk and then draining the thick sour milk in a bag or cloth. Sometimes bags are placed on top of each other to increase the removal of whey.

After draining, the curd has a crumbly structure. By stirring or using a blender you can make the product smooth again. There are various kinds of curd cheese in which moisture, fat and salt content and size of curd particles vary. Fresh cheese has a fresh sour taste, especially when it is prepared from skimmed milk.

By adding cream, the taste will become milder and richer. Curd can be kept for only a short time and must be stored at cool temperatures. During storage, further whey separation can occur; this is the result of further souring of the product.

Curd from Whole Milk

Pasteurise the milk 30 minutes at 63°C and then cool it to 20°C. Add per 10 litres of milk ¼-½ litre of starter culture or fresh sour milk or buttermilk; yoghurt can be added if desired. Add 2 drops of rennet-if available. It is advisable to dilute this small amount of rennet with several ml of water to improve its distribution through the milk. After stirring well, leave the inoculated milk to stand for 24 hours at 18–20°C.

During those 24 hours, souring and coagulation will take place; the milk becomes a rather firm mass. This thick mass is subsequently poured into a cotton or linen cloth or a bag so that the whey can drain through the cloth. The cloth is placed into a large colander or cheese mould beforehand so that the whey can thoroughly drain.

After 24 hours, sufficient whey will have leaked out and the remaining curd can then be mixed, for example with a spoon or blender, until it becomes a homogenous mass. The curd can now be consumed. When kept in a refrigerator, curd can be stored for 1-2 weeks.

Bag Cheese

You will need a sieve, small basket or cheese mould and a cheesecloth or tea towel. Let 10 litres of buttermilk with low fat content drain through a cheesecloth until 1.5 litres of bag cheese, or curd, remain. Place a cheesecloth in a sieve, small basket or cheese mould and press the curd firmly into it. Let the curd drain for several hours, then turn it. About 1.5 kg of bag cheese has then been made, which contains no salt and hardly any fat. It can be kept for only a rather short time: 1 to 2 weeks. Keep it cool, preferably in a refrigerator.

Fig. Bag Cheese

Krut

For making krut one needs buttermilk, cheesecloth and salt. This is a way to make cheese from any leftover milk. Add some sour milk or buttermilk to the leftover milk and mix. Boil the mixture until the milk curdles. Separate the curd from the whey by pouring it through a cheesecloth. The curd is then kneaded with 2-4% salt and dried in the sun.

Rasagollas

You will need raw milk, a fire, pan, spoon, lemon juice or sour whey, cheese-cloth, bowl, knife and concentrated sugar water. Rasagollas is a sweet dairy product originally from India. Traditionally it was formed into sweet curd balls, but because of the way it is prepared here, the curd can only be cut into cubes and not formed into balls. The milk is boiled with lemon juice (10 tablespoons or 150 ml per 10 litres of milk) or sour whey (1.5 litres per 10 litres of milk) while stirring continuously. Sour whey can be obtained from drained sour milk after the production of curd.

The curd is separated from the whey by pouring the mixture into a cheesecloth, which has been placed over a bowl. The slightly elastic curd is cut into cubes with sides of about 2.5 cm. These are then boiled for about an hour in a sugar solution of 600 g per litre of water. 1 litre of sugar solution is needed for each kilogram of curd. The cubes can be stored quite some time and are very sweet.

Feta

You will need sheep, goat or cow milk, starter culture or fresh sour milk, rennet, cooking-salt, knife, cheese moulds, cheesecloths and cans or a plastic container to store the cheese. Feta is a sharp, salty cheese originally from Greece that is made of sheep and goat milk. You can also use a mixture of sheep and cow milk, but then the cheese will not have its typical white colour. Feta is kept in a solution of whey and brine.

Heat 10 litres of pasteurised milk mixed with 200 ml of a starter culture, sour milk or buttermilk to 30°C. After 1-2 hours, rennet is added; use 2 ml of rennet per 10 litres of milk. After allowing it to coagulate for about one hour, the curd is cut into cubes of about 2.5 cm, after which it is carefully stirred for another 20 minutes. The curd must then be carefully transferred to the tubs covered with cheesecloth.

This can be done either by scooping the curd directly out of the whey into the moulds lined with cheesecloth, or by letting the curd settle, pouring off the whey and only then putting the curd in the cheese moulds. After a few hours the cheese must be turned. The curd mass is carefully removed from the cheesecloth and replaced upside down. After one day, the lumps of curd are cut into cubes of about 10 cm.

Salting can be done by sprinkling the blocks several times with salt or by placing the blocks in brine for 24 hours. If the cheese is kept for several days at about 18°C, it must be turned regularly and washed with cold water at the end of the storage period. The cheese can be kept for some time by piling blocks of cheese closely on top of each other and covering them with brine. The cheese should have a smooth and soft consistency.

Queso Blanco

The so-called *queso blanco* is manufactured in many ways in Latin America. Typical for this cheese is that salt is added directly to the whey/curd mixture. This has the advantage that slightly soured milk can be used to make *queso blanco.*

A much-used method is the following:

- Take raw (unheated) soured milk of 32°C, or take 10 litres of pasteurised milk and add 50 ml of sour milk, buttermilk or starter culture. Add 1.5 ml of rennet. After 45 minutes the curd is cut and stirred. Leave the whey/curd mixture to settle for another 30 minutes at 30-36°C. Pour off the whey and compress the curd to remove more whey. Mix 30-50 grams of salt through the curd. The salt can also be dissolved in water before being added. 100 grams of salt dissolved in 50 ml of water must then be added for each 10 litres of milk.

Transfer the salted curd into cheese moulds and press the cheese. During the first hours, turn the cheeses occasionally. Press them until the following day. To improve rind formation, pour whey heated at 50°C over the cheese while being pressed (after one hour). Cheese made with rennet can be kept for 2 months at 10-15°C. As a variation to this method, you can add acid instead of a starter culture and use no rennet. Take raw milk, which may already be a little bit sour. Heat it to almost boiling. Acidify it with 300 ml vinegar per 10 litres of milk until a precipitate is formed. The acid can be partly neutralised with the addition of some sodium bicarbonate (double soda). Pour off the whey.

Fresh Goat Cheese (in Oil)

You will need pasteurised goat milk, a heat source, a pan with lid, a thermometer, sour milk (or buttermilk or starter culture), rennet, a spoon, an insulated box or blanket or newspapers, cheesecloth, salt, cheese moulds, a cool storage place, greaseproof paper (if available), a large pot, herbs and olive oil. Bring the pasteurised goat milk to a temperature of 20°C. Per 10 litres of milk, add 0.5 litre of fresh starter or sour milk or buttermilk. \

Take 20 drops of rennet per litre of milk, dilute this in a little water and stir this through the milk. Place the pan in the insulated box or in the blanket or the newspapers to prevent it from cooling down. Check the next day to see if the milk has curdled sufficiently; a little whey on top is acceptable. Cut the curd into cubes the size of a matchbox. After 2 hours transfer the mass into a cheesecloth and let it drain for 12 hours at room temperature. Mix the dry curd with some salt and put the cubes into cheese moulds. Press the curd into the moulds so that no air holes remain and place the moulds in a cool (15°C) place.

The next day remove the cheese carefully from the cheesecloth and replace it upside down in the cheesecloth and mould. Leave the cheese for a further 24 hours in a cool place. Remove the cheeses from cloth and mould and turn them daily. Should they become too dry, wrap them tightly, for example in greaseproof paper.

If you wish to store the fresh goat cheese cubes for several weeks, place them in a large (glass) jar, which can be closed. Sprinkle a mixture of different herbs over them, such as rosemary, basil, thyme, bruised juniper berries, a finely chopped piece of garlic, several pepper kernels and a chopped up hot pepper. Other herbs can also be used.

Pour olive oil over the cheeses until they are just covered and add a few twigs of dill or rosemary to the oil. Close the jar and put it away in a cool and dark place. Before using the cheeses, let them drain well. Use the leftover oil for salad dressing.

Fresh Goat Cheese (Salted)

You will need pasteurised goat milk, a heat source, pan with lid, thermometer, sour milk (or buttermilk or starter culture), acid, spoon, rennet, knife, colander or cheesecloth, cheese moulds, pressing equipment and salt. Heat the pasteurised milk in a pan to 30°C, stirring continuously. For each 10 litres of milk, add 0.2-0.5 litres of sour milk or buttermilk or 0.2 litres of a starter culture and 30 drops of rennet (diluted in water). After 45 minutes, cut the coagulated curd with a knife; after another 10 minutes, the curd will be the size of a marble.

The top layer of whey can be poured off after leaving the mixture to stand a bit. Leave the curd in the carefully closed pan with the rest of the whey for a further 30-45 minutes. Then transfer the curd into cheese moulds in which cheesecloth has been placed. Press the curd; one hour is sufficient. The cheeses must then be pickled in brine. For a cheese of 500 grams, 10 hours of pickling is long enough.

Fresh Sheep Cheese

You will need pasteurised sheep milk, a heat source, a pan, a thermometer, a starter culture or fresh sour milk or buttermilk, rennet, a spoon, a knife, a cheesecloth, some salt (if desired) and cheese moulds. Sheep milk contains more fat and protein than cow milk and therefore only 4-4.5 litres of sheep milk are needed to make 1 kg of cheese. Because of the higher content of dry matter in the milk, sheep milk coagulates firmer than cow milk.

Heat the pasteurised milk to about 30°C, stirring continuously. Add 300 ml of a starter culture and 40 drops of rennet to each 10 litres of milk. After 45 minutes the milk will have coagulated sufficiently to be cut. Cut the curdled, thick mass carefully; continue till the curd particles have the size of a pea. Bring the curd into a cheesecloth.

If desired mix in some salt, and let the cloth hang until the cheese has the desired firmness. You can speed up the draining of the whey by opening the cheesecloth after several hours, scraping the thick part from the cloth, and mixing it in with the rest of the curd. You may want to make a less sour sheep cheese, which is a little bit firmer and with some lower moisture content. For this, you must leave the curd for a longer time: about 15-30 minutes in the cheese vat where the curd treatment is done.

After a short period of rest, pour off part of the whey, stir the curd carefully again and fill the cheese mould using a cheesecloth. Add some salt to the curd, if desired. Press the curd: about 4 hours of light pressing is sufficient. Store in a cool place. Sheep cheese can be kept for at least one week in the refrigerator.

Matured Sheep Cheese

You will need pasteurised sheep milk, a heat source, a pan, a thermometer, sour milk (buttermilk or starter culture), rennet, a spoon, a knife, colander, a cheesecloth, cheese moulds and pressing equipment, salt, a tightly sealed pickling tub, coarse cheesecloth and a cool storage place. 10 litres of sheep milk yields about 2 kg of ripened cheese.

After adding 60 ml of starter culture or sour milk (or buttermilk), leave the milk to stand at 30°C for 30-45 minutes. Only then add 60 drops of rennet, diluted with a little water, per 10 litres of milk, and stir it thoroughly through the milk. After allowing it to curdle for 1 hour, cut the coagulated milk for about 15 minutes until it is divided into particles of about 1-2 cm. Then stir it for 10 minutes, pour half of the whey off and heat the curd to 35°C by adding hot water with a temperature of 80-100°C.

Stir the mixture again for about 15 minutes, after which time the curd must be left to stand for 30 minutes in the pan. Keep the pan warm as well as possible but never place it on a fire. Remove the whey that has separated, and pour the curd with the remaining whey into a colander. After the first draining, the curd must be transferred by hand into cheese moulds covered with cheesecloth.

Index

H

I

L

M

N

O

P

R

S

T

V